P9-AOP-445

WITHDRAWN
WALLINGFORD PUBLIC LIBRARY
WALLINGFORD, CONNECTICUT 06492

HOW TO SURVIVE THE IRS

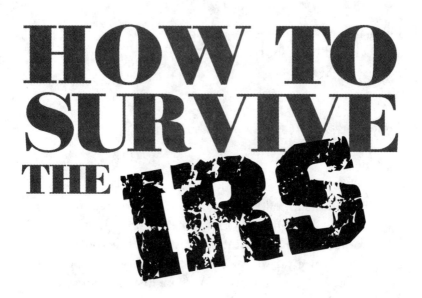

HOW TO SURVIVE THE IRS

My Battles Against Goliath

MICHAEL LOUIS MINNS

with a foreword by U.S. Congressman Ron Paul

BARRICADE BOOKS

Fort Lee, New Jersey

WALLINGFORD PUBLIC LIBRARY
WALLINGFORD, CONNECTICUT 06492

343.7304
min

Published by Barricade Books Inc.
185 Bridge Plaza North Suite 308-A
Fort Lee, NJ 07024

Copyright © 2001 by Michael Louis Minns
All Rights Reserved.

No part of this book may be reproduced, stored in a retrieval
system, or transmitted in any form, by any means, including
mechanical, electronic, photocopying, recording, or otherwise, without the prior written permission of the publisher,
except by a reviewer who wishes to quote brief passages in
connection with a review written for inclusion in a magazine,
newspaper, or broadcast.

Library of Congress Cataloging-in-Publication Data

Minns, Michael Louis.
    How to beat the IRS : my battles against goliath /
Michael Minns.
        p. cm.
        ISBN: 1-56980-170-3
        1. United States—Internal Revenue Service 2. Tax
        protests and appeals—United States—Popular
        works. I. Title
KF6324.Z9 M56 2001
343.7304/2 21   63-055
                                             CIP

Printed in the United States of America.
10 9 8 7 6 5 4 3 2 1

Table of Contents

Dedication:

This is dedicated to the memory of Linda "L.R." Robertson.
Born July 25, 1948
Died March 9, 1995
Without L.R. this book would not have been possible…and several of the innocent defendants would have served time instead of being acquitted.

and

To Percy Turk
Born June 1918
Died September 1987
The first client who told me I needed to charge more…without him I wouldn't have been able to keep the doors open.

Foreword
by the Honorable
Ron Paul

axation is hardly the price we pay for civilization, as Oliver Wendell Holmes claimed. In fact, taxes are often an attack on civilization, undermining the peaceful exchanges and the division of labor that makes civilization possible.

Is any taxation compatible with a free society? Yes, if it is indirect and mild, as the framers of the Constitution knew. What horrified them was the idea of direct federal taxes on individuals. Such a system, which they outlawed, could lead to tyranny.

How prescient they were. Since we amended the Constitution to allow income taxes, our government has grown into a monstrous welfare-warfare state that, in the words of the Declaration of Independence, is eating out the substance of the people and to an extent that George III could only have dreamed of.

Working in the tradition of the framers is attorney Michael Louis Minns. He has defended many Americans against the tax police, and argued for a fair and constitutional system in place of the personal income tax.

The case studies outlined in this book should make you angry and determined to change a system that wreaked such havoc on the lives and liberties of so many good Americans.

If we are to pass a free and prosperous society on to our children and grandchildren, we must abolish the federal income tax and bind down the central government once again with the bands of steel that the framers forged.

That is a great task, but surely one worthy of all our effort. For its goal is nothing less than the restoration of the original America, and her freedom and promise.

—Ron Paul
U.S. Congressman from 1976 to 1984 in the 22nd District,
U.S. Congressman 1997 to Present in the 14th District,
Doctor of Medicine, specializing in Ob/Gyn,
and Author

Preface
by Professor
Richard Davis
Rieke

Michael Minns coined the term "underground lawyer" to describe those people, whether trained in the law or not, who actively seek justice in their life experiences through effective advocacy. An underground lawyer understands the role of rhetoric in developing ideas and resolving problems. Identifying the role of rhetoric in legal contexts has been the primary focus of my career as a university professor. As I read this book, I saw evidence in each chapter of what I have been professing.

Rhetoric is the practice of effective communication in negotiation, mediation, interpersonal dialogue, and persuasive advocacy. It rests on the assumption that reality is inherently uncertain, constantly changing, and largely the product of what people choose to believe. It acknowledges that language does not have certain meanings. Meanings are in people, and there is no "correct" meaning of a word apart from the people trying to use it to understand each other. Language isn't even language until people use it to communicate.

Underground lawyers can tolerate uncertainty because they understand its inevitability. A good deal of their work is trying to resolve conflicts with people who think there are certain answers to life's problems that just happen to coincide with whatever it is they believe at the moment. People with this kind of authoritarian thinking seem to be heavily concentrated in governmental positions. Minns introduces us to such people in every chapter.

It is only in recent times that people have come to acknowledge the rhetorical element in their lives, and there is no better place to demonstrate this than through the study of the behavior of the IRS. As you read this book, you will become increasingly concerned over the absence of certainty, unless you are already an underground lawyer. Like most people, you probably believe that the tax laws and codes can be read and understood in a way that produces a clear-cut understanding of what the law requires. Like most of us, you may accept the fact that you don't understand tax laws, confident in the knowledge that trained professionals can do so. Just go to an accountant, a lawyer, or the IRS itself and they will provide certainty, right? Wrong! Most of us act as if such certainty exists because it is just too frightening to consider the alternative. When you finish this book, you will no longer be able to fool yourself.

The cases Minns presents here demonstrate that even well-educated and well-intentioned professionals cannot overcome the inherent uncertainty in complex issues, and that is the best case scenario. In many of the chapters, the people involved are not well intentioned. There are as many mean, selfish, ambitious, and downright nasty people among well-educated professionals as there are in the rest of society, and these are the ones Minns tackles in this book.

In the early 1960s, when I wrote my doctoral dissertation, *Rhetorical Theory in American Legal Practice*, law schools taught that rhetoric had no place in the law. In fact, law professors perceived rhetoric as shady trickery used to make falsity appear truthful. Do your homework, know the law, and present facts scientifically, law professors lectured, and you will do well. Truth and justice have no need for rhetorical strategies. This was a time when law professors talked about the "science" of the law. The textbook most commonly used to teach evidence was titled, *The Science of Judicial Proof.* Legal decisions were claimed to be as objective and certain as the findings of nuclear physicists (now, physicists will be the first to admit that their research is anything but certain).

In my dissertation, I argued that what the law schools were teaching was almost pure fantasy. Young lawyers were sent into practice effectively unprepared for the real, extremely rhetorical, world. Those who stuck to what they had been taught, turned out to be mediocre lawyers, retreated deeply into an office practice that allowed them to make believe the law was certain, or both.

However, many young lawyers quickly recognized that they had been taught a lot of nonsense as they watched successful senior attorneys in practice. They learned to practice law by watching experienced attorneys at work, just like the old apprentice system. Now, the honest ones admit that they learned lawyering at the expense of their early clients.

That kind of learning is better than what the law schools provided, but it still falls short. If you learn law practice through observation, you will pick up bad habits along with the good ones. Physicians do a lot of their learning by watching seniors, but they also study the latest research. Young attorneys rarely are educated in the rhetorical elements of their practice, and neither were the seniors they watched.

Michael Minns and I met when he invited me to work on one of the cases described in this book. He wanted me to provide insights from my training in rhetoric in the selection of a jury. In other cases, I act more broadly as a communication consultant, helping to shape the case to the jurors and the jurors to the case.

Attorneys are increasingly using communication consultants, largely for three reasons. First, lawyers still graduate law school almost completely ignorant of the rhetorical skills they will need in practice. Communication consultants respond to this need by working alongside lawyers to supply insights and suggestions that come from their training and experience. They also conduct regular training sessions to help young lawyers develop rhetorical skills. My book with Randall Stutman, *Communication in Legal Advocacy*, was written to assist this training.

Second, lawyers use communication consultants because they are simply stretched too thin to do everything that should be done to win a case. The lead attorney directs the overall effort and chooses what assignments to delegate to investigators, accountants, scientists, psychologists, and communication consultants. All this expertise comes together as the lead attorney conducts the trial.

Finally, lawyers use communication consultants because of the very uncertainty of the law. Anything that holds even an outside hope of improving the chances of success will be employed as long as there are sufficient funds.

In this book, Michael Minns shows himself to be a consummate legal practitioner. He has developed effective rhetorical skills and regularly employs a variety of experts. Most important of all, Mr. Minns understands the rhetorical nature of law, its uncertainty and reliance upon human understanding for good or ill. He opposes those who try to use power and authority to pretend that the law is certain and objective. His clients benefit from his skilled determination to slice through bureaucratic posturing to get at justice. This book will shock and scare you. If you pay attention, it will also enlighten you.

—Richard Davis Rieke
Teacher and Director, University of Utah Honors Program,
author of *Communications in Legal Advocacy*

Prologue

There cannot justly be any objection to having rail-roads and canals any more than to other good things, provided they cost nothing. The only objection is to paying for them....

—-Abraham Lincoln

A great civilization is not conquered from without until it has destroyed itself from within. The essential causes of Rome's decline lay in her people, her morals, her class struggle, her failing trade, her bureaucratic despotism, her stifling taxes....

—-Will Durant

Scriptures discuss the division of Israel and Judah as a result of taxes. Historians argue whether taxes caused the destruction of Rome or were merely a contributing factor. Taxes can make or break a country.

A large black basalt stone sits in the British Museum in London's Russell Square. The stone dates back to 196 B.C. Napoleon's soldiers found it in 1799 outside the Northern Egyptian town of Rosetta (thus the name Rosetta Stone) and carted it away with tons of other Egyptian treasures. When England defeated France in Egypt they kept up the looting tradition and the stone reached British soil.

The Rosetta Stone is one of the most important archeological finds of the ancient world because it enabled linguists to break the centuries-old code of ancient Egyptian hieroglyphics. The stone was engraved with hieroglyphics, below them was demotic Egyptian, and below that was Greek. Three separate languages saying the same thing. Known words in one language could be compared to unknown words or symbols. The stone became the key to two lost languages of antiquity and helped foster the adage, "Engraved in stone."

The rest of the Rosetta story is not as well known. The text is a decree of Ptolemy V (reign: 205-180 B.C.), announcing that he had reached his majority and acceded to the throne. Previous to his accession, the usual practice of the Ptolemaic kings was to hire tax collectors to go onto the land and collect from the farmers. Often they would hire Greeks who spoke little or no Egyptian. Sometimes too much tax would be collected, or more than one collector would come and the tax was collected twice, or a collector would claim the farmer had not really paid. Sometimes the tax collector put the money in his pocket and lied to the government. The penalty for noncompliance for the farmer could be death, or torture, or a child taken into slavery. (Things haven't changed that much. Today, many IRS agents are noncitizens who haven't yet mastered the fundamentals of English. Horror stories abound about collection agents who have trouble with basic math and fifth-grade grammar fundamentals. Also, their collection practices and penalties are about the same.)

In part, the Rosetta stone is a tax document. The stone declares that the new king has remitted some taxes and revenues in whole and others in part to lighten the burden of taxation so that the people may prosper during his reign. *This is something our own rulers might consider.*

A. J. Lowery, a former landscape artist, and his wife, Anita, published *The Justice Times* for well over a decade to complain about government policies on tax. The IRS had stolen twenty-six dollars from his checking account without explanation. Thirty years later the Lowerys still don't know who authorized the seizure that launched their publication.

One client of mine, with canceled check in hand showing she paid taxes, was accused of not filing. She sent checks with her return. The IRS computer says she only sent in checks. Why would someone pay and not file? The penalty for not filing is higher than the penalty for *not paying*. You're right—it is a stupid question and it is worthy only of a bureaucrat.

Down the street from my one-story building sits a modern multistory pink building where my client's vital numbers had been mixed up, the IRS Building, which they call the HAL Building. (You actually must put HAL on the envelope to mail them things.) When I discussed my client's case with an IRS agent, I congratulated him on the agency's sense of humor using the acronym HAL (IBM, each letter is moved up one). In Stanley Kubrick's movie *2001: A Space Odyssey*, HAL was the name of the government computer that went out of whack and killed all but one of the space crew.

That one man survived by disconnecting HAL. I expected some type of human reaction from the agent, like a laugh, but he only got exasperated and told me that the IRS computers never make mistakes. He was unfamiliar with the movie and its reference. And he definitely had no sense of humor!

A Brief U.S. Tax History

We all know about the Boston Tea Party. It was about a tax on tea. As a protest, patriots dumped tea into Boston Harbor in December of 1773. In 1794 the tax on whiskey caused the famous Whiskey Rebellion by Pennsylvania farmers. The federal troops came in and controlled them, but when Thomas Jefferson took the office of President in 1801, he abolished the system and fired the four hundred revenue agents.

On July 1, 1862, Lincoln signed the Internal Revenue Service Act, creating the office of Commissioner of Internal Revenue to finance the Civil War. In 1872, with the war long over, and Congress finally ended the income tax.

During that taxing time, Mark Twain on March 19, 1870, published "A Mysterious Visit" in the *Buffalo Express*, satirizing his horror in dealing with an IRS agent. Twain wrote, "It was plain that the stranger had enabled me to make a goose of myself.... At the legal five percent, I must pay to the government the sum of Ten Thousand Six Hundred and Fifty Dollars income tax! (I remark, in this place, that I did not do it.)"

Twain continued, "I am acquainted with a very opulent man, whose house is a palace, whose table is regal, whose outlays are enormous, yet a man who has no income...to him I went for advice, in my distress...he took his pen, and presto! I was a pauper...."

While this was occurring, Twain's benefactor's son sneaked two dollars from his wallet and Twain remarks, "...I would wager anything that if my stranger were to call on that little boy tomorrow he would make a false return of his income."

Twain was telling us the income tax system encourages and nurtures dishonesty. In my travels, I have visited two tax havens, the Netherlands Antilles and the Cayman Islands, and the truth of this was confirmed. In the Antilles, they have a haven for foreigners but a high personal income tax for citizens who live there. The island also harbors gambling, widespread unemployment, drugs, and rampant crime. In the Cayman Islands, where the haven works both ways, and there is no personal income tax for its citizens, there is little or no gambling or prostitution, virtually no crime, and full employment.

The tax Twain complained about was brought back in 1894 only to be determined unconstitutional in 1895 by the United States Supreme Court (*Pollock Loan and Trust v. Farmers*, 158 U.S. 601). Throughout most of the history of the United States we have not been burdened by a tax on income, legal or illegal. As Americans we have always protested against taxes.

In 1913, the government decided again to tax income. Representative Cordell Hull's words in the April 26, 1913 Congressional Record reassured his nervous constituents. "Every good citizen should be willing to devote a brief time during some one day in the year, when necessary, to the making up of a listing of his income for taxes to contribute to this government, *not* the scriptural tithe, but a *smaller percentage of his net profits.*" Very few Americans would actually pay an income tax until it was significantly increased during World War II, ostensibly as a temporary victory tax, which has never left us. Our extremely high tax rate has only been around approximately fifty years, less than a fourth of the country's age.

The dreaded "scriptural tithe," which may have caused the civil war in Israel over 2000 years ago, was 10 percent, double the amount Twain railed about. No decent man or woman would steal that amount from any neighbor. This tax in 1913 was graduated up to a maximum of 7 percent. It barely passed.

George Bernard Shaw's oft-quoted comment in 1944 seems more honest, "A government which robs Peter to pay Paul can always depend on the support of Paul." No one ever put it better than Daniel Webster (speaking before the United States Supreme Court), whose words were lifted by Justice John Marshall in his decision *McCullock v. Maryland,* 17 U.S. 327(1819), "An unlimited power to tax involves, necessarily, a power to destroy."

Shaw's contemporary American tax was the temporary victory tax, passed under the authority of the Sixteenth Amendment, for the purpose of winning World War II. Unlike the Civil War tax, it never went away. It was rewritten and codified in 1954 and then it was changed with each new administration and made more confusing and complex.

United States v. Joseph Nunan (236 F.2d 576)

When looking through the IRS hall of shame, one is tempted to pull a picture out like the federales holding a gun on the little boy Elian Gonzalez. Although no violence occurred in Joseph Nunan's case, it perhaps more typically demonstrates the history of an IRS employee's character, the complexity of the code, and the politics involved.

Mr. Nunan was the collector of the IRS in Brooklyn, New York from 1941 to 1944 when he became commissioner of Internal Revenue in Washington, D.C., until June 30, 1947. During Nunan's "reign," cries of corruption in the IRS hit Washington and Nunan left suddenly during the end of Truman's first term. Some have argued that only Eisenhower's administration in 1952 was interested in prosecuting Nunan for income tax evasion in 1954. The trial transcript, however, disagrees. Nunan *pled the Fifth Amendment* and did not take the stand, but testimony as far back as September 12, 1951, while Truman was still president, was elicited. The indictment was made February 18, 1952. It was Democrat Truman against Democrat Nunan. Pre-trial work got Nunan a two-year reprieve, and the Eisenhower administration took over and secured five convictions for income tax evasion.

Nunan had large sums of cash, in excess of $170,000, without adequate explanation. Essentially, revenue agents found $160,000 in excess of what he should have if he saved all his income. Nunan conceded he may have underreported but he had a good defense. *He denied that he was a tax expert*, said he became commissioner through politics, and never really understood the code.

Bear in mind, the code the commissioner did not understand in 1950 was the less complex Code of 1936. Not the tough one in 1954 during his trial, or the nonsense we are supposed to understand today. The court instructed the jury not to focus on the fact of a lot of cash. An instruction they no doubt ignored. Was Nunan innocent?

My guess is that Nunan didn't think so, Eisenhower didn't care, and the public was angry over the outrages. If Truman had run and beaten Eisenhower (highly unlikely) would Nunan have been prosecuted in 1954? He probably would have. Out with the old (Nunan), in with the new, the 1954 code. What is surprising is how little anyone in 2001 cares that the commissioner of Internal Revenue in 1947 said the code didn't make any sense—right up until 1954 when he went to jail.

The purpose of the Internal Revenue Code is to tax work. As Shaw said, Paul wants to tax Peter, thus, politicians try to tax the other guy's constituents. The genius of stealing the labor of a man or woman's work is that *workers* produce the most wealth. By getting it before it leaves its source, Americans could be taxed at higher effective rates than the Romans, Israelis, or Egyptians. By having the most confusing tax code in the history of the world our politicians could guarantee more arguments and puzzlement than the tower of Babel.

The Book

Every other year a new IRS book comes out by an "expert," a journalist, or a former commissioner. These writers talk about "stories I've heard," "stories without real names," or worse, act as apologists for the IRS.

A *Money Magazine* writer joined me and an accountant for a show about taxes on the *Geraldo* TV show in 1993 and told America, "With that many people and that much responsibility, there are bound to be mistakes." She implied that IRS mistakes were honest and forgivable. I disagreed with her.

The "mistakes" include: an IRS raid on a day care center where children were held hostage for money; a two-year old who got to see her mom and grandma sprayed by lethal combat mace because IRS agents were trying to collect money; and a false-evidence scam to indict a businessman the IRS knew was innocent. They also indicted another man who saw commercials the IRS ran telling people who had not filed, "Come in and file and get amnesty." This man came in, filed, and got indicted. After the *Geraldo* show, *by pure coincidence*, the IRS audited Geraldo Rivera.

I am no apologist for the IRS. I am not neutral. I am not a journalist or a tax preparation attorney, sitting on the side watching, crunching numbers, or intellectually philosophizing economic possibilities. I am a veteran of courtroom wars against the IRS.

The IRS and their "HAL" computer are out of control, and we

need to pull the plug. Taxing *work* is a concept straight out of Karl Marx, and it is an unnecessary evil. Tax alcohol, cigarettes, and prostitution and you will see less of it. If you tax work, call it a four-letter word and a disease (workaholic), and teach Americans to covet and not to earn, you'll see less work.

Every year the IRS puts people on trial, vilifies them in a circus-like atmosphere and keeps the entertainment going on long enough to pick the crowd's pockets. These show trials are staged every year right around April 15 just to put the fear of the government into the people so that they will comply with the "voluntary tax." Just remember, as Will Durant observed about Rome, while the show is going on, no one will be willing to keep the coliseum in repair, no one will go into the jungle searching for the lions to fight the gladiators, except slaves, and soon there will be an unavoidable decline. Then there will be no gladiators.

IRS agents lie, commit crimes, and destroy families. That's the story in this book. Since most of the stories in this book are about surviving the IRS, there are a lot of hard-earned tips in here, too. All of the stories are real. Nevertheless, no one wins them all. So unlike stories where the hero always wins, you'll read when I got my butt and my client's butt kicked too! You are getting the stories directly from the trial lawyer who handled them. None are second hand. I've *seen with my own eyes* the blood, the privacy invasions (like seventy-year-old Mrs. Buford's pictures in her pajamas taken through an IRS pervert's spy lenses), the cruel brutality, the injustices, and *heard with my own ears* the bald-face lies of IRS agents under oath. I've seen dreams, families, and retirement plans pulverized into dust while sadistic IRS agents laughed about it.

If you want to read a book about how our dedicated public servants run the world's best tax system of voluntary compliance—*don't buy this book*. The whole concept is political malarkey. The people who call this a voluntary system are scam artists who belong in jail. Many of them work for the government.

When I began my law practice, I never had any intention of handling tax cases. Through a series of incidents, I ended up defending Norma Ginter for the capital murder of Sheriff Gene Matthews in Arkansas while he was supposedly trying to capture the alleged tax protestor, Gordon Wendal Kahl.

Kahl was convicted for not filing tax returns. Afterward, he was in a shoot-out where two U.S. marshals died in North Dakota and Kahl's son was wounded. He drove his injured son to the hospital and then left the state. The authorities said he killed both marshals. Actually it is more likely he killed one. Scared poorly trained government agents probably killed the other accidentally.

In 1983 he was found in the Ginter home in Lawrence, Arkansas and *murdered*. He had been living for four months with Arthur Russel and his daughter Karen Russel and her two children. Karen turned him and her father in for a $25,000 reward paid to her by Special Agent Knox (code name: Fort Knox). A *New York Times* reporter discovered Kahl's severed foot. Arms, head, and feet had been cut off the burned body. Sheriff Matthews, joining the federal effort to capture Kahl, was also shot. (I believe by friendly fire, but that's another story. A book and a movie blamed Kahl for Matthew's shooting, even though Kahl was already dead at the time of the incident.)

Sheriff Matthew's wounded body was delivered to a hospital where the surgeon (whose wife Matthews was allegedly involved with) failed to revive him. The death report says he was dead on arrival—perhaps so.

Norma Ginter was charged with Matthew's murder. She was offered a plea bargain for life imprisonment to avoid the possibility of the death penalty, but she refused it. I defended her and she was acquitted. Rather than brilliant legal work, it was persistence that prevailed. She was innocent. Before the trial, she spent a year in jail. Judge Andrew Ponder ruled that this innocent housewife, who had never before received so much as a traffic ticket, was too dangerous to walk the streets. Since her acquittal in 1984, she still hasn't gotten any tickets. Apparently, Ponder was wrong. The voters tossed him out of office. Her home, however, was burned to the ground. It seems that a police officer, Tom Lee, sitting on the top of her roof, poured kerosene down the vents.

The Gordon Kahl-Norma Ginter incident was the first in a series of modern federal actions like Waco and Ruby Ridge where people *died*. In 1983, however, the media was completely on the government's side. Norma Ginter was portrayed as a dangerous gun-toting nut, when, in fact, she did not even own a gun. (Her husband did own a .22 rifle, which was, of course, confiscated.) It was after this incident that I began helping people with IRS problems.

In 1991, I was featured in the then chief Houston magazine, *Houston Metropolitan*. They were intrigued by my maverick stand against the IRS and proclaimed in bold print, "Minns Advocates the Abolition of the IRS." It was considered radical in 1991—a cause I had espoused for twenty years. It was still a radical thought in early 1994, when I met with a group of airline pilots in Washington, D.C., before a committee under the supervision of Congressman Bill Archer, to express our dissatisfaction with the IRS.

The committee told us everything would be on the table if the Republicans took Congress. I was forty-three-years old at the time and in my lifetime I had seen a unicorn (which turned out not to be real) and a two-year Republican Senate, but no Republican Congress. All I could say was "sure." I didn't believe it would happen. Recent history has proven me wrong, as the last decade has proven Ponder wrong.

Today the abolition of the IRS is mainstream conversation. In 1976 Congressman Ron Paul voted against the IRS. His was the lone vote. Today, back in Congress, he won't vote alone and there will be some Democrats also voting against the IRS. Will they succeed? Frankly, I don't know, but I'm skeptical.

I am a trial lawyer, but frankly, I couldn't personally represent a mass murderer, child abuser, drug dealer, or a divorce lawyer. I wouldn't feel comfortable getting them off. To do my best, I have to like my clients and want to win for them. For that reason, I am not a trial lawyer in the classic tradition. I am glad there are others to carry that necessary banner.

While I believe everyone is technically innocent under our bizarre tax laws, since no one understands them, I really don't care. Guilt or innocence is irrelevant. I'd like everyone accused of tax crimes to be found not guilty. I want the heinous laws forcing us to keep burdensome records repealed. I want jurors to free people from tax burdens like they freed slaves and abolitionists during the era of slavery.

For my part, I'll try to keep people out of jail, support political office holders who are enemies of the IRS, and be available for public debate. It is a major uphill battle. Most of the people, who know the system best, profit from it either by having power, a job, or an income stream. Most support taxing income, not because it's a good thing for America, but because they profit from the evil. If a doctor can pray for an end to cancer, a tax preparer should be able to condemn the IRS, but I wouldn't wait for H & R Block to campaign against the income tax. That's a large part of the problem. We'd have some temporary unemployment of tax professionals, but we don't have horse-manure removal experts in metropolitan areas anymore, and the last coal scuttler has left the railroads. We'd adjust to a world without IRS agents very quickly. A switch to a less intrusive tax, like a sales tax or value-added tax, would be a far better choice.

There is *nothing* of value in our present system of taxation, *nothing* worth saving, and *nothing* to admire—only a code to be ashamed of.

In this book, as we talk about the new and improved IRS for 2001 and investigations of corruption, let's not forget Commissioner Nunan and the fact that the investigations have been going on as long as the IRS has existed and the problems *still* exist. The solution is not to fix the beast. The solution is to *execute it.*

Introduction
Understanding the IRS Code

So that there isn't any confusion in the reader's mind from the outset of this book, if you earned $7,200 as an employee in the year 2000 as a single individual, or $500 through self employment you are *required* to file a tax return. There are five different types of people who are charged with tax crimes in the United States.

First are people who don't file. They may believe they don't have to file. They may want to play ostrich and not pay taxes in hopes that no one notices. They may just forget to file. They may not have the money to pay and hope to catch up by not filing. They may not be able to figure out the complex return and don't have the money to hire someone else to do it. They may deliberately not file as part of a political protest against any number of government policies or actions.

Second are people who file forms that don't fit the rules. Examples are returns with all zeros or returns that claim the protection of the Fifth Amendment (sometimes even for the name). Another example of this is simply using the wrong form.

Third are people who make honest mistakes and file returns that violate rules for themselves or others. They often rely on professional advisors who made honest mistakes or who intentionally sold them bad advice.

1

Fourth are people who make dishonest entries to hide or falsify deductions for themselves or others.

The fifth group consists of people who do everything right but the IRS mistakenly believes the taxpayer did something wrong and persists in prosecuting them mercilessly.

From the first and second groups, every year con artists dupe thousands into not filing and sell people kits on how to avoid paying taxes. The con artists usually escape with the victims' cash into the night, and, occasionally, the victim who listens to them goes to jail. As regular as flowers that bloom in the spring each year, a new theory or two blossoms forth as to why you do not have to file and pay income taxes. In the early 1990s, one that got considerable attention was "The Pilot Connection." For several thousand dollars, the promoters guaranteed they would take you out of the system so that you would never have to file again. People all over the country called us to ask how these guys could get away with it if it was not legal. The leaders appeared on the talk show circuits like *20/20*, expounded their theories to America, and signed up a lot of people. The questions remained. In 1993 a number of the program's founders were indicted. They were tried in San Francisco. The jury could not reach a decision, so they were re-tried and *convicted*. Do not worry. There will soon be replacements to sell "snake oil" cures for the IRS.

Lest you be tempted to purchase some "snake oil," be aware of this: while the requirements to file a tax return vary from year to year (essentially, if you earn $7,200 in a calendar year as an employee, or $500 through self-employment) you are *required* to file a 1040 form of some type. If you do not, and if you know you are supposed to file, you are guilty of a violation of 26 U.S.C. 7203, a misdemeanor. For *each* unfiled year you can be *fined $25,000 and sentenced to one year in jail*. If the government alleges that in addition to willfully failing to file, you have committed an overt act motivated by an intent to conceal the income you did not report, the charge against you can be boosted to a *felony: income tax evasion*, 26 U.S.C. 7201.

An overt act can be something as simple as checking the box marked exempt on your W-4 form if you are not exempt, or as complex as setting up a lot of trusts to funnel secret money through. Often, the only difference between someone charged with a misdemeanor or a felony is the attitude of the IRS special agent or his understanding (or lack thereof) of the criminal law. *The government convicts 95 percent of the people who are charged with the crime of failure to file.* Only the best cases (from the government's viewpoint) are brought to trial. The only other crime with a higher conviction rate is mass murder. *Everyone* who has ever been charged with mass murder has been convicted.

If you *understand the law* and *intentionally put the wrong numbers on your form*, or *don't even file a tax return—you have committed a crime*. If you do not understand the law and violate it by accident, you have not committed a crime. Nevertheless, even if criminal intent is disproved, you are liable on civil charges and must *still pay taxes, interest, and penalties*.

The third group of tax violators are those who misinterpret the tax code. How can that be? Isn't the law written down clearly? When you start to read it and try to analyze the tax code you find out that no one understands it—*no one*. Former Chief Justice Richard Neeley of the West Virginia Supreme Court said it very well when he honestly shared with us, "The Internal Revenue Service lawyers responsible...confessed...they did not understand the Tax Reform Act ... they opined that the Congress, which wrote it, did not understand it ...the court would make it up as they went along and pretend to understand it." (Neeley, Richard, *How Courts Govern America*. Yale University Press, 1981, p. 25.)

One root cause of the confusion is the fact that politicians, who steal from us to give themselves lifetime positions, larger-than-life pension funds, and the legendary, supposedly non-existent "free lunch," wrote this complex code. If professional writers or English teachers wrote the code, and if politicians were prevented from mis-

3

using words, fewer people would get into trouble. One of the most pernicious lies is that the Internal Revenue system is based on "voluntary compliance." It was probably intended to sugarcoat the bitter medicine of taxation because we were "volunteering" to calculate the dose ourselves. It's true there is no such thing as a "free lunch." In reality, people are forced into picking up the bill by trickery and bullying. You can find tons of government printed literature and propaganda describing our wonderful "voluntary" tax system. Often someone, who misunderstands official government literature that uses the terms "voluntary compliance," can wind up in a great deal of trouble. *Compliance with the tax code is no more voluntary than is secondhand smoke in a small room.*

We volunteer as a nation to give billions of dollars and work hours to charitable organizations; we volunteer to put our kids through school and to feed them. Very few volunteer to pay taxes. We pay because we follow a law that we almost universally dislike. Every president elected in my lifetime got elected in part by complaining and protesting that the tax system was unfair and he would fix it. Only two presidents in my lifetime actually "fixed" part of it by making significant tax reductions: Kennedy (whose proposals passed after his death) and Reagan. Each reduction was followed by a massive upsurge in the economy.

Contrary to the assumptions of some denizens of Washington, D.C., we are not stupid. When they tax alcohol, we reduce consumption of it. If they raise the taxes on cigarettes, our smokers cut down. If Nevada taxes prostitution, it declines. By the same token, if work is taxed, we get the message and cut down on work. If the tax on work is reduced, we work more.

It is very easy for an intelligent person to figure out that taxing work is immoral and that the dumbest guy on the planet often spends his own money more intelligently than the best so-called public servants. At the very least, the average person on the street spends money on items he wants to spend it on, as opposed to watching the

4

government indiscriminately fritter money away on outrageously wasteful projects no one really wants—not even the government. It's a big leap, though, to go from cherishing these widely held opinions to making the momentous decision of letting April 15 come and go without filing an income tax return.

It's a decision no ethical lawyer or CPA would counsel a client to take because it is a blueprint for personal punishment. If you don't file and are charged with a crime and are very fortunate to win a not guilty verdict, *then you may still be attacked civilly.* Civilly, there is no state-of-mind defense to not filing a return. That means that if you are required to file and you do not, you lose when you get to tax court, which determines how much you will have to pay in taxes, interest, and penalties. You do not get a jury, and the judge will probably rule against you before trial. It's a waste of time and money to proceed in tax court if you have not filed a return at all.

How Did This All Start? Or, More Spurious Reasons Not to File

Where do people get the idea that they do not have to file a tax return or have to pay income taxes? Generally it starts with the Sixteenth Amendment to the Constitution and then goes in ever more bizarre directions from there. The Sixteenth Amendment, passed in 1913, allows income to be taxed. There are those who assert that the amendment was not properly passed. The most believable exposition of this theory was written by Bill Benson and Red Beckman, entitled *The Law That Never Was.* Benson, a former state tax collector, became convinced by his own research that he was not required to file a tax return.

Benson and Beckman discovered that there were substantial irregularities in the ratification process of the Sixteenth Amendment. Some of the states counted as having endorsed the prospective amendment had not really done so, or had voted on a slightly different version. According to Benson, since the amendment was not prop-

5

erly enacted into law, in effect it "never was." Well-researched and documented, Benson's book was quite popular as a source of reliance for many people who claimed it as their reason for not filing tax returns. Federal courts did not share Benson's fans enthusiasm. *No court reviewed the actual evidence produced by Benson.* Unfortunately, we do not have the legal right to second-guess the courts except by appealing their decisions. The Supreme Court has *never* overturned the affirmations handed down by various circuit courts of appeals, upholding convictions of defendants whose reason for failing to file was based on their belief that the Sixteenth Amendment is not law.

Do the federal trial and appellate courts make mistakes? Yes and no. If they do something obviously wrong, it may be a mistake, as the word is literally understood, but whatever ruling the Supreme Court makes is the last word on the subject until the justices change their minds. Logically, we do not have much of a choice other than reliance on the finality of the rulings of our appellate courts. If every one of our more than 250 million citizens made his own independent decision on what the law was and felt free to ignore the courts, we would have anarchy. So, right or wrong, the court has made its ruling, and the Benson argument is "wrong." If I were on the court, I would have been convinced that the Sixteenth Amendment was not law, but I wasn't, and Benson, honest as I believe he is, *served time in a federal penitentiary.* Lawyers who advise people, for money, that they don't have to file a tax return are stealing from their clients.

Compared to some of the theories that other non-filers espouse, Benson looks positively mainstream. There are those who argue that the presence of a flag with gold fringes around the edges invalidates the jurisdiction of a courtroom, because that flag indicates that "maritime law" is in force. Proponents of these various theories cling to them fiercely, and declare that the defendant or his lawyers just did not know how to plead the issues properly. Whenever someone pronounces the "magic words" just right, the judge will be "compelled" to let him go.

Some say that having a social security number places a citizen on a contract basis with the government. They say that anyone can opt out by simply notifying the government that he has been deceived in the past, and he is now rescinding his social security number! Others allege that money not backed by gold is not legal tender and therefore money earned in Federal Reserve Notes does not give rise to a taxable debt. An old favorite argument is that wages are not income, because income means profit, not an even exchange. No employer would pay an employee more than he is worth. Therefore, what is commonly known as employment constitutes an even trade of labor for money. This is not a taxable exchange, and therefore no return is required. *Warning: Some of these theories sound attractive, but believing them can be hazardous to your liberty!* I am merely parroting numerous failed theories so you can get an idea what's going on. *None of them work. The courts have rejected all of them!*

The tax, allowed by the Sixteenth Amendment, had to be created by a statute. The politicians obliged immediately, creating the first post-Sixteenth Amendment statute in 1913. It affected very few people, i.e., only those people in high-income brackets were taxed. The income tax, as we know it today, began as a so-called "Victory Tax" to help finance the war effort during World War II. It was unpatriotic not to be part of the system. The use of the term "voluntary" to describe mandatory filing requirements crept into the language of American taxation. Another widespread myth is the "government need" argument, which most of us have bought these last fifty years, that the government has always needed and gotten an income tax and we all have to pay our fair share. The government relies on this "voluntary" effort to meet the "need" as a placebo to keep the populace from getting angry. The fact is that income taxation is a very poor method of raising money compared to other methods. The gasoline tax, the cigarette tax, and excise taxes all raise lots of money, but don't force us to do slave labor keeping records for the benefit of government snoops. What is our fair share of costs incurred by the most wasteful government we can imagine? As much as they can take.

Most of us just accept certain things as facts, such as, "The government can not get by without an income tax." These persons ignore American history that, following the tax rebellion at the Boston Tea Party, had nearly two hundred years of prosperity without an income tax!

Most of us just accept as a matter of faith that we are legally required to file tax returns, because we have a nationally recognized tribute day when we formally make a sacrifice, April 15. The Mayans had days when they sacrificed virgins to the gods, and because of their tradition, they knew they were supposed to keep doing it. Both cultures required conformity or exacted punishment for disobedience.

Criminal versus Civil Charges

When someone who is required to file an income tax return does not do so, is he guilty or not guilty of a crime? The key distinction is found in the defendant's state of mind. Is the accused honestly trying to follow the law, or not? There were two theories as to how much evidence you needed to show your mistakes were not willful.

One was that the evidence had to be objectively reasonable. If your excuse was not reasonable, then you were guilty even if you really thought you were doing what the law required. That's a tough two-pronged test. First you had to convince the judge. He had to let the jury decide because in the United States, without a plea of "guilty," no judge can order a defendant convicted, but he could tell the jury, "You may not consider the defendant's claim that he deducted his poodle as a guard dog as a defense. The court instructs you that is not objectively reasonable."

Now you may be saying, "So what? I do not think that is reasonable." If you are on the jury you can say, "I don't think that is reasonable and therefore I don't believe it. I think the defendant intended to commit a crime." The problem comes when the judge makes the decision for you or even changes the rule a little. You might say, "Hey,

I think he actually believes he can deduct the poodle but I don't care—that's not reasonable. I will convict him."

The other standard for instructions was subjective. No matter how unreasonable the reason for believing that the claim was legal, if the defendant sincerely believed it, that was a defense. The trouble was that different courts had different instructions and some demanded an objective test while others a subjective test. Several court decisions have clarified some areas of the "state of mind" defense.

U.S. v. Cheek

In *U.S. v. Cheek*, Cheek was a pilot who thought he was not required to file his returns, so he did not do so. He had a jury trial and was convicted. Then he appealed to the Court of Appeals in Chicago (Seventh Circuit) claiming that the instructions of the trial court, that his opinion had to be objectively reasonable, were unreasonable. The Seventh Circuit disagreed with him and he went up to the U.S. Supreme Court, which said the standard must be subjective and that Cheek must get a new trial with different instructions. A long story follows, which will not fit into this book.

U.S. v. Powell

While Cheek was on appeal, two other cases went to trial and resulted in convictions. One was Dixie Lee Powell, a sixty-year-old retired Mormon school teacher from Tucson, Arizona. Each and every year the IRS would completely disallow Dixie's returns. Each year she would be audited and her deductions disallowed. Finally in desperation she began to do her own research. She found a statute, 6020b (which has since been repealed), which said, "If any person fails to make any return required by any internal revenue law or regulation the Secretary shall make such return from his knowledge and from such information as he can obtain." Consequently, she wrote the IRS and asked them to prepare her returns for her under the statute. She would no longer do so since she had the right to let the IRS do it for her. The problem was that the courts have said that with regard to 6020b "shall" means "may." The IRS ignored her letter and charged her and her husband with failure to file.

Mrs. Powell represented herself at trial and her husband Roy followed. Roy, a seventy-year-old triple bypass survivor, said at trial, "Whatever Dixie says, that's fine with me. After fifty years of marriage I can't go against her." Roy had no idea whether or not they had filed. Dixie had done all their financial planning and tax preparation for years. The judge gave the jury instructions on "objective intent." Dixie wanted to show the jury the statue upon which she had relied. The judge said no. The jury asked to see a copy of the statute and the judge told them that it did not say what Dixie said it said. The judge was wrong. The jury returned a verdict of guilty and both Mr. and Mrs. Powell were sentenced to time in a Federal prison.

They were allowed out pending appeal. Mrs. Powell continued to do research and found the published case *U.S. v. Buford*, (see chapter 5), which had my name in it and she called me. She was interested in the IMF (Individual Master File) because she wanted to know what had caused her to be the subject of intense observation by the IRS. In a computer in Martinsburg, West Virginia, every American citizen or legal immigrant is listed under his social security number in an Individual Master File, which contains a lot of private information. (For more information, read the chapter on the Bufords. Also see *U.S. v. Buford*, 889 F.2d 1406, and *U.S. v. Powell*, 995 F2d 1206.)

She read *Buford*, learned of the IMF, pulled her IMF, and discovered she was cross-referenced with an accused drug dealer who did not pay her taxes on the illegal drugs. Dixie's name was the same as a suspected drug dealer in Phoenix, Arizona. To this day the IRS claims it did not mix these two women up, but Mrs. Powell's IMF shows that it did. Because the IRS agents confused her with the other woman, they disallowed all of Dixie's deductions, including her eleven children and her farm with her husband Roy.

She called me to handle her appeal. I did. I was very impressed with the way Mrs. Powell had protected the record, making all of the necessary objections at the trial. You can generally only appeal on things offered or kept out and objected to at trial. Lots of pretty good trial lawyers are nevertheless bad appellate lawyers and do not set up things for appeal. In a tax case that is pretty important since there is a very good chance of a conviction no matter who is trying the case or what the facts are.

The Ninth Circuit Court of Appeals handed down an opinion reversing the conviction, ordering a new trial, and ordering the court to allow Dixie to read 6020b to the jury and to give subjective instructions to the jury instead of objective. Shortly thereafter the IRS office sent out interoffice memos saying that this case only affected the Ninth Circuit and that even there, it was not the law and that it would be reversed soon. In fact, a new *Powell* case was rendered, slightly changing the holding of the court, but that's another story unrelated to this effort.

U.S. v. Willie

The third key contemporaneous willful case was the *Willie* case in the Tenth Circuit out of Denver. It was handed down within days of the *Powell* case. In fact, the government offered it to the panel in Powell to get them to change their mind, but it failed to offer *Powell* to the *Willie* panel. Willie was an American Indian who did not file. He had a treaty with the U.S. government saying that his tribe was exempt from income taxes. At trial he offered the treaty to the jury to prove what he had relied on. The judge said no. Willie could testify about the treaty but the jury would have to rely on his word. They could not see the treaty. The jury convicted Willie and he went to jail. I would have loved to argue the Willie case on appeal. Nevertheless, that is the law in the Tenth Circuit.

Whenever I have been faced with a fight between using the arguments of *Willie* and *Powell*, I have successfully persuaded the court

11

to go with *Powell*. *Willie* is not only another of our country's sell-outs of Native Americans and the violation of another treaty, it is also a sell-out of our basic right to face a jury with the taxpayer's side of the story. So far *Powell* has won over *Willie* in every jurisdiction that I am aware of except, of course, the Tenth Circuit.

Why Big Brother Wins and You Lose

One of the reasons for the unusually high conviction rate of income "tax offenders" is the fact that most people accused of tax crimes *plead guilty*. In order to convict a defendant of the crime of willful failure to file (the easiest conviction for the government to win), the government must prove three elements:

1. The duty to file: The government must prove that the defendant had the threshold level of income to be required to file a tax return. This can be proven through the introduction of W-2 forms or 1099 forms, the reconstruction of income through bank records, and the testimony of individuals.

2. Non-filing: The government must prove that the required tax return was not filed. Normally, the government has an IRS employee make a diligent search of the computer records and come up with a document that certifies that no return was found for that particular year.

3. Willfulness: Willfulness is defined as ... a voluntary intentional violation of a known legal duty ... and not because of mistake, accident, or other innocent reason or motive. In other words, if you know you are supposed to file and you do not file; then you are guilty. The government often uses a defendant's previous tax returns to show that the defendant was aware that he had a duty to file.

What criteria does the IRS use for selecting its lucky three thousand candidates for criminal prosecution each year? There are no absolute formulas, but certain generalizations can be made. The IRS wants to make an example out of public figures, and they want guaranteed convictions. They want to appear invincible. They are also rather lazy and would rather have a case handed to them on a silver platter than have to work hard to prove it. That is why *vocal opponents* of the IRS are more vulnerable than hidden ones.

The easiest target in the world is the so-called tax protester, who identifies himself by writing letters to the government espousing any or all of the unusual theories discussed in this chapter. That is just like taping a "kick me" sign on your posterior. These people, often filers in the past, are on the national computer. The IRS keeps dossiers on all of these people for future possible criminal selection or civil audit. On the other hand, someone who has been out of the system for so long that his social security number may never have been entered in the IRS computers is unlikely to be selected for prosecution because the IRS may not know he exists. (Less than a decade ago IRS did not have the capacity to link up 1099s and W-2/W-4s with social security numbers. Certainly someday soon most of the people still outside the system will be traceable on IRS computers.) Someone who works for cash and never gets a 1099 or a W-2 form, especially if he moves frequently, is difficult to find and difficult to trap. A lot of the snake-oil no-tax salesmen fit this category. Unfortunately, their customers are likely to be easy pickings for the IRS.

Sometimes a criminal indictment comes like a bolt from the blue, but generally a target is notified in many ways, sometimes subtle, sometimes not so subtle. The usual procedure, when the IRS says you owe them money, is that they send you what is called a thirty-day letter. You have thirty days to disagree in writing. You can argue for a while and compromise, but ultimately if there is an unreasoning government bureaucrat on the other end, you may lose all administrative arguments and the IRS gives you its final decision. That final decision is called a ninety-day letter.

If you have received the ninety-day letter, you have three options. One, you can agree to pay the tax, and then pay it. Two, you can do nothing. In that case, in ninety days, the letter becomes a final, unappealable judgment and you owe the money. Three, you can file a petition in tax court. Then you get another chance at the appeals level where you can enter into more negotiations or offer a compromise. Today, thanks to the 1986 Taxpayer's Bill of Rights, along with the ninety-day letter, the IRS must send you information telling you how serious this letter is. Often in the past, people did not understand it, waited too long and had huge judgments assessed against them that they may not have owed. Even now lots of people fail to read all the small print. Generally, people who receive thirty-day letters settle up with the IRS and are not criminally indicted. The IRS can, however, at any time, bring forth a criminal indictment. If they feel that they can convict you of the crime of tax evasion, there will be no thirty-day letter.

This is where some of the not-so-subtle ways the IRS notifies the taxpayer come into play. There might be the armed special agents knocking at the door reading him his rights. The owner of a house-cleaning service might find that an IRS special agent, demanding copies of checks or records of cash payments made to the business, has contacted her customers. An undercover agent, pretending to be a customer who wants financial privacy, might visit a coin dealer.

The IRS also often cracks down on organizations promoting tax shelters, both legal and illegal, and then raids their main offices, seizing customer lists. Then, at their leisure, like Roman emperors reclining on couches and idly plucking grapes, the special agents can select some hapless soul to undergo criminal investigation or audit.

There are two reasons why membership lists of tax shelter investment groups or organizations that advocate tax protest are prized. First, these lists offer ripe easy targets. Second, destroying, impoverishing, or just chasing away the clients of someone they want to take down is an effective way to hurt the major target economically.

Often they will also seize the assets of someone they suspect of wrongdoing in advance to prevent him from using the assets to hire competent private counsel. Many wealthy people are reduced to using public defenders because their assets are seized pending further study, which sometimes never takes place.

Suppose the IRS has narrowed down its potential targets in an area to ten people. One of the ten has "poster" potential. Every other year or so, the IRS will select a high profile individual to be its "poster child." This person's job is to be crucified and vilified publicly, just to put the fear of the IRS into the rest of us. It may be a civil prosecution or a criminal prosecution or sometimes both. The poster child must lose in court or graciously submit to a plea. Past poster candidates have been Leona Helmsley, Willie Nelson, Daryl Strawberry, and Joe Louis, who all either capitulated or did some jail time. IRS public relations plans cases to be tried, convicted, and sentenced by April of that year, just in time for the annual tax season publicity campaign brought to us by our government to scare us to death into what the IRS likes to call "voluntary compliance." The "poster child," if he cannot pull strings and get out of it altogether, and if there is a good case, is definitely going to be indicted.

The next case may be questionable. He may not even be guilty, but he can be shaken down to plead guilty to save his wife, friend, or other loved one from indictment. Sometimes this poor soul will plead guilty merely for vague suggestions of leniency, which seem good against an invincible enemy.

That leaves eight second-tier targets. One of them will be charged. The reasons for indictment vary: perhaps the target filed five years ago, then stopped, and signed up with a group that advocated non-filing because the Trilateral Commission was assaulting the national integrity of the United States; perhaps the target sent in strange letters to the IRS threatening not to file ever again; perhaps the target makes an above average living, or better yet, is a wealthy person or a small business owner of whom the jurors may be induced to be jealous; these are all reasons for becoming a target of the IRS.

These guys are easy to convict. Sometimes they are victims of con artists. Sometimes they are a little greedy, looking desperately for an answer that ordinarily would not make sense. Often they are people who had a run of bad luck and got behind on their taxes for any one

15

of a myriad of reasons: an illness, a bad year without enough money to cover the taxes, or an accidental overlooking of a neglected return that everyone thought had been filed. People are so intimidated by the IRS that they often incorrectly assume that if they get outside of the system due to no intentional fault of their own, they are still at fault and are perpetual criminals.

There are a number of ways to handle the defense of this type of case. One is taking the posture that the law is wrong, the judge is wrong, and the defendant should walk because he alone is right. This is, in fact, the most *common* defense to a failure to file charge, and it is *universally unsuccessful*. Sometimes a lawyer handles it, but most lawyers who assert these types of defenses have been *disbarred*. Often, individuals raise their various theories on why they do not have to file. Even if they do a very good job of arguing their case, they still can not get their evidence in (like the *Willie* case) and/or figure out how to instruct the jury or get the judge to do so. They get convicted, go to jail, and contribute to the invincible posture of the IRS.

That's where people like me come in. I am an advocate defending families and people the IRS has tried to destroy. I am a veteran of courtroom wars. Frequently, judges are extremely vindictive to the lawyers who defend these guys. Obviously I'm prejudiced, but I think, that in a country where everyone is guaranteed a lawyer (perhaps not a competent one, but a lawyer nonetheless), the person who takes the job should not be attacked for taking the job. If there are those of us who have represented people accused of making mistakes on their returns (or even failure to file a return), we certainly should be given at least as much courtesy as the person who upholds the constitutional rights of people accused of murder or child abuse. It isn't an easy job, but somebody has to do it.

Score Card

By the way, this isn't Perry Mason. This is real life. Of the criminal tax cases discussed in this book, indicted clients faced a total of approximately 211.5 years in prison. Of that, they were sentenced to a total of 3 years.

Total charges	51
Acquittals or dismissals	46
Pleas	1
Convictions	2
Total appeals	5
Wins on appeal	4
Losses on appeal	1

That's the record on the cases discussed at length in this book. While you read, try to think about who went to jail and who stayed out. It will help you get the feel of this work. These criminal cases combined with the two civil cases should give you a good survey about how tax court works.

The most difficult decision about the book was leaving stories out. Despite the fact that all the stories are very important, you won't read about Sammy Lott, the quadriplegic whose wheelchair the IRS stalked, but you should get a stomach-full, anyway.

Chapter I
Hobbled in Boston:
The Commonwealth v.
Linda and Cheri Hobbs

"Men stumble over the truth from time to time, but most pick themselves up and hurry off as if nothing happened."

—Winston Churchill

BOSTON TRIAL — OCTOBER 1993

Jim Hobbs was no saint. He was a veteran of the Vietnam war and a recipient of a couple of air medals for combat (which he describes as no big deal). Jim got shot at many times but was never hit (which he describes as lucky). When Jim came back to the United States, he became a war protester of a different stripe. Lots of war protesters did time in jail. Jim was one of them. Vietnam had made an angry young man, an angry older man, and Jim would never stop protesting again.

He was thin, lanky, with brown hair draped over his forehead, and bore the self-righteous conflict of someone who came from a matriarchal home (his dad had died when he was nine) with no help and no money. Jim cut a macho-like liberal figure, and women came easily to him. At twenty-five, Jim met the love of his life, Linda, who went by the nickname "Cookie." She was a short, feisty, brown-eyed, full-figured beauty with black hair and a voice as loud and filled with protest and argument as Jim's. They were a match, made not in heaven or hell, but in the realities of the hard life each had independently known, now seeking love and commitment in a world that had let both of them down.

It was a passionate match, one destined to lead to lots of fights and lots of physical appetite. Cookie had two kids (Cheri and Howie) by a former husband, no child support, and both of her parents were deceased. When Cheri was seven, she asked Jim to adopt her. He told her she was too young to make the decision, but that if she felt the same when she was twelve, he'd do it. On December 9, 1981, she felt the same, and the man who had raised her and been her dad for eight years adopted her and her younger brother. The marriage of Cookie and Jim added two boys to the family: Jim Jr. in 1976, and Kevin in 1978.

Of the group, Cheri had inherited her mom's passion and height. Cheri weighed in at less than a hundred pounds ten years later and would soar up in height to all of five-foot three, an inch taller than her mom. She was pretty and vivacious, with jet-black hair and mysterious brown eyes, the best features of her mom. In 1990, those gifts of beauty and independence led to a child.

As pretty as Grandma Cookie and mom were, baby Angela had even bigger brown eyes and an angelic round face that prophesied lots of exciting moments with the feisty spirit of her mom and grandma. The eyes sparkled with a mixture of innocence, mischief and fun. The baby was the crown of the Hobbs family's new good fortune; they had gone from nothing to middle class. At the time this story started for me, the two boys, Jim Jr., 17, and Kevin, 14, were both in high school. Their older brother was at the University of Massachusetts, and their sister Cheri was a waitress, supporting Angela, depending on her parents for baby sitting and diapers.

Jim Hobbs was nothing if not independent. While he had stayed away from active protest and jail for the nearly two decades of his monogamous marriage, he couldn't work in a nine-to-five job.

He worked as an independent trucker, the modern version of the cowboy. Truckers make more than average bucks when work is good, go hungry when times are tough, and run their own business, keeping their truck up and their union dues paid. They are on the road long hours and cross the country night and day. They also have frequent drug checks. Contrary to popular misguided opinion, random and two-year checks make most drivers of the big rigs pretty safe and usually drug free.

One of the times that the old Hobbs temper flared up was when his daughter came home from eighth grade and told him a teacher had told the class that truck drivers all run around on their wives and take drugs. Our temperamental vet went to the school venting his considerable anger and received an apology and a retraction.

One event occurred with Jim and the law during this period. Cheri's boyfriend had been arrested for an outstanding three-year-old ticket and Jim went to post a bond for him. He paid the twenty-five dollar bond and demanded a receipt. Jim didn't trust authority. The officer refused to give him a receipt, and Jim made a scene, demanding one. He was arrested for his conduct and had a date set for trial. Jim demanded a jury and, representing himself, told them what had happened. They found him "not guilty." The next day the police station began a new policy: to issue receipts. Jim had not made any new friends, but typical of Jim, he had not backed down.

JIM AND THE IRS

The baby was two and a half on Friday, February 12, 1993, when this story begins. The Hobbs family owned a home, a truck, a couple of cars, and a lot of furniture. Their circumstances were upwardly mobile. In eighteen months Jim and Cookie would celebrate their twentieth anniversary.

21

Unhappily, Jim was audited by an overzealous IRS agent. The auditor had a problem with Jim's truck deductions for 1985 and 1986. In each of those years Jim had nearly $15,000 in repair bills. Trucking is a business that relies on keeping a truck in good shape. An investment of $70,000 buys you a vehicle that will deliver about a million miles, if you caress it and take care of it. It could last ten years on the road. If you don't take good care of it, cut the mileage figure in half and you have to buy a new one in five years.

A trucker cares for his truck before he puts food on the table, because if the truck goes down he can't *put* food on the table. Jim's truck was kept in A-1 condition, and he had the receipts and records to show what he had done to the truck in those years. Taking $30,000 from Jim's pocket in those two years changed their lifestyle from steak in the house to spaghetti, but with the truck back in shape and business up again, Jim's fortunes improved and the family again prospered.

Unfortunately, the IRS agent told Jim that he was going to disallow his repair deductions for 1985 and was suspicious about 1986. Jim was furious, but he hired a lawyer and the three of them went back to the table in a follow-up to the audit. The agent wanted to review not just 1985, but 1986, too, and he wanted to look at everything Jim had on his return, not just the repair deductions. Jim laid his well-organized folder on the table and proudly showed his documentation to the IRS auditor. Notes on napkins, carefully hand printed explanations on receipts, all neat and orderly and laid out chronologically. Motel bills (whenever Jim couldn't sleep in his truck), cash receipts for on the road meals, all "I's" dotted—a careful, easy-to-follow map of Jim's expenses and travels.

Jim went to the bathroom. His lawyer left to take a phone call. When Jim got back to the room, a $3,000 truck repair bill, the proof of a business expenditure, was missing. The very first repair bill at the top of Jim's neat folder for 1986 had been for a radiator repair. There was no doubt in Jim's mind what had happened, and he let the agent know in no uncertain terms that he wasn't leaving that room without the bill.

The agent denied that he knew where it was. The lawyer, hearing the raised voices, came back into the room and questioned the agent. The agent looked into his own notebook and noticed that he had "accidentally" put the radiator repair bill in the back of his ledger book.

"Oh," he said. "*That* bill. I set it aside to keep it from getting mixed up." The agent returned the bill, but the pretense of cordiality was over. The agent told Jim and his lawyer that they were both suspicious characters. He not only disallowed the deductions for the repairs, he disallowed the deductions for fuel and even Jim's dependents. Apparently he didn't believe that Jim had kids or was married. The meeting degenerated further as the hostile agent, trying to reassert himself in light of his hapless exposure as a liar, began to ask one personal, unrelated question after another. "Where is your wife right now? How much money do you have in your wallet?" Jim's lawyer wisely terminated the meeting.

The next step he took was tax court. He could have appealed to the agent's supervisor.) Tax court is highly technical and has no jurors, only a tax court judge. Under the circumstances Jim elected to go to tax court, and his attorney was going to stay in the saddle for a very small fee.

The IRS agent had personally threatened the attorney. He told him that he would get him, too. By now, Jim had been terminated at his trucking connection as an independent contractor. The contractor that he subcontracted for told him, "We can't use you until this is over. The IRS agents are making us uncomfortable and we just can't risk an audit. Sorry."

Big Jim was determined to go all the way. He felt pretty good about his position and his lawyer, until he called him and told him that the IRS was offering to settle for $15,000 and that Jim had to take it. "Do I owe the money?" Jim asked.

"Hell no," his lawyer admitted. "In fact, they owe *you* money... you're entitled to a small refund. It's just that it's hard to win these cases and I think you need to put this behind you." The lawyer didn't know Jim Hobbs.

Jim had never learned to compromise and he ordered counsel to fight to the end. Counsel filed a motion to withdraw. Jim opposed it in court, telling the judge that he didn't know what to do and he needed to keep the lawyer on the case. The judge ruled against him and Jim was left alone to fend for himself.

Why did Jim's lawyer abandon the case? I can only speculate. Up to this point the lawyer had been doing a very good job for him. If he hadn't, I would give you my opinion. (My other "day" job is suing crooked lawyers.) In this case, I want to give this guy the benefit of the doubt because of the fine work he had done prior to quitting. Maybe he was threatened and couldn't stand the heat. It is often the case that IRS agents, who are often frustrated former high school bullies or the victims of the bullies, threaten to use their presumed power to imply horrible personal possibilities to the lawyer or CPA for helping the taxpayer. Perhaps he had offered Jim a fee lower than he could afford to handle the case. This is not uncommon. An honest lawyer wants to help out, and sometimes if he knows the client can't afford him, he offers his work cheaply. While he abandoned Jim, he didn't cheat him, so I am excluding his name from this work.

Imagine someone who just raped your next door neighbors, male and female. He carved them up into sausage and ate them to hide the evidence. He got caught because the police found his video tape of the entire affair, and he cannot afford counsel. He is entitled to a lawyer for free. Unfortunately, the law doesn't work that way for taxpayers. If you are involved in an IRS dispute and can't afford to pay what they want, you not only lose your right to a jury trial, you also lose your right to a lawyer—unless you can borrow the money to pay an attorney or get one to work for free.

Jim's lawyer was allowed to withdraw and Jim was faced with handling his own case in the hyper-technical tax court. At his criminal trial, Jim had listened to the police officer lie and then told his version to the jury. The judge didn't help him, but he got the simple truth across. Could he have done the same thing in a complex case? Maybe not.

This time it was *his* job to start the case. The government doesn't have to prove you owe a tax in tax court. You have to prove you *don't*! (The new tax bill of 1998 switches the burden of proof starting in 1998 but there are a lot of obstacles in the way.) Jim had no idea what to do, how to start, or how to proceed. Additionally, in tax court, most of the evidence is stipulated to on paper before trial. Jim didn't know how to introduce his deductions. He told the judge he didn't know what to do. The judge said, "Then, Mr. Hobbs, the case is dismissed."

Jim was astounded, elated, and confused. He thought that meant he didn't owe anything. Unfortunately, it was just the opposite: it means that the petitioner (the taxpayer who files in tax court) *loses* the case *as if he had never filed anything at all.* Jim now owed $60,000 that he shouldn't have owed. He would later learn his mistake when they came unannounced to take his paycheck. The bill would be larger with the interest.

This story, however, is not about Jim Hobbs. This is only the background you need to understand the story. This story is about Cheri and Cookie Hobbs—*my* case, which has less to do with tax court and more with IRS abuse.

Here's how I got involved. It was September of 1993. I was in Boston, appearing on radio and television, discussing a subject close to my heart—IRS abuses. My wife Michelle was with me. After the broadcast, we returned to the hotel to find a fax waiting for me from my right-hand assistant, L. R.

L. R. Robertson (Linda Roderick Robertson) came to work for me in April, 1985. She was Magna Cum Laude from Hunter College, had a photographic memory, and at five-foot five weighed over three hundred pounds. The biggest part of her was her heart. She told me she believed God had sent her to apply for the job as a paralegal with me, so I put aside my prejudice against her weight and hired her. I was afraid to either suffer the wrath of God or turn down a blessing, and I believed this woman. She was a woman of great virtue and truth. She became one of my great blessings. One of the few sincere Christians I've ever met, L. R. told me that sending a Christian to a law office was like sending Daniel to a lion's den. Ten years later, on March 9, 1995, after nearly a hundred trials together, and becoming my close friend and confident, L. R. died of a heart attack. After her death, I couldn't work. We closed the office for a month. L. R. wrote the introduction to my first book *Underground Lawyer* and edited it. This book, my practice, and our clients all suffer the loss of her.

Jim Hobbs, who lives in Boston, had called my Houston office asking for a free consultation. Jim told L. R. that he'd been considering calling me for some time, though he knew he didn't have the money to pay a retainer. He had seen me on another television show where I was doing essentially the same thing as in Boston—talking about the IRS.

He hoped he could convince me to take his case pro bono, which means without a fee. I get about fifty similar requests a month. I wish it were possible to fill them, but it's financially impossible. Still, I do handle more pro bono cases than many of my peers, especially those cases involving IRS abuses. L. R., having listened to Jim's story, had a feeling I'd be interested in Jim's case. The fact that I was in Boston seemed like divine intervention to her, so she sent the fax to the Boston hotel.

After I received the fax, I called Jim Hobbs. Michelle and I met with Jim and Cookie Saturday morning. We talked for three hours. I found his story so fascinating I lost track of time and missed a second television appearance. As for Jim and Cookie, they missed a rally being held in their honor. I listened as they related the story of IRS bullies trying to bludgeon them into submission with every intimidating weapon in their considerable arsenal.

One common occurrence is that IRS agents, angry over effective counsel, occasionally make veiled (often, not so veiled) threats. They are a vindictive lot. One day after Geraldo Rivera did his 1992 tax exposé show, he was informed he would be audited. Coincidence? Is there really a tooth fairy? Did Jim's lawyer drop the case because of threats? Had Jim lost his job because of IRS intimidation? I was sure of it, and all of this played a part in my decision to take the case pro bono. But the clincher was Cookie's story.

Jim and the IRS were at war, but our case had nothing to do with Jim. The defendants were his wife and daughter.

At 9:10 in the morning on February 12, 1993, while Cookie was alone at home and Jim was out, revenue agent Ralph J. Devito showed up with two other agents demanding from Cookie entrance to her home and $60,000, or he was going to take Jim's truck and her car.

Devito was a stocky powerful-looking guy about five-foot nine or five-foot ten with an olive complexion. Armed agents Kydd and Morris accompanied him. From this point onward, there are two very different reports about what happened, so I'll start with the one I believe is true and then give you the Commonwealth of Massachusetts' and the IRS' version.

The IRS agents were later joined by a local police officer. He was about six-feet tall with short blond hair and a wiry muscular body: the spitting image of the powerful humanoid robot in *Terminator II*. Part of the reason the government's position is so incredible is that the "Terminator" had to use a weapon on the two Hobbs women. He admits to that. The question is, *why?*

Devito knocked on the door and Mrs. Hobbs opened it, leaving the chain on. Like any normal citizen she inquired, "Who is it?"

Devito, raised his voice loud enough so that the next door neighbor could hear him, shouted that he was with the IRS, and she needed to let him into her house so he could collect $60,000. Mrs. Hobbs didn't know what was going on but she did know that these guys weren't nice guys. Her husband told her about the IRS's sneaky dishonesty regarding the Hobbs's finances. Her family was then living off of her income from part-time retail clerking of about $1,100 for 1992. Devito then shouted out words to the effect that the Hobbs are tax cheats and she and her husband were in a lot of trouble. "Open the door and let us in!" he commanded. Would the three little pigs let in the big bad wolf? What is more important: were they legally required to do so? Mrs. Hobbs didn't know and this was worse.

"Do you have a warrant or a court order?" she asked.

Devito bellowed, "We don't need it. I have papers." The papers he had were a lien attachment not signed by his supervisor and not naming Mrs. Hobbs, only Mr. Hobbs. Later, in court, the government would produce an attachment properly filled out with Devito's supervisor's signature on it and a statement that an inventory had been made. It was dated February 12. How did the second lien come about? How did it get altered after the fact? These are good questions. Take these questions to the wolves.

Devito then did what IRS collection agents are famous for: he attached the paper to Cookie's car, saying it was his. He did the same to Jim's truck. The original which showed up later in court, was properly filled out, the photocopy of the original wasn't. How was this possible absent fraud? It isn't. The "original" was backdated. There is the smell of IRS perjury in the air.

Jim was out looking for a job and couldn't be reached. Cookie, terrified, phoned her daughter who hopped in her car with the baby, Angela, and drove over. Devito, apparently wondering if violence was going to take place and afraid that the three armed IRS agents would be unable to protect themselves from the towering five-foot two Cookie Hobbs, called in the "Terminator." With police siren wailing, he rushed to the scene of the crime (or perhaps more accurately, rushed to the scene to *commit* a crime). Devito had already stopped by the Billerica police force to alert them of his upcoming activity in the event that backup or heavy arms would be needed. Little did the alert public servant know that soon unarmed five-foot three Cheri

28

would arrive on the scene. Perhaps if he did he would have called out the Marines.

When Cheri arrived (beating the "Terminator" to the scene), her mom rushed out to embrace her. Together they told Devito that the sticker on Mom's car had to go. Maybe they could take Jim's truck with this piece of paper, but they couldn't take Cookie's car. Mom had paid everything the government said she owed on her taxes, and her name is the only one on her car.

Enter the "Terminator." Cookie opened the trunk of her car and started to remove $4,000 worth of dresses that belonged to her employer. She signed for these dresses to use for a fashion show and was personally responsible for them. She had to get them out of the car.

When Cookie took the dresses out, Devito's face turned red and he screamed and shouted that she was supposed to stay away from the vehicles. Could he tackle the two women with his armed escorts? Before anyone could give any explanation, the "Terminator" arrived and faced the women eye-to-eye. The trunk of the car contained the high school textbooks of both Hobbs boys, and, equally important, the baby stroller for Angela, along with a big box of Pampers and some baby clothes, including Angela's tap shoes. (In April 1994, three-and-a-half year-old Angela would remember the theft of her tap shoes and her uncles' schoolbooks for Geraldo. Afterward, as Geraldo walked away from Angela, she grabbed him back to add "and then they handcuffed my mommy." There wasn't a dry eye in the audience.)

The total value of everything was probably less than $200 (except for the dresses), but when you live on minimum wage and tips, your mom makes $1,100 a year, and dad has been unemployed for several months, you don't toss the baby stroller out without getting a good explanation.

Cookie had given up on keeping the car. Cheri did not want her mother, who was in remission from life-threatening cancer, to get hurt. Both women appealed to officer "Terminator" for justice. If necessary they would give up the truck that might be liened, the car that wasn't, keep the uninvolved baby stuff and textbooks, and end the nightmare.

"My grandbaby's stuff is in the trunk." Cookie said gesturing at the car.

"Shut up," the "Terminator" told her, and the IRS agent warned both women to get away from the car. Terrified, Cookie went over to the car, silently obeying the officer's instructions to shut up but sat on the rear bumper to get attention and, hopefully, permission to pick up the diapers and clothing for her grandbaby from the open trunk. Officer "Terminator" roughly grabbed her by the arm and pulled her away. Cheri figured out what was going on, went to the car and sat on the bumper. Officer "Terminator" then grabbed her and pulled her away. Mom then took up the post on the bumper. All the while, Devito was encouraging the "Terminator" with not-so-nice sign language. The "Terminator" then grabbed mom and jerked her away.

Cheri screamed, "Please don't hurt my mom." Mom decided she had to tell the "Terminator" about the baby things—but mom was wrong. This disobedience to the law apparently caused the "Terminator" to fear for his safety. He pulled out a can of mace while Mrs. Hobbs was trying to talk to him, even after he ordered her to shut up, and he sprayed her in the mouth. Enough chemicals to kill all the bugs in a couple of homes streamed down Cookie's open throat, burning and tearing her up. Devito encouraged the "Terminator."

"Arrest her!" he ordered. Arrest who? The now very helpless Cookie, or the enraged Cheri, or perhaps the next door neighbor who was watching the whole government joint effort? Where was the FBI when you needed them? Would "Terminator" be safe? Would the IRS agents jump in to protect him and prevent the perpetrators from rescuing the baby things? No problem. Our trained law enforcement officer flung a choking, startled Cookie to the ground, face down, and cuffed her hands behind her back and then lifted her up in the air by the cuffs, leaving welts on her forearms. Perhaps Cheri was not quite so dangerous as the "Terminator" feared because now, the baby things forgotten, and terrified about what the chemicals might do to her mother, she simply broke down and cried.

30

"Terminator," not to be taken off guard by this tactic, walked over to crying Cheri, pulled out the mace can, and from a distance of three inches covered her face with the chemical. The fight was over. Mom wanted to tell Cheri not to worry about her, but Mom unfortunately wouldn't be able to talk for quite some time. Cheri was stunned. She was blind. Her face was stinging. The closely sprayed chemicals, meant to be used at a distance, have covered her hair, her eyes, her face, and her neck. "Mom, are you all right?" she screamed. "What's going on? What did he do to me?" Mom wanted to reassure Cheri, but her throat was gone for the time being. All she could do was shudder from the pain, try not to vomit on herself, and hope they wouldn't do anything more to her daughter.

At this point, Cheri's three-year-old daughter could have easily taken her mom down now. A martial-arts expert would have been incapacitated. The mace used on Cheri and Cookie was military issue, much stronger stuff than normally used by street cops, and of questionable legality. They were filled with pain and fear. They were paralyzed. The "Terminator," however, was not finished. At point-blank range, at the urging of IRS agent Devito, he shot the mace again into Cheri's face, and then, to the complete amazement of the on-looking neighbors and Cheri's terrified mom, the "Terminator" shot Cheri right in the face for a third time. One Vietnam veteran who had the same chemical sprayed in his face from a foot away described it as feeling like you had put your face in a frying pan filled with hot grease and held your breath until you passed out. This stuff was not for children. Now it was safe for "Terminator" to tackle the important job of arresting the second Hobbs woman. He threw her to the ground, cuffed her, and tossed her into the back of the police car like a sack of potatoes, up against her mom.

The two women could hear and see each other only to the extent their remaining limited senses allowed. Cheri was trying to ask how Mom was (she still couldn't see) and Mom was trying to tell her that she was okay (she still couldn't fully vocalize). By somehow contorting themselves, they could touch each other. Cheri became more afraid when she could touch mom, but couldn't hear her. Was it the chemical in her ears or in her mom's throat? Would it aggravate the cancer?

Devito took the truck and the car and shouted out to the Hobbs women before the back door of the police car was shut, "I'll be back for your home. You haven't seen the last of me." That was certainly the one piece of advice Devito gave which had the ring of truth to it. (My sister, Mitzi, a mother of two, reading a rough draft of this chapter, asked me "What about the little girl? Who took care of her?" All too typical in these types of situations is the total lack of concern for the children. Was Angela traumatized? Yes! Who was left at the house to watch her? Her Aunt Peggy came over to sit with Angela. Devito could have cared less. Maybe that was a blessing. At least she wasn't taken to Children's Protective Services, another nightmare I wrote about in *The Underground Lawyer*.)

At the police station the two newly apprehended suspects were thrown into a dirty cell with human feces and blood on the floor. Officers laughed as Cheri rubbed her eyes, only making things worse. One woman officer had enough and brought her out to a sink and put her hands into the water and instructed her, "Wipe the stuff off your face with the water. Don't rub it into your eyes or it will get worse. Hurry! I've got to lock you back up fast."

Cheri managed to get some of the chemical out of her eyes and could see a blurred vision in a mirror. "Oh my God," she thought, "I know that's not me."

The face in the mirror had frost all over it, some bruises, and looked like a street person. It's amazing what thirty minutes of brutality could do to a person. "Okay, time's up," the friendly woman announced and dragged her back to the cell. "I still have burning and pain in my eyes," Cheri said, "I couldn't get enough water to my face." All that was too bad. Cheri had to get back to the cell. However, she could see a little. Mom actually looked better than Cheri had imagined and even more important, she could now speak with a little rasp. Things could be a whole lot worse. In fact, at that point Jim Hobbs was at the station making arrangements for his women to be released. Soon they would get out and be charged with the heinous crime of disorderly conduct, punishable by a maximum of six months in jail. In the Commonwealth, this doesn't really mean six full months; it really means only about five and a half months.

The Hobbs women went to court and had a short trial with two court-appointed attorneys before a judge and were convicted and sentenced to do thirty days in jail. What were the rules for an appeal? They were entitled to a trial de novo (a new trial) in front of a jury (this right has since been taken away), but if they were convicted everyone in the courthouse said the judge would give them the full six months. Counsel recommended they do the thirty days and feel lucky.

Although it's unconstitutional to do that to a person who demands to have a real trial, it's customary all over the United States to punish someone for demanding that the government prove they are guilty. The government wants the accused to "kiss up". In the federal system it's called acceptance of responsibility and it means you'll do less time. The extra punishment time for demanding a trial is often called "rent" for the use of the courthouse. What if you are innocent? What if you plan on appealing? What if even a minute in jail is a gross injustice? Tough. If you demand a trial, you do harder time. Kissing up is a very important part of the criminal justice system and now, in America, it is actually written into the federal sentencing guideline laws. (These guidelines effect all federal criminal tax trials but do not legally relate to state charges such as this case even though it is tax related.)

It is a barbarous practice that dates back to torturing a confession out of the accused. During the Inquisition in Spain, it was important not to kill or imprison innocent people. The only way for certain that you could know if someone was a crook, or worse, a follower of Satan, was to have them confess. Fortunately, there were people who were available to help you do just that. Once you did confess the torture stopped and the punishment began. The punishment was not nearly as bad as the torture. It was either imprisonment or death and your heirs, if you confessed, sometimes got to keep their property.

I agreed to take the Hobbs case and asked if they could cover my plane fare and the hotel bill. They agreed to try. I got Alice Weiser to come up for the same non-fee to assist on jury selection, a field in which she is unparalleled.

In the Commonwealth of Massachusetts, in a misdemeanor case, the information you get from the jurors is so ridiculously limited that it makes the federal system look like a smorgasbord of information (which it is not), but you do get a handwriting sample in the form of a jury information sheet (which contains three lines and almost no information). Alice is the best in the world at handwriting interpretation.

Neighbors of the Hobbs got together and raised money for the plane tickets with an auction and a bake sale. Unlike my other cases in 1993, these clients couldn't raise much in the way of expenses. They still got the most important element I can put together, even for a very large fee, me. I reviewed the paperwork and talked to the two local court-appointed lawyers.

Mr. Chance, Cheri's court-appointed attorney, had some valuable pre-trial discovery for her. He and Cookie's court-appointed lawyer had not gotten together. Cookie's lawyer had set up a meeting at the Hobbs house but failed to show up. Cookie's case was the tough one. The Hobbs wanted to get rid of both lawyers and have me handle both cases alone. I explained that Chance was doing a lot of quality work (although it would have been nice if his very busy schedule had let him personally interview the neighbors who had been witnesses), so I recommended that they keep Chance. There was no money for any of the extras so helpful in winning a case. Local counsel was important.

I had flown back to Houston on Sunday, had a hearing Tuesday morning (Monday was Labor Day), signed papers, finished my work on two pending briefs, and flew back to Boston on the 6:00 AM flight

34

Wednesday morning so I could get there in time to meet the witnesses, read the file, and get over the jet lag. When I travel, a one hour time change really means almost nothing but even the almost is something. Trial work is stressful and draining. Conserving energy so you can work and think is important. A tired lawyer is often an ineffective lawyer.

On Thursday morning I showed up for docket call dressed in a sweater and no tie. I had also failed to pack a white shirt. I am a horrible packer and reluctant dresser. I had to ask the court for permission to appear as I was. Jim would go and get a shirt for me later. At least I had my pants. Once, when my suitcase went to a different city, I appeared in court in Honolulu in my jeans, a shirt I picked up at the hotel, and a very Hawaiian tie. The Hawaiian judge was very understanding. He said, "No problem. We're relaxed here. Sometimes lawyers have to come to court from the beach. I understand." The Boston judge, Doherty, didn't seem as friendly as the Hawaiian judge had. However, she said it was okay with a little bit of a growl and then proceeded to decide if we were going to trial at all.

The "Terminator" wasn't there because he was at a funeral. I had filed a motion *pro hac vice* (Latin literally, for this thing), which simply means I was asking permission to appear in the courts of the Commonwealth of Massachusetts even though I don't live there or have a Commonwealth license. My request showed that I was licensed in the First Circuit Court of Appeals (the federal appellate court that has jurisdiction over all federal issues in Boston) and a bunch more. Murphy, a very competent and pretty lawyer, who asked for a continuance because of the funeral, represented the government. The judge barked at me since I hadn't been allowed yet to appear and ordered me to sit down. I sat down near the bench, and the bailiff gestured to me that I should leave the area in front of the bar. Basically, as lawyers, we own tenant rights to the area right in front of the judge, sandwiched between the judge and the public area. These are better seats than the public gets. We are entitled by this leasehold right to more respect than the public. Is this right? Sorry—that's not the subject of this story. You can decide, but it's fact. I stood up and asked the court. "Your honor, am I ordered behind the bar?" The judge said, "Of course not," and I sat down. The bailiff was a little embarrassed.

Previously, Chance and the other local lawyer had asked me what was going on. Hadn't the case been continued? I was under the impression that it hadn't, and that the only thing that had occurred was that the government had asked for it to be continued. "Well," they asked, "What's the difference?"

The difference I explained was that I had flown in from Texas at a great expense of a day of travel each way plus plane fare and that I wanted to get the trial done. Could the Hobbs bring us back again? Could I afford not three days, but six or more on the case *pro bono*?

I had already asked my worthy opponent to waive the continuance request because I was here for free to do a good deed. This wasn't a capital murder case. The officer could come back when the funeral was over. She still had three IRS witnesses. (Perhaps you law enforcement junkies are saying to yourself, sure, but who would believe the sworn testimony of an IRS agent? That's a good point, but you'd be surprised how many people worship government—even IRS agents).

She refused. Polite or not, prosecutors are often not sympathetic to the reality of being a real human being. We are all merely criminals waiting for our cell, trying to reduce our time in it by bargaining but in this case, the prosecution had asked for the continuance.

Chance was very straightforward about it. "If you want to raise the argument go ahead. I have to work here and we have to cooperate. You're going back to Texas. You don't have to get along with the prosecutor's office."

No one had asked the clients what they wanted. Can a public defender simply agree to a continuance without even asking his or her client what he or she wants? Actually even the privately hired counsel routinely go ahead and go along. Since I would be running the case and since I had come at considerable inconvenience from a long way away, I hoped I could informally resolve the issue. It seemed a foregone conclusion.

The prosecutor seemed surprised that I was even questioning her position. She apparently thought I was ignoring her, as well as the unwritten local rule, and the general consensus in the room that these continuances were routinely granted. She felt it strange that the continuance had not already been granted *ex parte* (only one side heard). I went ahead and objected and demanded that the court rule on it.

After the court had me seated (she hadn't allowed me yet to appear and was apparently still mulling over whether or not I was qualified to try a case with a six month penalty at stake on a misdemeanor), she asked the prosecutor about her witness. "Is it a relative's funeral? How long will it take? Is it set for morning or afternoon? Why does the officer need to be there all day? Is he still in the state?"

The funeral was in Boston, it wasn't a relative of the officer, and the government had no idea if it was set for morning or afternoon. The court asked me if I had any questions. "Your Honor," I responded, "I did but you just asked them and I'm satisfied that the officer, if they need him in addition to the three IRS agents who were witnesses, can get here in time today for trial."

The court agreed. "There are a lot of lawyers here to try this case. The defendants have a right to get this over with. I'm denying the continuance and setting this for trial in front of Judge Milan. Counsel's motion to appear *pro hac vice* is granted."

I thought the judge had been fair (she had ruled in our favor) and used some uncommonly good sense. I regretted that she wasn't keeping the case to try herself. I felt we would get a fair trial with her.

We moved into a small courtroom across several hallways and corridors and awaited the Honorable Judge Milan, who agreed to give me thirty minutes before he brought in the jury so I could wait for and then put on my soon-to-arrive shirt with matching tie. (Jim confided later that he knew my failure to bring the proper lawyer uniform and appear, in his words, "like a country bumpkin," was a tactic which helped get the other side off guard and which nudged the judge to deny the continuance motion. Years have passed and we are now close friends, but

I have never been able to convince him that it wasn't a plan of mine to look like a fool in front of a judge I had never met).

On the way to the other courtroom the bailiff came up to me and apologized for our encounter. We made friends. He was basically a nice guy doing his job and, hey, what if I wasn't really a lawyer sitting up in one of those front row seats? If everyone could sit up in the front, who would want to be a lawyer?

In the courtroom, now dressed in the appropriate uniform, I asked the prosecutor if any offers were still on the table. After a few insulting comments like, "Well, you should have asked me earlier," and "this is such an insult," and "well, your client is so terribly guilty; she should really spend some time in jail" prosecutor-type talk (actually less than the norm), she offered both of them the right to plead guilty and take probation. I told her I would recommend a no contest finding of guilty and then after six months dropping the charge. She said they would consider it.

No contest means it can't be used against you, and dropping it in six months means that you have no record, and all of it means the client doesn't have to go through the degrading routine of admitting to a crime which is often very difficult, especially when the client is innocent.

Mom said no. She would not plead under any circumstances. Cheri said okay. She'd take the deal. Now you ask, "How can an innocent person plead guilty?" Simple. Cheri didn't want to leave her three-year-old daughter for six months, so she was willing to plead guilty even though she was innocent to avoid the chance of going to jail. It's done every day. I told her that I would go to trial anyway if she wanted. It was her record, her decision, and her life. I was there to try it, but I wouldn't be going to jail if we lost.

"Would we win?" mom, dad, and daughter all asked.

I gave the same answer I always give, structured to the moment. "So far this year I've won every case I've tried. I didn't come here to lose this, but I could lose this case and every case I try for the rest of my life. I'm here to try this and win it for both of you, not just your mom. I'm here because I want to help, but I think this is your dad's fight more than it is your fight, and if we lose *you* go to jail, not dad. You make the decision and no one will disrespect you for it, or if they do, they don't deserve your respect."

Chance had found a local counsel for me who had drawn up the form for *pro hac vice* (this allows an out-of-state attorney to plead a local case) and would sit with me but, frankly, although we had some differences in opinion on procedure, I wanted to keep Chance. He was a good lawyer. He would clearly fight for the client in the courtroom. He had already done a lot of good pretrial work and gotten a lot of helpful documentation. Also, he knew this courthouse like the back of his hand. I asked him if he would stay with me as co-counsel after Cheri pleaded guilty. He agreed to do so. Technically, I was representing Cookie, and he was representing Cheri, but in reality the clients wanted us to work for both of them. Chance agreed in spirit.

We went into the courtroom. My opposing counsel complained that I had not followed the local rule and filed a list of all my witnesses. I had earlier that day gone to the main clerk's office and asked to purchase a copy of the local rules and had been told that there weren't any. I had also gone to the clerk of the first court and had been told to go to the main clerk's office. I informed him that I already had. When the clerk in the last courtroom confirmed that I was violating local rules, I asked to know which one I was violating. Local rules often mean simply local unwritten custom. Sometimes they mean whatever the judge wants them to mean. The transcript of the first trial (a written record of everything the witnesses said) was missing. No one could find it.

The court then said he would not accept Cheri's no contest plea. She could only plead guilty, get probation, and have a record. Her other option was to go to trial and risk six months in jail. I told both of these brave women that the custom, when you get this good of a deal, is to take it, guilty or innocent. Chance told them another of the unwritten local rules. If they went forward and lost, they would go to jail for the maximum six months. Everyone in the courthouse knew it. Most people start off saying that they would never plead guilty to a crime they didn't commit, and it is unethical for a lawyer to encourage his client to do so, but in the real-life courtroom, the innocent and the guilty alike kiss up to get the best deal, and a no-prison-time deal is the best.

Alice Weiser asked me what I would do in the same circumstances. I told her I'd want my wife or daughter to take the deal; that for myself I'd rather do the time. (Of course, while I said that, I wasn't facing the time.) That confirmed what she thought from knowing me and, of course, from my handwriting. Would Cheri take the new deal? Yes, Cheri pleaded guilty. Her mom would then go on trial without her.

Before Cookie's trial, the prosecuting attorney read the government's version of what happened for Cheri to agree with and be convicted. This was the government's version: The IRS agent calmly came to the scene after previously telling the local police they might be called for backup. Devito asked Mrs. Hobbs if she would allow them to peacefully take the vehicles. She flew into a rage, refused to look at their papers, and threatened them. Her daughter came out of the house and was clearly potentially violent. It was necessary to call for backup. Officer Daniel Doyle (the "Terminator") arrived at the home and attempted to calm them down. Suddenly, for no reason at all, the two women both jumped into the trunk of the open car and refused to get out. The daughter, after being gently pulled out of the trunk, jumped on the back of the officer with the intent to create a public disturbance (in their private front yard). Neighbors began to gather around and, fearing a possible uprising, Officer Doyle used the mace to control the unruly women and then escorted them into the vehicle and took them to the station. Devito took a careful inventory of the cars, writing basically that there were two cars (nothing else was on the inventory not the baby stroller, schoolbooks, etc.), and invited Mrs. Hobbs to assist in the inventory preparation, but she refused. The two women were then driven to the police station where they were immediately tended to and the effects of the necessary mace were gently removed.

Cheri looked stunned. "I can't swear to that," she said.

The court inquired. "Why not?"

"Because it's not true," she said. "I don't want to go to jail. I have a three-year-old daughter to take care of. All I know is that lawyer lied."

The court wasn't pleased. Was it because an innocent person had been pushed to confess? Was it (more likely) because things weren't going forward expeditiously? I honestly don't know but the plea was rejected and we both proceeded to trial. Sometimes a person has too much character to do the "right" thing, and so a trial goes on.

We had seven witnesses: Mr. Hobbs, Mrs. Hobbs, Cheri Hobbs, and, if necessary, three neighbors who would testify to what the "Terminator" had said in the first trial and a neighbor for rebuttal, only if necessary to impeach government inconsistencies. Generally the names of rebuttal witnesses don't have to be given to the other side because you only use them to impeach testimony already put on. Impeach means to disagree with, to say that's not what he said earlier, or that's not true. Impeachment is only necessary once a witness has taken the stand. Chance had already complied with the unwritten local rule, so I apologized to the court and the government attorney and told them I had only been of record for about a half an hour and did not have the time to comply, but that I would go with Chance's list. After getting chewed out by the court for my failure to abide by the unwritten local rule, which probably didn't apply to rebuttal witnesses anyway, we continued.

Next my "co-counsel" (Cheri's lawyer) and the government asked that we "invoke the rule" that the witnesses be sequestered. That means they can't watch any of the trial and are not supposed to discuss any of the details of the case with each other. This is fairly common, especially in Texas, but this time I objected. The only one who knew anything about the tax case, which was in fact the underlying case, was Mr. Hobbs. He also had prepared a detailed report, had put the conflicting lien papers together and had from all his experience become a very effective underground lawyer in his own right. I wanted him in the courtroom to help. Overruled.

Okay. I wanted my three impeachment witnesses in the courtroom to hear the testimony of the officer and agent Devito. If they said the same things they said in the first trial I wouldn't need them, but if they didn't, I'd need to put my witnesses on the stand for impeachment to testify that the story was different. I also felt obligated to them. They were among the neighbors who had raised the $2,500 for plane tickets and hotel room to see the Texas lawyer and Alice Weiser work. They had paid the price of admission. They also added to the moral strength of the audience. This misdemeanor was being tried to a full courtroom of spectators.

The court instructed me that there were lots of other ways to impeach. I replied that the only other way I knew was with the actual record, but due to the court reporting error, it didn't exist or if it did, it was missing. Tough. They had to leave. With that I asked that they be released from the witness list. I would not be able to bring them in to impeach testimony they didn't hear so I'd take a chance and make a record for appeal if the testimony was different. Every criminal case needs to plan for the potential of a conviction and an appeal. Now my co-counsel spoke up and said they were still on his list and he wanted them to stay on it. They were kept out. I instructed the witnesses not to talk to each other in the hallway about the case. They left.

The trial started. Alice, Chance, and I picked the jury. It was a pretty good jury. Lots of feeling people on it. The jury was asked to leave the room while a strange motion was taken up. The government wanted to put Devito on but wanted us severely restricted in the questions that we could ask. How strange. The IRS had what they called an informational officer to tell the court, under oath, what Devito was allowed to testify about.

Basically, he couldn't say anything about the tax return or anything about the background story between Jim and the IRS. Well, Devito's conduct was pretty important. Did the tax records on these two people indicate that they might be potentially violent? If so that would show a predisposition on the part of the IRS agent Devito and would tell a lot about his testimony. The Sixth Amendment to the United States Constitution *requires* cross-examination. If it is restricted, you can't get to the truth. How can it be fair for one witness to say whatever he wants for the prosecution, but be severely limited when he answers the defense questions? The judge passed this professional witness over to me.

Minns: Did you see anything?

Witness: No.

Minns: Have you reviewed any of the records?

Witness: No.

Minns: Pass the witness, your honor—because he's *not* a witness. If we're going to conduct some sort of hearing about this court following the regulations of a governmental bureaucracy that has *no* authority in your court, at least put the real witness on and ask the relevant questions.

Incredibly, after apparently understanding the issue, the judge ruled that we couldn't have full and complete cross-examination on the issues of the returns, but that if it came up we would deal with it later. The government gave its opening and I gave ours. Chance reserved his for later. Ordinarily that's not smart, but when you have two competent lawyers arguing the same side (and I argued on behalf of both mother and daughter), then it makes good sense. The first impression often wins or loses the case. In this case Chance and I were beginning to pick up a tempo and work well together. After the government's case was over, Chance would get to rise and reinforce our position before he put on his case.

43

Basically, I told the jury that there were two very different versions of what happened. One was true, the other improbable, but even
if they agreed with the improbable version of the IRS and the
Commonwealth, there was no criminal intent to do anything wrong
and nothing was done publicly. Everything occurred on private property. I also went up to jurors and held my hand three inches away and
"maced" them with it.

The first witness was agent Devito. "I was calm in a voice just like
I'm speaking in right now," he said. "I knocked on the door and...."

His testimony was interrupted by the bailiff, now my friend, who
brought an important matter to the judge's attention. Barbara Butler
(Mrs. B. to the Hobbs family), one of the Hobbs' neighbors, had come
to court to give spiritual support. She had brought more than that. She
watched Devito and "Terminator" discussing the case and demanded
to know what the bailiff was going to do about it. The bailiff decided
what to do—he would enforce the law—the sequestration rule had
been violated. The "Terminator" and Devito had used the time that
the information officer was on the stand to discuss the intimate details
of the case. "When did you see me? When did you call?" the
"Terminator" asked Devito. Their two stories and the paperwork
record were about two hours apart and the two public servants were
busy closing the hours so they jibed, getting their trial watches and
trial sworn testimony synchronized. Is this unusual? Heck no. Is it
illegal? Yes. Especially after the government's request for sequestration. Government witnesses routinely violate the sequestration rules.

Three things were unusual: First, they had been blatant about it.
Second, the overflowing neighborhood witnesses and others were
standing around listening, and three people reported this conduct to
the bailiff. Finally, the bailiff actually reported it to the judge. Now
what would happen?

The "Terminator" and Devito each swore oaths to tell the truth
and each gave different versions of what had happened in the hallway.
Both admitted there had been at least some discussion of the case.

44

The bailiff volunteered that he hadn't actually told the witnesses outside the courtroom they couldn't talk to each other. I consoled him.

"Your honor, it's the responsibility of counsel to tell her witnesses not to violate the rule. In this case you have a peace officer who has been in court many times and an IRS agent who probably took a course in testifying. (Many IRS witnesses take courses in testifying and are professional witnesses.) It is inconceivable that they didn't know they were violating the law."

The judge was a little angry. "I don't want to point the finger at anyone. I just want to hear what each party thinks should be done." Chance thought that Devito should be struck and not allowed to testify. The government prosecutor thought she should be allowed to break the rule. I thought that since I was the only one who had asked not to even have sequestration, and that only my witnesses had been following the Court's sequestration orders, that both witnesses should be stricken. The court agreed.

"What do I do now?" the prosecutor asked.

"Any other witnesses?" the court asked.

"I guess," she said meekly.

She would call the two other IRS agents. Unfortunately they weren't listed.

"Is the local rule only for out-of-town counsel to follow?" I wondered out loud.

The court, having reamed me out on the "list" rule, wouldn't back down now. If the names were not on her list, they were not testifying. There would be no other witnesses. The prosecutor said she'd like to re-file and dismiss at this time. The court wouldn't buy that. "Either put on another witness or rest." Judge Milan ruled.

"Well, under the circumstances," she conceded, "We rest."

I made a motion for a judgement of acquittal. Basically this means that since there is no evidence, there is no need to have any more trial and a "not guilty" verdict should be entered. Would we have won anyway? Frankly, Alice and I thought we were way ahead, but you take

45

your wins any legal way you can get them. This one was sweet and it was over. Mom and daughter were found "not guilty." Happy ending.

The Hobbs still have problems with the IRS. The local police have since been shining lights in their home for no reason other than nuisance. There is a very good chance that a civil rights suit will be successfully filed for the unnecessary violence inflicted on the Hobbs women by the "Terminator." In February of 1994, I began a search for a co-counsel to file a civil rights suit against the "Terminator." I hired Andrew Aloisi of Boston, Massachusetts, a top-flight plaintiff's counsel, who, as co-counsel, filed suit against the villains. I had to pick someone with the guts and staying power as well as experience to stay the course.

This case is typical of IRS abuse. A hard-working man is arbitrarily disallowed his legal deductions on the whim of an IRS agent and then circumstances snowball out of control. It escalates to the point of seizure of property, without which the taxpayer cannot earn a living, and includes the police brutalizing two small women. Just to receive their basic rights as U.S. citizens, the Hobbs have had to endure years of affliction, apprehension, and anxiety during the numerous confrontations with the IRS both in court and out of court. Somehow, I don't think this is what the Founding Fathers of our country envisioned when they formed our government. It's supposed to be a government *for* the people not *against* the people. It's ironic that these events happened in the Boston area, the cradle of liberty in America.

Chapter II
Businessman: Undercover Sting

"It is error alone which needs the support of government. Truth can stand by itself."

—-Thomas Jefferson

BIRMINGHAM, ALABAMA

When Rey Spulak came to my office with his friend "Nebraska," (I have not gotten permission to use Nebraska's real name) he was depressed and disappointed after a nearly ten-year struggle with the government. An honest, formerly successful entrepreneur, Rey was now facing financial ruin and a federal indictment of two counts of bribery of an IRS agent, which carried a possible penalty of ten years in the federal penitentiary. He was not a happy guy.

His friend Nebraska, who had been charged with the same offenses, was more optimistic. Both gentlemen wanted to put up a fight and save their skins from a powerful, unsympathetic government. Both men had tried to follow the law. Both had been led astray by dishonest government officials and both Rey and Nebraska hoped their jury trials would result in acquittals.

The friends differed in that Rey intended to adopt a more conservative approach to his legal defense, while Nebraska was pinning his hopes on a pet theory. He had already filed some pleadings with the court on his own. If all else failed, Nebraska was convinced he would be able to convince the jury *or* the judge *or* the appellate court that no matter what else the government proved, it would fail to prove that it had jurisdiction over him. You see, according to Nebraska and his well-paid legal researchers (none of whom had licenses to practice law), he didn't have to pay taxes at all! He was a citizen of the sovereign state of Nebraska, and people born in Nebraska, if they were also free, white, and male, were not Fourteenth Amendment citizens— they were "Preamble" citizens.

In our office, we are privileged to hear just about every theory in the country as to why a person might not be required to file a tax return or might be exempt from income taxes. Every year there is usually at least one or more of these popular theories and, coincidentally, a new organization that sells the theory or a variation of it (or a book or a "kit" or a complete course). Often the information comes with a money-back guarantee or a promise of free legal protection, in the "unlikely event" that it is needed.

Unfortunately, by the time the indicted purchaser gets to our office, his "guarantor" has often gone underground or left the country. The tax guru tells people (if they will listen) exactly how the unfortunate defendant failed to follow his instructions to the letter and is, therefore, doomed to failure, or at least unworthy of the tax guru's further protection.

We have a lot of different classifications for these people. Sometimes they are honest but misguided. Sometimes they are sad little sheared sheep. Sometimes their theory once made sense but no longer does.

One such example is continued reliance on the 1895 *Pollack v. Farmers* case in which the United States Supreme Court ruled that the taxation of income was unconstitutional. Good so far. However, after the passage of the Sixteenth Amendment in 1913 established the constitutionality of the federal income tax, reliance on *Pollack* was outdated.

Then there is another theory. Some raise the objection that the Sixteenth Amendment was not properly passed. There are some good arguments for this position that have been meticulously researched. For example, the state of Kentucky voted against the amendment, but Secretary of State Philander Knox counted it as a vote for the amendment. Unhappily, the Supreme Court and every other federal court for the last fifty years that has considered the issue or a similar issue has found the argument to be without merit.

Some people have simply quit filing income tax returns in order to protest what they see as inappropriate government actions, which they do not want to fund with the fruits of their labor. Often these protesters are high-minded moral individuals whose causes run the gamut from left- to right-wing: opposition to the Vietnam War, banning the proliferation of nuclear weapons, preventing the destruction of the environment, cutting foreign aid and domestic welfare spending, protesting run-away government waste and inefficiency, opposing government-funded abortions, or religious persecution. Every president in my lifetime has gotten elected by, among other things, complaining about IRS collection methods and promising reform. We are a nation of protesters. Protesting taxes is very high on our list.

However, some of these protesters are simply selling silver bullets to kill IRS vampires. It's a mistake. Silver bullets don't kill bloodsuckers; they kill werewolves. We call these promoters "protesters for profit." They usually aren't prosecuted, are seldom in court to protect their followers, and seem to accumulate lots of non-traceable cash.

Finally, our most beloved, technically innocent, but often horribly abused creature of civil disobedience is the simple uncomplicated fruitcake kind of protester. He relies on a theory that a con artist couldn't sell to a fifth grader.

Nebraska was such a guy: the devotee of an exotic theory to

49

explain why he was exempt from federal taxation. He was white, of freeborn parents, and a sovereign of the great state of Nebraska. Aside from being a really strange concept, the theory was so offensive that if a judge were to let a jury hear it, and if the jury could understand what it meant, it would probably alienate every liberal, most educated conservatives and every minority on the jury to the point where they would convict him out of indignation.

Proponents of the theory embraced by Nebraska believe there are two classes of American citizens. One class was created by two acts of government: The Thirteenth Amendment that freed the slaves; and the Fourteenth Amendment that ordered due process and guaranteed certain rights that the states could not abridge. Through an interpretation of the combined Thirteenth and Fourteenth Amendments, a new kind of citizen was "created." These "Fourteenth Amendment citizens" received the "privilege of citizenship" *from the government* and therefore had "a duty" to pay income taxes.

Nebraska and other adherents of this theory believed that this inferior class of citizenship was the only one available for those of minority races. In contrast, according to this hypothesis, there was another class of citizens who could claim inalienable rights *granted by God*, as described in the Preamble to the Constitution and the Declaration of Independence. As the supposition goes, a native-born American white male could claim to be a "Preamble" citizen and a citizen of whatever "sovereign state" of the union in which he was born or resides. However, if someone is entitled by birth and race to make this declaration and fails to do so, or "volunteers" by taking on social security and other Fourteenth Amendment government services, he becomes just another Fourteenth Amendment citizen.

Our office has actually had telephone calls from prospective clients wanting to know how much we would charge to file the correct papers to change their citizenship status and cancel their social security number! (By the way, you can't rescind your social security number. You can refuse to accept money from social security, but can't refuse the obligation to pay.) I don't know if we have been able to dissuade many from this philosophy through our standard explanation that our office will not consider filing frivolous legal documents for *any amount* of money. I would hazard to guess there are at least one hundred thousand adherents of this postulate, many of them highly educated, although some of them live in their own private world. Rey's friend Nebraska had swallowed the "citizenship" theory, hook, line, and sinker. Rey, on the other hand, was just looking for a legal way out of his serious difficulty.

For years, Rey Spulak owned and operated a farm equipment dealership. He was farsighted enough to perceive the downward trend of farm income, so he elected to sell his dealership. The proceeds of the sale were to be paid out over a period of time, secured by a promissory note. Unfortunately, the purchasers of the dealership became insolvent soon after the purchase. The promissory note became worthless. He lost his business and the note.

Nevertheless, the IRS assessed taxes on the transaction as if Spulak had received the full cash value of the promissory note. In addition, Spulak had another tax problem. When his tractor dealership was thriving, he had invested in some limited partnerships in the music business. He and the other partners deducted the losses they sustained. It was no secret in those days that the primary reason these partnerships existed was to act as tax shelters. It was presumed to be perfectly legal, and highly respected CPAs and lawyers routinely recommended them and often got commissions—or kickbacks. Lots of people utilized similar tax planning devices, did not get audited and did not have a problem. In fact, many got audited and their IRS auditors approved the deductions. In Rey's case, however, the auditor disallowed his losses and he was charged huge tax penalties and interest retroactively!

When the IRS says you owe them money, they send you what is called a thirty-day letter. You have thirty days to disagree in writing. You can argue for a while and compromise, but ultimately if there is an unreasoning government bureaucrat on the other end, you may lose all administrative arguments and the IRS gives you its final decision. That final decision is called a ninety-day letter.

If you have received the ninety-day letter, you have three options. One, you can agree to pay the tax, and then pay it. Two, you can do nothing. In that case, in ninety days, the letter becomes a final, unappealable judgment and you owe the money. Three, you can file a petition in tax court. Then you get another chance at the appeals level where you can enter into more negotiations or offer a compromise. Today, thanks to the 1986 Taxpayer's Bill of Rights, along with the ninety-day letter, the IRS must send you information telling you how serious this letter is. Often in the past, people did not understand it, waited too long, and had huge judgments assessed against them that they may not have owed. Even now lots of people fail to read all the small print.

If you elect to pay the taxes that the government says you owe (which in cases like Rey's are often double, sometimes up to ten times as much as the maximum amount possible under *any* construction of the law, conveniently giving the IRS and you or your lawyer room to negotiate), and you feel you have been aggrieved, you have the option of going to U.S. district court to sue the government for a refund plus interest. You are entitled to a judge or jury trial (your choice) in federal court. The "full payment now, sue later" option is very rarely taken. Most taxpayers, regardless of how many horror stories they have heard, think that justice will eventually prevail and choose to proceed in tax court. It is cheaper and you don't have to "pay now, have trial later." Another reality is that most taxpayers simply don't have the available cash to pay everything the government says they owe. Finally, if you pay it all and then lose the judge or jury decision, the money is gone. There is no room to negotiate. Once a collection agent has your money, be it the IRS or a Mafia thug, negotiations for bucks are really tough and usually unproductive.

The option selected most often by taxpayers who fight is to sue the commissioner of Internal Revenue in the United States tax court. In tax court, there is no provision for a jury trial. The judge is the finder of fact as well as the applier of law. Most tax court judges are former IRS lawyers. The burden of proof is usually on the taxpayer. (Since 1998, under certain circumstances, the burden of proof has shifted to the IRS.) The lawyers who practice there are among the most expensive in the legal business. The government will often enter into a compromise settlement before the case actually goes to trial, but many cases still go to trial. There is a substantial waiting period, and if you ultimately lose, you lose really big, because the penalties and interest continue to build up while you wait for a decision. If you lose, the judgment is often catastrophic.

Rey Spulak was facing the possibility of being ordered to pay the IRS more money than he had made in his lifetime. A typical taxpayer, he filed in tax court. Like anyone with any sense, he spent many a night awake, worrying about what would happen if he lost. He was absolutely devastated when he learned that the attorney he had trusted and hired to represent him in tax court had lost his license. Now he was a sheep about to face the wolf without even a shepherd bearing a stout stick to help ward off the attack!

It was this desperation that propelled him to attend a seminar in the Bahamas. There are seminars given all over the world to help people with IRS problems. The customers range from doctors looking for pension help to wild-eyed rabid fanatics looking for a lawyer to defend them if worse comes to worst and they end up killing a particularly nasty agent. The seminar speakers range from legitimate authorities to con artists to fruitcakes or combinations of both.

In the Bahamas, Rey met the undercover IRS agent Moussalem, a real wolf in sheep's clothing. This secret agent sold a complex legal solution that caused four men to serve prison sentences and got Rey and Nebraska indicted. Like a typical "protester for profit" (as opposed to a protester for ideals) he was selling "bad law." Unlike the typical tax con, he was selling for the IRS! After being convinced that the undercover IRS agent's scheme was legitimate, Spulak introduced a lot of his friends to this "gentleman," including Nebraska.

Nebraska's situation was somewhat different. He was a long-time friend of Spulak's. Nebraska had some tax shelter investments, too. He was a college professor with wide-ranging tastes in literature—from Shakespeare to tax conjecture publications of mixed varieties. Nebraska had attended meetings in the United States and became convinced that he was not a person required to file.

He had heard a lot of theories, and unlike some people who come to the same decision by deciding on a particular theory to the exclusion of others, Nebraska was convinced by a lot of different theories. He wasn't 100 percent sure exactly *why* he did not have to file a return, but he knew one or more of the theories applied to him. In practice, it is always easy to sit back and laugh at victims such as Rey and Nebraska. In reality, the cruel and unequal way the IRS selects victims often causes normal middle-class people to crack under pressure.

Authority figures proclaim a certain loophole is foolproof. You watch it work for half a decade and decide to partake. You're in. Suddenly, you're audited, your home and savings account are seized, and the five-thousand dollar deduction you took is a fifty-thousand dollar—or maybe a five-*hundred*-thousand dollar tax and penalty that the IRS now demands from you. An illness in the family causes you to get behind. You become afraid, and you quit filing. Ten years later you don't know what to do. These are not isolated events. People fall into these types of traps every day. When honest people fall into a hole they perceive as too deep to crawl out of—then it is. The perception becomes a fact—and a belief that yesterday seemed bizarre suddenly becomes more reasonable!

As time went on, Nebraska began to rely more and more on the theory that the federal courts had no jurisdiction over him because of his citizenship status. If you were an heir to your civil rights under the terms of the original Constitution, the *Preamble* defined you. Your rights were *inalienable*—not a *gift* or *privilege* handed out by the government. You did not have to use the Fourteenth Amendment, which is some type of contractual agreement with the government to become a citizen. You were a citizen without it! Does this make sense? Perhaps it is a little clearer than Nebraska's earlier description. Maybe not. When the Fourteenth Amendment was ratified in 1868, it stated, "Citizenship rights are not to be abridged." It followed the Thirteenth Amendment that freed the slaves. The Sixteenth Amendment, ratified in 1913, spelled it out in terse language: "The Congress shall have power to lay and collect taxes on income, from whatever source derived...."

So the Preamble defense qualifies for what we call, in our office, the "fruitcake files." It would be impossible to sell to a judge. Only a compassionate jury would even listen—and eggs would fly. Insanity as a defense would be a better option.

Lots of people find themselves in trouble with the IRS for a myriad of reasons. Some meet the wrong IRS agent at a party. Some knowingly break the law, hoping they won't get caught. Most of the time they don't get caught—they simply sweat a lot worrying about it. Often they have tried to follow the law and unwittingly end up in a tax shelter that either was not set up properly or had no legal basis in the first place. Or, often, the tax shelter *was* set up correctly but the IRS doesn't care or recognize it.

The seminar Rey attended in the Bahamas was put on by one of the very few off-shore tax-shelter promoters who actually made good on his promises. He absolutely guaranteed the participants that his plan would keep their money out of the hands of the IRS. He convinced nearly a billion dollars worth of investors to put their money in his offshore insurance company. Unlike so many other promoters, he even made good on his guarantee. To this day, as far as I know, not one dollar of the nearly one billion that left these shores to be invested in that enterprise was ever recovered by the IRS. Of course, the flip side was that most of the investors lost their money. The offshore guru never sent it back.

Undercover IRS agents looking for indictment "volunteers" almost always attend these large seminars. They are tax collecting or enjoying an educational holiday at taxpayers' expense in Switzerland, the Isle of Man, the Netherlands Antilles, the Cayman Islands, or the Bahamas. These offshore tax-haven countries are very often beach resorts and/or gaming capitals. Just the place for a public servant to tan his public posterior. The seminar explains the program of the promoter and others. Some are legitimate, but many are far from it. The undercover agents are there to "pick some clients." Rey was "captured" by Robert Moussalem.

Moussalem was a convicted felon. (The IRS loves to work with convicted felons. There are lots of ex-cons whose morality fits right into the program.) He convinced Rey Spulak that he could put him in touch with an IRS agent in Birmingham, Alabama, who could guarantee that Spulak's tax problems would vanish.

The only setback was the pending case in tax court. Rey would have to drop his case there and take a voluntary judgment against himself before the Birmingham agent could get involved. Scary? Yes, but absolute trust was required in these situations.

Moussalem had the full approval and assistance of the IRS. He worked undercover with taxpayers' dollars to entrap allegedly guilty taxpayers. His motive has not been made public: Reward? Reduction in sentence? I can't tell you. The tragedy is that most of those entrapped were not guilty and most of them were not inclined to commit crimes. Moussalem would work to overcome this problem.

Rey reminded Moussalem that he was a Nebraska resident, considerably removed from Birmingham, Moussalem's city of operation. Moussalem was so convincing, however, that Spulak agreed to meet with this seemingly magic IRS agent in Birmingham. Devastated by the desertion of his former attorney in the face of his imminent tax court trial and puzzled by the numerous conflicting theories of a multitude of so-called experts in the Bahamas, Spulak was desperate to cling to any straw that offered a glint of hope—and Moussalem offered more than mere hope.

Rey Spulak went to Birmingham, where Moussalem introduced him to "Bob Cooper," also known as "William Cooper," an undercover IRS agent. In fact, we will refer to him as "Undercover." Undercover assured Rey that he liked him and would be able to help him. He explained that Rey would have to drop his case in the Omaha, Nebraska, tax court and move to Alabama. Undercover further assured him that the "offer in compromise" he was about to enter into was perfectly legal and quoted portions of the Internal Revenue Code to prove it. There actually is a section called offer in compromise; and Rey actually had a chance to win some of his arguments in court. Undercover's scheme flirted with it and abused it. If not for the intervention of Moussalem and Undercover, Spulak would have had an excellent chance of winning some elements of his Omaha tax court case, but no one will ever know. So that the matter could be referred to Undercover's collection office in Birmingham, Spulak signed papers agreeing that he owed the IRS all of the disputed money and dismissed his case in Omaha.

Nebraska had a lot less to lose by giving up his right to proceed in tax court under the citizenship premise. His citizenship theory had less chance to win than Charles Manson has to get a pardon. However, with both of their civil tax court cases dismissed by them, Spulak and Nebraska were in the same civil boat together, just as though they had both gone to court and lost. There was no difference between the fruitcake and the bonafide case. Meanwhile, down in Alabama, the events, which would lead to the criminal case against Rey and Nebraska, continued to unfold.

Undercover met privately with both Rey and Nebraska. Each meeting was very similar to the one I described for Rey. Several other victims went through similar initiations. Some may still be in jail. Undercover first showed Rey the actual statute that allows the taxpayer to make an offer in compromise. To understand what happened, first let's take a look at a hypothetical situation depicting how a legitimate offer in compromise might be reached, in the case of an alleged

57

million-dollar tax debt, and then a facsimile of the real McCoy in Spulak's case.

IRS agent: Okay, you owe us a million dollars.

Taxpayer: Okay, you got me. I really thought the law allowed me to take business deductions when my pigs died and we had to eat them. I spent my last penny losing this case in tax court. Still can't believe I lost. How about a compromise?

IRS agent: Okay, what do you have in mind?

Taxpayer: I thought I'd agree to pay five dollars a week for the rest of my life.

IRS agent: No way. Your $50,000 home is paid off, and you make $100,000 a year. I say, give me your home and pay all of the $50,000 you have left over after taxes for twenty years.

Taxpayer: No thanks. I'll just let you steal the home, take the shirt off my back and then I'll file bankruptcy and wipe out the tax debt. How about $25,000 cash now, then $25,000 a year for five years?

IRS agent: I think we can prove the pig was fraudulent and therefore you can't wipe out the debt in bankruptcy. If you have $25,000 in cash, I want it now anyway.

Taxpayer: Well, actually, I don't have any cash. I was going to put $10,000 on a charge card and get my uncle Abe to lend me the $15,000 balance.

Sometimes the taxpayer doesn't have any assets in the United States and he lives on the Isle of Man where they have no extradition for taxes and no income taxes and no way to collect the money except by negotiating with the taxpayer's lawyer. The lawyer says his "Man" inhabitant would like to come back to the USA occasionally to visit, without worrying about being robbed and perhaps incarcerated while the IRS interrogates him about the state of his fortune and its location, but only if it's not too expensive. This type of deal can often result in as little as two or three cents on the dollar as opposed to a more normal requirement of seventy or eighty cents on the dollar.

Essentially, the offer-in-compromise statute codifies what actually existed before: that you can bargain on your alleged tax debt and like any other type of negotiation, the individual bargainers and specific facts allow for various different logical solutions. Some practitioners have clout, like the last commissioner who still knows everyone in the treasury, or a former senator, or even better, the ex-agent who is bargaining with his former friend who is about to retire after twenty years and is looking for a job in the free market.

If the government would bargain like a capitalist in most cases, settle whenever settlement was wise, and forgive some of the horrendous penalties that have accrued against people who got out of the system, they could eliminate the deficit! Unfortunately, bureaucrats usually do not negotiate intelligently. They take to trial tax cases against indigents who could not pay if they wanted to, and they rob people of most of their income, forcing them to go underground or leave the country or, often, go on public assistance.

Most of the people desperately in need of help against the IRS are unaware of two great secrets known by all competent persons who work in the field: First, under the right circumstances, you can wipe out income tax debt in bankruptcy court (though credit card companies can be expected to push to modify this legislation in 2001). Second, you have a legal right to bargain with the IRS and if the bargain is reduced to writing and signed (the word of an IRS agent is not worth the paper it's *not* written on) you can settle for less than you actually owe.

When Undercover showed the statute to Rey, he was overwhelmed. When Undercover convinced him to drop his case in tax court before settling, he was getting him to drop his best chance for fair bargaining, that is if Undercover had any authority to bargain at all, which he didn't. Undercover's only job was to find criminals and get them convicted. If he could not find them by such methods as sending his associate Moussalem to lurk in exotic places like the Bahamas seminar, then he could do the next best thing: he would *create* criminals. If he struck out there, he would lie and indict wholly innocent people such as Rey or complete "fruitcake" victims—IRS's easiest targets—the Nebraskas of this country.

Undercover then set up a private meeting with Rey in true Hollywood fashion. Only, Rey was the "good guy," being set up by the bad guys. Undercover was wired like a Christmas tree; not with lights but with more bugs than an Orkin commercial. The conversation was carefully structured. It went something like this:

Und: Do you have the money?

Rey: I do, but I want to make sure this is perfectly legal.

Und: No, Rey. You have to say "Yes." Nothing more. Do you have the money?

Rey: Yes.

Und: Are you willing to compromise me?

Rey: That sounds so funny! You mean, do I have the money for the offer in compromise?

Und: You have to just say "yes," Rey. The law is very particular. Are you here to compromise me?

Rey: Yes.

Und: Where's the money?

Rey: Here it is. I'm going to need a receipt and something in writing.

Und: No, Rey. You have to say, "Here's the cash." You don't get a receipt. You're not dealing with the Mafia. You're dealing with your government and we have certain ways of doing things. You have to trust me. Now, where's the money?

Rey: Here's the cash.

Und: Okay, Rey, I'll take care of everything. You can forget about Uncle Sam. It's all settled and over with.

Rey: I'm sure lucky I ran into you, "Undercover." There are so many crooks out there. All I ever wanted was to follow the law. I just don't understand why one of the other government workers didn't settle this years ago!

(Most of the quotations in this book are exact, taken word for word from transcripts or testimony. This section has been altered, keeping the flow but greatly reducing it. The actual transcript took a long time for Undercover to trap Rey. The results are intact but greatly abridged and over-simplified. These are not taken directly from the text but from memory. Our office was broken into in November 1993 and this file could not be found. The tapes were also missing. We have since installed extensive burglar alarms and motion detectors.)

Rey was indicted a few weeks after this conversation with the undercover IRS agent for two counts of attempted bribery of an IRS agent, and faced a potential ten-year imprisonment. With a similar conversation and transaction, Nebraska was also indicted. Four other citizens who had the misfortune of dealing with Undercover were also criminally prosecuted. Two were already in prison at the time I met Rey and Nebraska.

I could not represent both Rey and Nebraska. Their defenses would be very different and possibly hurt each other. I declined to do so. I did agree to prepare most of the discovery pre-trial motions for both, which were very similar, and I recommended that Nebraska plead insanity. I thought Rey had a very good case. In fact, I did not understand how the government had gotten convictions of other people in similar situations. Sometimes, of course, your clients are not completely frank with you: one of the worst things that can happen during a trial is getting hit by a "surprise" that is a surprise only to you, and possibly to the jury. Especially if the government always

61

knew what was coming. Nebraska filed his own additional motions for dismissal based on the "fact" that the court had no jurisdiction to even have a trial since Nebraska was a citizen of the state of Nebraska and *not* the United States *after* the passage of the Fourteenth Amendment and therefore also the taxing amendment. I filed extensive discovery motions on behalf of my client and gave the co-defendant copies he could file himself; then I referred Nebraska to another fine lawyer for trial.

The court granted our motions for discovery and, lo and behold, we were given a transcript of the conversation between Rey and Undercover. It read something like this:

Und: Do you have the money?

Rey: (inaudible)

Und: Do you have the money?

Rey: Yes.

Und. The law is very particular. Are you willing to compromise me? (Inaudible) Are you here to compromise me?

Rey: (Inaudible) Yes, here's the cash. (Inaudible exchange.)

Und: Okay, Rey, I'll take care of everything. You can forget about Uncle Sam.

Rey: I'm so lucky I ran into you. There are so many crooks out there. (Sounds of walking.)

Und: We're all crooks, Rey. No choice in the matter.

Would that be enough to get a grand jury to indict someone? You bet. In fact, Justice Richard Neely of the West Virginia Supreme Court once remarked that a grand jury would indict a peanut butter sandwich! In this case, any jury would convict Rey based on this partly audible, partly inaudible tape. That is, unless they wondered why the richest government in the world would rely on such a cheap tape system that failed to properly pick up sounds. That was "explained" by the government. The conspirators whispered so much because they were nervous, but their intent was clear. Undercover had secreted himself into a world of criminals just waiting for IRS agents to come forward and take bribes.

A trouble-making defense counsel, who was a stickler for the rules and unwilling to trust his government in a simple transcription interpretation, might also wonder why these "criminals" had to go all the way to a seminar in the Bahamas to find a corrupt IRS agent, coincidentally wired for poor sound mixed in with some very good sound. Strangely enough, although we were familiar with deceit by the IRS on a regular basis, at this time most of my staff was convinced by the tape transcript that this would be one of our toughest cases and that our client was guilty. My only feeling was that Rey was guilty of great gullibility.

I kept pressing for the production of the original tapes, noting that, frequently, the government's interpretation of a tape or document was different from the one a jury might have. The court agreed, and, after obtaining a signed judicial order for production, we got back on the plane for Houston. Our hearing had been in front of a federal judge visiting from Florida.

I always try to learn a little about my trial judges before the trial. In this case, I had recently had a hearing in front of that same visiting judge on another case in his home state of Florida. I was the only lawyer in a room full of local Alabama lawyers who knew something about the judge. I was, of course, not local. I particularly wanted to have Rey's and Nebraska's cases severed, i.e., tried separately. My client had a reasonable case, based on mistake—and hopefully, a different transcription when the newly acquired tapes were played in court and became "audible." I did not want to try Rey with Nebraska, whose theory smacked a little of racism and would undoubtedly rub off on Rey. I lost the motion for severance but won the discovery requests.

A few weeks later we received the first set of tapes. They were not the originals that I had requested an opportunity to review. They were,

63

however, after an independent engineer did a little amplification work of the "inaudible" sections, brought up to the point where they could be heard. The actual tapes were similar to our first version. In short, the partly inaudible version was a complete fraud.

The tapes exonerated Rey and Nebraska, but there were a lot of tapes still missing, and the government had been ordered by the visiting judge to produce them. What was in them? Was our once *bad* case, now a *good* case, about to become an even *better* case?

It was clear now to everyone in the office that both Rey and Nebraska had been framed. Lots of questions still weren't answered. What was the motive of Undercover? Why was this "sting" operation set up? What was Moussalem's role? Was his participation an element of a plea bargain he had entered into due to his own conviction? Had Moussalem's trial and conviction been a sham? What was Moussalem being paid with—besides free trips to the Bahamas? Why had four other attorneys relied on the government version of the tapes? Were four innocent people in jail? What was the government still holding back? What would the last tapes reveal?

Again, our judge ordered the government to produce more tapes. Their deadline was the Friday before the Monday when the trial was scheduled to begin. The government prosecutor called and offered us a continuance of the trial. Defendants usually want to postpone the trial as long as possible. Until trial occurs, no one is ever convicted. On rare occasions, wishes come true and as time passes and potential trial settings pass, the trial never comes up. In this case, I said, "No, let's get on with it and give me the missing tapes."

Many questions raised by this case will never be answered because we never got the tapes. Without ceremony, the government just dropped the charges against Rey and Nebraska on Friday. The media called and asked for comments, but Rey did not want to have anything to do with them. He was exonerated and was not going to jail. Happy days!

Nebraska was a fish with a different smell. He gave interview after interview and, believe it or not, is now teaching others how to avoid filing tax returns! On the front page of one paper, the headlines read, "Tax Evasion Case Dismissed...Defendant Claims Court Recognized Citizen of Nebraska Exempt from Income Taxation...." Needless to say, the court, if interviewed, would likely not agree.

I like to think that the cause of our victory was my discovery work and steadfast devotion to the pursuit of truth and justice. Nebraska has his own version. I admit, his probably makes better press copy.

Following Nebraska's victory, we got calls from all over the country on the jurisdiction issue. "I'm from Kansas. Do I have to file?" "I'm a Texan, surely we have more freedom from federal jurisdiction than a Nebraskan?"

Whenever there is a victory against the IRS, a dozen axioms surface testifying to the reason for the victory. Each hypothesis is likely to land a few people in jail. Nebraska is on the way to everlasting fame in the history of fruitcake theories.

Moussalem, who originally introduced Rey Spulak to Undercover, was found dead under mysterious circumstances, allegedly a suicide. Undercover is not in jail and may still be working his IRS scam.

Rey Spulak endured ten tension-filled years worrying about arbitrary sanctions placed against him at the whim of an IRS agent who claimed Rey owed money that he didn't really owe. To compound the injustice, the IRS tried to illegally entrap him into a false bribery charge. When their clumsy and heavy handed attempts to convict Rey failed, the government conveniently dropped the charges and made the incriminating evidence against them "disappear." A good man went through a decade-long ordeal and nobody was punished for ruining ten years of his life. If you still harbor any illusions as to the beneficient nature of our government, I suggest that you remember Rey Spulak's lengthy nightmare.

Chapter III
The Absent Minded Professor

"I'm a mathematician, not a philosopher."
— Albert Einstein,
responding in the negative
when asked if he prepared
his own tax returns.

SALT LAKE CITY, UTAH, JANUARY 1993

My absent minded professor's leg was bouncing up and down. His right hand thumped on the wooden counsel table, his paisley tie jerked a little as he fiddled with it as though it were too tight for him to swallow. Dressed in conservative brown, he raised his left arm to his head to smooth his wavy hair as he listened to undefeated Jeffrey Breinholdt, United States attorney from Washington, D.C., explain to twelve jurors why Geoffrey Alan (a pseudonym requested by the client) should be found guilty of tax crimes for 1985, 1986, and 1987. Because the law requires the jurors to act in partial ignorance, and because it would hurt the government's case, he left out the fact that, once convicted, Geoffrey faced the possibility of fifteen years in a federal prison.

I casually put my left arm around Geoffrey Alan's shoulder, smiling nonchalantly at my co-counsel, Mark McLachlan, a gray-haired, distinguished local Salt Lake man, and suggested with a whisper and a wave of my hand that Mark pull up a file. I opened the file for Geoffrey, then put my left foot over his right foot with force, and in a low voice, while pointing at the irrelevant file, I explained to Geoffrey, "Innocent people sit up, don't fidget, don't bang their knees, look concerned, perhaps occasionally outraged, but mostly under control and humble. You're creating background guilt pictures while Breinholdt crucifies you."

A little child-like, my absent-minded professor smiled back, saying without words, "Oops, I forgot."

Winning a criminal tax trial requires that you do everything right 99 percent of the time, get lucky, and close the case right. A client of mine was once convicted in his second trial in Muskogee, Oklahoma because, after difficult deliberation, a juror who wasn't sure she should convict merely because the judge obviously wanted her to, saw my client, head down, shoulders slumped in the hallway. His demeanor suggested dishonesty to her. He appeared to be "sneaking around."

Geoffrey Alan was scared; and frankly, so was I. This peach of a man was facing hard time and personal destruction.

The courtroom is a pressure cooker. You must watch the jurors, the judge, the court personnel, the audience, the opposition, and the bailiff. You must listen to the noises in the hall and the testimony and argument, evaluate it all, re-evaluate it, and devise and re-devise strategy. If you lose a criminal tax case, your client goes to jail. Federal judges are also notorious for threatening to put vigorous defense counsel in jail. In fact, the failure of the judge to hint his or her outrage by describing his or her powers of contempt during a long trial is the exception—not the rule.

The threat is rarely carried out, but is very much a sword of Damocles hanging over counsel's head. The government claims victory in an overwhelming percentage of its tax cases. There are about ten lawyers I know who regularly defend clients accused of tax crimes and who can count all the victories of their combined careers on one hand. Two have been disbarred recently (one unjustifiably; the other was practically clinically insane) and a third jailed.

I had forewarned Geoffrey and my team not to shake and rattle at counsel table, not to show signs of concern as Breinholdt ripped apart the life of Geoffrey Alan to these twelve strangers, but instructions before trial are easier to take than to follow. L. R., my right hand, comes across unassuming and kind, which she is, but more than one foe has fallen to defeat by underestimating her brilliant forensic talents and near-photographic memory for dates, names, and statutes. A veteran of more trials than most full-time trial lawyers, even L. R. had trouble keeping her composure listening to Breinholdt's cunning opening argument.

Of three thousand tax-related indictments a year, three hundred actually go to trial. The rest give up and go directly to jail or, depending on the statute and bargaining, probation. Of the three hundred, about ten are acquitted nationwide, according to A. J. Lowery, editor of the *Justice Times*. Each minor city has its specialists in criminal tax defense. Often it is an ex-IRS lawyer, equally often, a lawyer who seldom if ever has faced a jury. Frequently they charge large retainers and then push for a plea. Often they quit before trial because the client—having spent a fortune flying them to Washington for consultations and coffee—is broke. More often they just bow out, preferring to avoid the undignified process of trial combat.

On the opposite end are the ones who guarantee victory with vague suggestions of constitutional passages to ward off evil IRS spirits, or theories that wages are not income. These guys put more people in jail than the IRS could ever hope to do on their own. Whenever there is a legitimate victory, these heroes pop up and sell versions of the victory, which often don't even relate to the real reason for a dismissal or acquittal. (See Spulak case, Chapter II.)

We were set for trial before the Honorable Judge J. Thomas Greene on January 4, 1993, in the federal courthouse in downtown Salt Lake City, Utah. Paul Des Fosses, a former IRS agent, now devoted to blowing the whistle on corrupt IRS practices, surmised IRS public relations planned both cases to be tried, convicted, and sentenced by April of 1993, just in time for the annual tax season publicity campaign brought to us by our government to scare us to death into what the IRS likes to call "voluntary compliance."

Contoured as though he were going to a *Gentlemen's Quarterly* photo shoot after the trial, tall elegant Jeff Breinholdt glided like a ballet dancer to the podium, gracefully avoiding enough government diagrams, blow ups, and exhibits to fill a Hollywood backyard prop area. He nodded magnanimously to our motley table with just a touch of scorn and then with a broad warm smile, faced the jury. Well dressed and handsome with short black hair, Breinholdt cut an impressive figure.

Court: Mr. Breinholdt, you may proceed.

Breinholdt: Thank you.

Judge Greene graciously nodded to this affable Greek god with his Harvard ring and thousand-dollar Hickey Freeman suit, and indicated that he could continue.

Breinholdt: "This case is about a man who was living a double life."

Our courtroom was a hundred years old. Hand-stained cherry wood paneling hung with the portraits of former judges. The jurors sat in reupholstered wooden chairs.

Judge Greene, in marked contrast to Breinholdt, was short, stocky and not concerned about how his hair fell on his face. Many trial judges have tried few, if any, jury cases as lawyers and often seek the power and salary of the federal bench (in 1993, $130,000) to escape an unsuccessful legal career.

Greene did not fit that mold. He relished being in the pit. He

70

thrived on the stomach pains and the verbal fisticuffs. He had made a living as a trial lawyer and loved it. Greene read the motions filed before him, read the relevant cases and digested them like a scholar. He had a fast and sharp temper but also a piercing intellect and an equally fast comprehension of complex legal matters. He also believed in the jury system and the constitutional presumption of innocence. He had accepted the bench not as a pulpit and not to escape personal inadequacies, but to explore intellectually the next step in his legal studies. At times he made it clear he missed private practice. He was demanding and tough, and tended to chastise. He was fair, however, and he was willing to give Geoffrey Alan a fair trial. Another mark of an excellent judge is that he would rule quickly, not forcing us to wait all day for decisions. He also had a sense of humor, a most welcome commodity in the heavy hard world of trial law.

At our table sat L. R., my heavy-set good-natured all-observant brilliant legal assistant adorned with a large silver cross but no make-up; Paul Des Fosses, CPA, founder of the Whistleblowers, former school teacher, former professional athlete, and a rodeo champion with a bad back, which had caused him to balloon up in competition with L. R.; myself, accused wrongfully of being too short, with a nose allegedly out of joint from boxing, well-dressed, (in my opinion!), but obviously no competition for Breinholdt's *G.Q.* looks; my absent-minded professor; and our local lawyer, Geoffrey's personal counsel, Mark McLachlan, a distinguished veteran of many campaigns.

At Breinholdt's table, placed right next to the jurors, was his colleague Eric Lisann, also flown in by "Justice" from headquarters in Washington, D.C. Lisann, who had short-cropped, curly hair, a tan, and a body builder's physique in tailored clothing, didn't exactly seem like Mr. Public Servant either. Smart, sassy, pretty with a strong jaw, Lisann could have been elected Yuppie of the Year. In a beauty contest against them we would have been disqualified, possibly even sanctioned for having the gall to compete with these guys.

Breinholdt: Mr. Lisann and I represent the Government of the United States. (Meaning of course the jurors too, *against those who would defile America*, meaning of course, *us*.) On October 26, 1986, Robert Underwood, who is a commercial loan officer at First Security Bank received a letter from the defendant that said.... "due to last minute arrangement with...decorators, painters, and carpenters. I must be in Salt Lake City at my new home....The business is doing well."...Later, LaDonna Crane,...a professional tax preparer received a letter...that...stated, "I have not had a good year due to heavy competition by others who have the same product as I have."...A month after that grim letter to LaDonna Crane,...Underwood received another letter. "The business is doing well and things are looking up for me"...Crane received another letter....It stated: "I've had another bad year."

Breinholdt began addressing Geoffrey as "Mr. Alan" and then subtly called him "Geoffrey", taking away a piece of this fifty-three year old inventor's dignity with the familiar form—and finally simply as "the defendant," always a demeaning appellation. Once you become "the defendant" you are only one step away from becoming "the convict."

Breinholdt: As Judge Greene has already told you, the defendant has been accused by the grand jury of not reporting his income.

Breinholdt paused, letting it sink in that this evil defendant had already been accused by a grand jury. A young woman, who may have been able to visualize herself on Breinholdt's Harvard arm, looked smitten and simultaneously puzzled. You could read it on her face. "I don't understand why we're here. It's obvious the grand jury found this defendant guilty." Geoffrey was viewed by half the jurors during this pause. No shock at our table. No show of concern. All was under control at least visually, although L. R., Mark, and Geoffrey all admitted later that the next words would shake them all up, and make even Geoffrey have doubts.

> Breinholdt: Their tone (the letters mentioned) was different for a very single reason. There would be no reason to misrepresent his financial situation to his loan officer who was well aware of his successful mail order business and the extent of the hundreds of thousands of dollars....

Breinholdt delayed a moment putting heavy emphasis on the words, "hundreds of thousands of dollars."

"The defendant, Geoffrey Alan, led a double life of deceit and dishonesty. He became obsessed with his treasures and his opulent lifestyle."

Breinholdt turned, pointed to Geoffrey, and paused for more dramatic effect. I had Geoffrey stand up and face Breinholdt. It caught Breinholdt off guard for a pinch of a second. Did any jurors catch it? I wanted Geoffrey to show the jurors he was not hiding from these accusations but facing them head on. Breinholdt quickly recovered and gracefully turned back to the jurors and returned to his melodic tempo.

> Breinholdt: The specific place of inaccuracy is on line 1(a) which asks for information relating to gross receipts or sales. The evidence will show that figure, which is slightly over $72,000, in that return was under-reported to the extent of about $239,000...about $800,000 over...three years.

Breinholdt nodded at the jurors, disgust now on his face, and again looked over at Geoffrey, nodded and returned to the pulpit.

> Breinholdt: It's about a man who, during the time period we're talking about, when he's reporting somewhere between $12,000 of adjusted gross income in 1985 to about $7,000 in adjusted gross income in 1987, bought a $495,000 home in the Mount Olympus Cove area of Salt Lake City and proceeded to spend hundreds of thousands of dollars for such things as home improvements, decorations, and antique furnishings. This is the

same house that was referred to so glowingly in the letter of October 26, 1986, to Robert Underwood. You will see that Mr. Alan, in decorating his dream home, went so far as to hire a full-time crew of workers to come to his house five days a week, eight hours a day for about thirteen months. The government will prove to you that these checks, (Breinholdt pointed to three boxes in front of the jury box) which took up enough room to fill two large hot tubs, came from customers of his from all over the United States, over a million dollars!

Breinholdt then pirouetted over to blow-ups of letters Geoffrey had sent his accountant saying that business was bad, and also representations that Geoffrey's date of birth was wrong on his driver's license.

Breinholdt: The defendant...bought $60,000 worth of Persian rugs from a rug dealer in Southern California and, in an effort to disguise his identity as the true recipient of the rugs, disguised himself as an interior decorator. According to these statements, the most significant assets that were acquired during this period were a Salt Lake City home that Mr. Alan valued at $1.5 million and $800,000 worth of items consisting of such things as Persian rugs, antique clocks, porcelain vases, antique paintings, and a $90,000 coin collection.

You will hear and see evidence of Mr. Alan's affinity for coins and silver. You will hear about a man who during the time period we're talking about, in addition to buying half a million dollar home and decorating it with those expensive items, still had the financial means to throw hundreds of thousands of additional dollars into a declining silver market...you will hear about a man who was very conscious—perhaps even obsessive—with his financial status, who would quibble with his silver dealers over such things as a $5 freight charge or with his bank over such things as a $23 interest payment.

You will hear about a man who frequently played games with his

74

Social Security Number, who would provide his correct Social Security Number on the returns he filed with the Internal Revenue Service, but when he dealt with creditors and other people who might have a more accurate picture of his financial status, would switch a digit. For example, 575 would become 537. This playing games with his Social Security Number was not an isolated occurrence. It happened so many times and over such a long period of time that, after a while, Mr. Alan actually developed an entire credit history under a false Social Security Number. You will hear about a man who frequently used false names if it meant saving money. He called himself such names as Robinson and Ken Jensen. He claimed to own businesses such as Great Basin Coin and Ye Olde Antique Shop, which, in fact, did not exist. You will hear about a man who in order to obtain wholesale prices, asked his banker to misrepresent his occupation and his name to vendors who were calling, checking on his credit.

As I've said, this case is about a man who was leading a double life, who would describe his financial situation in wildly different ways depending on who he was talking to.

Breinholdt gave another dramatic pause, looked each juror in the eye and returned to his table with Lisann.

Jeffrey Breinholdt had concealed most of the players on his team from the jurors, a million-dollar team of government witnesses, errand runners, special agents, FBI contacts, and subpoena servers who would all sit in the back or wander the hallways so our team of four (plus two jury experts) would look massive compared to their apparent team of two.

In chambers I had lost a key evidentiary ruling on which our case depended. The IRS had, during its multi-million dollar, five-year investigation, discovered false tax returns at Geoffrey's bank only two weeks earlier, or so they said. For the same years Geoffrey reported a small net income to the IRS, he had dummy returns for the bank showing lots of income. He had lied to the bank. He had, however, an

75

acceptable reason. I argued to the court unsuccessfully that the bank returns, which we conceded were false, would so prejudice the jurors that Geoffrey would not be on trial for his '85, '86, and '87 returns, but for the false bank returns.

Greene ruled that they were admissible to show bad intent, but agreed to instruct the jury that they were not evidence of the crime Alan was charged with, only possible evidence of Geoffrey's state of mind. I am perhaps least effective when trying to keep evidence out. I believe in the jury system and also believe the fairest trial is the one which allows the *most* evidence. In the pre-trial conference it became clear that this intentionally false 1040 form, the one given to the bank, would be the crux of the government's case.

Breinholdt's opening pushed four issues, all prejudicial, all mostly irrelevant:

1. Geoffrey made a lot of money;
2. Geoffrey spent a lot of money;
3. Geoffrey told the IRS one thing, the bank another;
4. Geoffrey had discrepancies in numbers, such as social security and birth dates on a driver's license.

The evidence was definitely against us, so far. Nevertheless, we had a few factors weighing in on our side: unlike the government public servants, we would work twenty-four hour days during trial (even dreaming about the case), and despite a brilliant opening by Breinholdt and some terribly prejudicial facts, we had the *truth* on our side: Geoffrey Alan was innocent!

My grandfather, George Minns, was fond of the adage "To tell half the truth and leave the other half untold is to tell half a lie." Most of the facts eloquently expressed by Breinholdt were true, but the conclusion he reached, and wanted the jury to join him in reaching, was false.

Over a hundred years ago a country trial lawyer up against a formidable Philadelphia lawyer explained this phenomena to a jury with a story about a farmer and his son and daughter. First, the country lawyer told the jurors in his pebbly, raspy voice, "I agree with my colleague from Philadelphia on his exposition of the facts...." (The jurors were surprised. Was he giving the case away?) " ...but I see that he has come to the wrong conclusion." (What did this mean, right facts, wrong conclusion?)

"The farmer's young son came up to him, breathing hard, and shouted to him, 'Pappy, Sis and her boyfriend are peeing on your fresh hay.' The farmer slowed the child down to get a better picture of the facts. It seems his son had seen his sister pull down her pants and her boyfriend pull down his pants and then the two of them dropped down on the loft onto the fresh hay where the young boy couldn't see them." The country lawyer dead-panned his jury, pointing first to his great Philadelphia adversary and concluded, "You see, like my honorable friend here from Philly, the farmer's son got his facts right but he's come to the wrong conclusion!"

The country lawyer who won the verdict quietly signed the court records with his name—A. Lincoln.

Before going more into the trial you need to know who Geoffrey Alan was and is. It is easy to assume a defendant is a criminal. The government's opening successfully dehumanized Geoffrey.

Geoffrey was born in 1940. He enjoyed art, weapons, and comic books. He knew these would be interests of his in later life. He would order weapons and games by mail as a child. A devout Christian, Geoffrey graduated from Brigham Young University with a master's degree in fine arts. Then he went on to complete three years in the Peace Corps and two years service in the armed forces before he got married. His marriage failed, but he buried himself in his various business pursuits and, later, in taking care of his crippled sister and elderly mother. All this time Geoffrey was tinkering with a concept for a new "hunting device."

Geoffrey also bought and sold antiques and eventually got into the rare coin business. For all of these pursuits he wrote and placed his own ads, and so legally had the right to open an ad agency and deduct the 15 percent commission that ad agencies traditionally get from the bill to make their profit. The assumed name he chose for his ad business was part of the government's complaint. He devised a number of different ads for selling weapons. To decide which ones were effective and which weren't he used a number of different names such as House of Weapons and others. All names went into the same account. Using different names sounded sinister when Breinholdt talked about it, but it is a standard mail-order practice. In fact, many companies like General Mills and others, package foods under their own names and also under other names. Macy's own brand, Amber Mouthwash, tastes and looks like Listerine, because it *is* Listerine, bottled under the Macy name by the Warner-Lambert Company. Multiple name use is a common acceptable marketing practice all over America. Geoffrey's banker verified these businesses because he legitimately and honestly was involved in them, and his banker knew it.

Two obstacles had kept Geoffrey from reaching the golden ring. First, he never patented his device. A dozen imitations, including Japanese and Taiwanese competitors, flooded the market and slowed Geoffrey's sales to a dribble. Second, the IRS decided to take him out.

Geoffrey began to launch his antique business as a standby venture by first purchasing (financed, of course) a run-down mansion in the posh area of town. He filled it with copies of antiques, grandfather clocks, and Persian carpets, all using legitimate assumed names. He also purchased bullion for resale from Monex, a commodities firm. He remodeled the house towards his goal of having a high ticket, invitation only, model home from which to sell antiques. Then as the icing on the cake, Geoffrey invented a new crossbow, smaller, with greater accuracy and range and beautifully handcrafted. This time he *did* patent it and could offer it as competitively as the earlier device without having to worry about being copied by foreign and local competitors.

Then, the explosion came. Monex was like a disease. They never clearly explained margin calls or markets. They never told Geoffrey that 90 percent of all commodities investors get wiped out of their positions. They only delivered bullion to Geoffrey once. As each day passed his silver dropped and they asked for more money. In 1985,

1986, and 1987, Monex took Geoffrey, along with hundreds of others, for a lot of money. Geoffrey alone lost over $400,000!

Geoffrey's bookkeeping system was terribly unsophisticated. He carried his records and notes in a plastic Rubbermaid laundry basket. He knew what was in there, but couldn't quite tell you why. If you asked for something he could find it, but you couldn't ask him what to do with it. He had rebuilt his 1973 Cadillac El Dorado convertible, manufactured his inventions, and could understand an interest charge he didn't deserve. However, he was so unsophisticated with his tax returns, the ones he was accused of willfully falsifying, that he didn't take deductions for his handicapped sister, business interest, or his home mortgage deductions for taxes and insurance. If Geoffrey had wanted to hide $400,000, he sure didn't do it the right way, which would have been with assumed names on multiple accounts or, even smarter, with foreign or offshore banks. Every penny, cash or check, went right into the same business account with the same bank that he had used for twenty years!

In 1986, while foreign invaders were attacking Geoffrey with the blessing and subsidy of *their* government, *our* government, through its unethical and out-of-control agency, the IRS, was stomping on Geoffrey, his employees, and future potential, with both feet. A full-fledged audit was conducted against Geoffrey Alan. Bank records were pulled, and all of his transactions were put under the magnifying glass.

At trial, Monex, whom we later learned had actually filed a report with the IRS against Geoffrey, was represented by a Canadian lawyer who, in my opinion, had scales like a serpent. I questioned him after his testimony against his company's former client, Geoffrey Alan.

Minns: As an attorney, did you notify your company's client, Geoffrey Alan, when you learned that he was the subject of an IRS investigation?

Attorney: No. Never thought of it.

Minns: Is that an unethical non-disclosure in Canada?

Breinholdt: Objection!

Court: Sustained, it's irrelevant.

Minns: I disagree your honor. Whether or not this witness is unethical is important for the jury to know to determine his credibility.

Court: Overruled.

My point was either made or lost, and I did not want to alienate the judge, so I moved on. The theory of law is that all jurors presume innocence (they don't), that all instructions to forget or remember are obeyed (they aren't), and that narrow issues of law are decided in a vacuum (they can't be).

A major part of our strategy was to let the jurors know that Geoffrey was one of us, and an important, functioning one of us. Geoffrey's business had been ruined in a war in which his own government was attacking him from the rear. By 1987, the devastating losses in Monex silver and the loss of business caused by his competitors had diminished Geoffrey emotionally. His health suffered.

Geoffrey's accounting system was simply to subtract the Monex losses paid out from the bank account and report the balance. The IRS doesn't allow you to do that. You must show all the money taken in, then subtract the losses if you are allowed by law to subtract them. If the losses are from an investment you can deduct it all, but only up to $3,000 a year (unless capital gains exceed that amount). If it is a business loss, you get it all right away. This distinction would determine whether or not Geoffrey even owed a tax.

$400,000 income

-$400,000 business loss

0 Net income: no tax

It was the IRS position that Geoffrey had put the "0" on the wrong line. The line he put the "0" in should have said $400,000.

The IRS also believed that his coin and silver businesses were not businesses but speculation, which would require him to write the $400,000 off over a period of years. This second position was only a civil position, an argument the IRS would use to make the jury feel Geoffrey owed a tax, whether he did or not. The IRS's position was that the silver was purely an investment. Ours was, of course, that it was a business to re-sell silver retail. Finally, the issue was really *intent*. Was Geoffrey intentionally defrauding the government? Or was Geoffrey to go to jail for up to fifteen years, based on a misinterpretation of tax law? If he went to jail, he would go for filling out a false return for the bank, an unrelated bad act.

The "bad act" occurred in 1987, 1988, and 1989. He went to H&R Block, got some "advice," used their forms, put his social security number on the forms, signed a couple and took four 1987, 1988, 1989 and later, 1990 forms to the bank proclaiming profits; profits he hadn't made. Adding injury to an act that already looked suspicious, he used the wrong social security number with the bank.

While Geoffrey's acts had the appearance of impropriety, I was sure I could convince a sympathetic jury otherwise. Picking jurors is one of the most difficult and most important parts of any trial. There are hundreds of books written on the subject and experts everywhere. In the end, you use your best judgment based on your experience, all the "experts" you can afford to hire, your client's gut feelings, observations, blind luck, and prayer.

Each side gets to kick people off without giving a reason, without cause, and then each side tries to get the judge to knock people off *for* cause. Cause means Juror A has already decided to convict or believes all government officials always lie on the stand. The decision is up to the judge with some case law boundaries to guide him. Every federal judge does it differently; some let counsel ask questions, most, like Greene, ask all the questions themselves. An unfair judge can hurt you badly in jury selection.

Before the trial starts, before opening arguments, you pick the jury.

We had twelve jurors and two alternates; since the alternates were released before judgment the make-up of the jury alone was important.

Of the six-man, six-woman jury, eleven were Anglos, one was Indian-American (not a Native American, but from the country India), six were self-employed, four were members of the National Rifle Association, and one was a fine arts expert. I expected good feelings from NRA, fine arts, and self-employed. We attached no significance to race on our panel.

Most government workers are the kiss of death in tax cases. If you sued Exxon, no one would consider letting Exxon employees on the jury, but no rule prevents the government from having its employees on the jury. Each side gets to ask the judge to kick unfair jurors off. However, even IRS employees are considered fair jurors if they say they will be impartial and, of course, they always do. On the other hand, people who hate the IRS will usually be honest and admit it and get kicked off as unfair. In a federal felony tax trial, the defendant gets to strike off ten and the government six and the rest are seated as jurors. Judge Greene agreed when I asked that in light of our pre-trial losses on the issue of admissibility of the false bank 1040's that I could have four extra strikes. He then gave the government three extra strikes.

After analysis of the jury, we were still a little short on strikes. L. R. had observed our adversaries seemed to be bending their ears over to hear our strike discussion, so Mark McLachlan and I had a slightly loud stage-whisper argument over two jurors. I said we had to have one remain, and we had to strike one. I guaranteed Mark that Juror A would vote for us. He said he didn't like him as much but saw him as neutral. Lo and behold our "friends" kicked Juror A off. I pulled our team together more quietly, showing concern; Breinholdt kicked Juror B. Did they overhear us? It seemed like it, but as a gentleman, I'll give them the benefit of the doubt and assume both sides disliked the same two guys.

One paper carrier turned out under exam by our skilled judge to be ex-CIA, which bothered me enough to kick him off. Our jurors sat in the jury box and we were happy campers. Once again I used Alice Weiser, the Houston jury selection expert and handwriting analyst who'd helped me with great success, as well as Dr. Richard Rieke, a Salt Lake City professor of Court Communications, University of Utah, and author of *Communication in Legal Advocacy*.

I met the professor on the plane going to Salt Lake City. He sat next to me. We talked about litigation, and I realized he would be a valuable addition to the team.

My method is "scientific." The other side always picks the people we don't like. Unanimous selections are dumped, then we painstakingly evaluate the pros and cons while guessing the strikes of our opposition. I make the final decisions.

The team of Weiser and Rieke may be the best I've ever used. In Salt Lake, you strike, the government strikes, and the list is passed back and forth. Some jurisdictions, like Texas, have each side strike blindly, which sometimes leads to fewer strikes if both sides strike the same juror. Mark, a local lawyer, gave me some added understanding of what the IRS had forfeited by using all Washington, D.C., lawyers.

My adversaries worked together with the special agent, a local summary witness, and a couple of times a note or two from their gallery of assistants. Their strategy of "hiding" the extra staff would later backfire. Our independent jurors didn't just look at the stage for evidence. They could see these guys getting reinforcements from every area of the courtroom.

Our jury was selected, and Breinholdt began with his dazzling opening argument, which left too much of the truth untold. It would be difficult for him to keep all of his credibility until the end of the trial.

The Court: All right. You may, Mr. Minns, now address the jury on behalf of the defendant.

Mr. Minns: May it please the Court, Counsel, ladies and gentlemen of the jury. I hope that everybody listened carefully to Judge Greene yesterday when he said that you begin deliberations only after you hear everything, because if you began deliberations before you heard anything else it would be a violation of your sworn duty. Of course Mr. Breinholdt is a very good speaker and very convincing. I'm going to present a little bit different version, as you might expect me to do so. I don't agree with the government interpretation of the evidence. With the court's permission, little things make big differences; for example, this is an invention of Geoffrey Alan.

I picked up Geoffrey's hunting device, assembled it and held it up for the jurors. "He is an inventor." I pointed out. "It looks a lot different when it's not put together." My point was two-fold: First, the working model is more impressive than the inert pieces sitting on the table; I didn't want the jurors to think Geoffrey had been selling worthless merchandise. Second, I wanted to preach my grandfather's sermon, showing half the story isn't a true story. I would repeat this theme over and over again in different ways throughout the trial. By the end of the trial, hopefully the jury would get behind the artfully created government version and see the truth. The unassembled pieces didn't add up to the whole. From there I shared with the jurors much of what you've already been told about Geoffrey.

Jurors are usually glued to the first words of the first witness. Following our openings, the evidence stage of the government prosecution began. The government gave us a break and slowed their momentum by putting on dry record-keeping people to testify to records we had already admitted to—like two million checks entered and cleared.

Breinholdt introduced pictures of every room of what he referred to as Alan's mansion, showing twelve Persian rugs. He also put on evidence of Alan's assumed names for his multitude of businesses.

The government's "killer" witness was to be Robert Underwood, Geoffrey's personal banker. He testified to the "tax returns" that Geoffrey gave him, which showed lots of money. If time permits I usually like to interview as many of the government's witnesses as possible. Sometimes the government tells them not to talk to anyone. OK. You can tell that to the jury (if the defendant refuses to talk he is accused of obstruction of justice). Sometimes the witness is simply worried that he shouldn't talk to you. Sometimes it is beneficial not to have talked to the witness. You can ask a witness you haven't met, "We haven't met before, have we?" The government will, of course, have interviewed him perhaps several times.

The banker waited in the hall during the lunch break after his testimony before it was time for me to cross-examine him. I grabbed him. "Is it all right to talk to you?" he asked. "Could I go up to Geoffrey and say 'Hi'—shake his hand?"

Of course he could, I told him. In fact, I suggested he do this in the courtroom as soon as he saw Geoffrey. He did, in front of the jury.

After a mellow direct by Breinholdt, Underwood was turned over to me. He admitted that occasionally clients exaggerate their success to their bankers. He agreed that while it was not good for Geoffrey to have lied to him, he could understand under the circumstances. He testified that Geoffrey was basically a decent, honest man. He also admitted that many social security numbers get out of order through computer mistakes. Had this happened to Geoffrey? He didn't know.

Lisann put on the social security administrator to show that Geoffrey used the wrong social security number. He also inadvertently showed the jurors too much of the stuff our public servants are all too often made of. Ms. Stone (not her real name) looked like a miniature lineman for a butch football team. She had short-cropped black hair, a body like a tank, and a face of stone, without love or compassion. She testified that Geoffrey was using false social security numbers and then gave the names and birth dates of six people, one in Puerto Rico, who actually had the various numbers. She was proud of her investigation. She and Lisann went over social security charts and blow-ups and lectured us on right and wrong numbers. I objected that her giving this information out was a violation of the Privacy Act. Judge Greene took over.

85

The Court: Counselor, do you represent these people?

Minns. No, your honor.

The Court: Overruled.

Judge Greene was technically right. I would pursue this on cross-examination and hopefully get my point across: the witness was willing to break the law to win the case. She hadn't violated Geoffrey's rights; but she had violated *these* citizens' rights.

Minns: Ms. Stone, does it appear Mr. Alan may have been using the wrong social security number for the past thirty years?

Witness: It looks like it.

Minns: Well, when you learned this, and realized he didn't have one penny of credit in his social security account for thirty years of payments, and you called him to let him know, what happened?

Witness: I never called him.

Minns: Why not?

Witness: It's not my job.

Minns: Ms. Stone, did you get permission from Mr. Jones of Puerto Rico to share his private privileged social security information publicly in this courtroom?

Lisann jumped up quickly and objected and was sustained. I asked one last question.

Minns: Isn't using this information without his permission illegal?

Breinholdt: Objection.

The Court: Sustained.

I disagreed with the judge, but his ruling was firm and I passed the witness. Greene is fair to both sides but rules his courtroom with an iron hand. I did not want to alienate him and I had made my point.

Lisann then offered to put on the witness stand a fired employee of Geoffrey Alan who wanted to testify that Geoffrey's crippled sister told her that Geoffrey had violated tax laws. Had she been allowed to testify she would have been the only one to testify adversely to Geoffrey's character. It was irrelevant, probably untrue, but potentially prejudicial.

It was also that highly objectionable creature that lawyers call *hearsay*. In the United States of America we are guaranteed by the Sixth Amendment to the Constitution the right to confront our accusers through cross-examination. If Mary gets to tell us what Dick said even though Dick isn't in the courtroom, we can't really examine what Dick said. We have to accept Mary's integrity and her memory. What if Dick is a compulsive liar or worse, but Mary is a saint? We'd hear the uncrossexamined words of a sinner through the mouth of a saint. Highly believable, but still not true. Hearsay is a statement made out-of-court repeated *in* court by someone or something (including a piece of paper) other than the person who actually made the statement, trying to convince the jury of something. Unless there is an exceptional reason, it should be kept out. The law is filled with legitimate exceptions, but Lisann didn't have one.

Breinholdt's letter from the fired employee continued a different version of her purported testimony. Before the trial, special agents try to tie down government witnesses. They interview them, type up select portions of the interview, have them signed, and then use them to keep their witnesses consistent by "reminding" them what they will need to say under oath. These affidavits are usually discoverable during trial before the witness is cross-examined. They were adding to it. I was outraged.

Essentially, there are two rules which require statements of witnesses to be given to the defense: *U.S. v. Brady,* a Supreme Court case, and the Jencks Act. *Brady* deals with exculpatory information. If the government has evidence that could be used to prove innocence, the Supreme Court requires it to show the evidence to the defendant. Unfortunately, government lawyers violate this law every-day. They want convictions. Exculpatory evidence increases the chances for acquittals. The Jencks Act deals with impeachment. If the witness says he is a license plate-maker, but his statement says he has never been near metal, that impeaches him.

Most of the government witnesses had signed statements con-cerning what they knew. This woman's signed statement had nothing to do with Geoffrey. He had fired her for not doing her job. Now the government was representing that she would testify that Geoffrey's crippled sister told her Geoffrey cheated on taxes. I asked the court to hold Mr. Breinholdt in contempt. I was overruled. If she said these things a year ago, why wasn't it in her statement? Judge Greene did-n't want to hear either of us on the statement controversy, only how the testimony was relevant. Lisann couldn't satisfy Greene and I sus-pect he couldn't satisfy himself. He fidgeted with irrational argu-ments. We all knew why he wanted her on the stand: to beat Geoffrey with his twelve-Persian-carpets prejudice. Greene denied the testi-mony and we moved on. Keeping out this type of unreliable evidence is not the same as keeping out evidence both sides agree is true. Hearsay is an opportunity to fabricate evidence to prove non-existing points. It is an opportunity to make a lie appear to be the truth.

The government then began a parade of sixty witnesses to testify where the checks in the baskets in front of the jury for Geoffrey's hunting device originated.

Breinholdt: Is this check # X from you?

Customer Witness 1: Yes.

Breinholdt: Did you buy a hunting device with it?

Customer Witness 1: Yes.

The check was already in evidence by agreement. We also agreed Geoffrey received the money. What was the point?

On cross I asked one question.

Minns: Did it work?

Customer Witness 1: Yes.

Minns: Pass the witness.

On the next witness I asked the same question and one new question to the witness.

Minns: Ready to go home?

Customer Witness 2: Yeah.

On the third the court responded to me.

Court: I bet I know what you're going to ask, counsel.

The jurors laughed. To this day no one has figured out why the government flew in these people. More money. More power flexing. The jury was getting a little angry.

After most of the week of testimony, the government concluded with Antonia White, the government tax expert who prepared numbers for '85, '86, and '87 for Geoffrey's alleged tax debt, and then their summary witness Ms. Haymond, who did the same. Neither witness had ever made a living preparing returns and their figures were so different it seemed as though they had audited two different people. I hoped that after my cross-examination of their testimony none of the jurors would have hired either of them to prepare their returns. Each had serious misunderstandings of the tax code. Who doesn't?

In my closing I would tell the jury that if God chose to breathe life into this code (I held the mischievous volume up) and it took the stand and swore to tell the truth, and if God further worked a miracle forcing it to tell the truth, it would say, "Nobody understands me." The two agents certainly didn't. A banker, a carpet salesman flown in from California, customers from around the country, the sellers of Geoffrey's home, an employee of H & R Block, Geoffrey's former bookkeeper, a neighbor, and others certainly didn't.

The government rested. I went to work reviewing the case with other witnesses and left Mark McLachlan to put on character wit-

89

nesses. Basically, character witnesses tell the jury your client is a good guy. It is a critical part of the trial. The lawyer must be able to solicit from them who they are, what their opinions are, and upon what they are predicated. Mark did a superb job. I was free to get the balance of the case ready. Frankly, we all thought cross-examination had turned the tide. Our case, the answer to the government's, would last less than a day.

Geoffrey's new CPA, Mike Davis, was also superb. Poised, honest and professional, his opinion was that our absent-minded professor was unsophisticated in tax matters and in fact, was due a refund. In cross-examination, he did even better. Breinholdt should have left him alone. His only potentially interesting damage to our expert was on fees.

Breinholdt: How much are you billing your work on this case?

Davis: About $5,000.

Breinholdt delivered a couple of more beat-the-fee-into-the-ground questions, looking knowingly at the jurors with a "What do you think about that?" smile. With one of his patentable flourishes, he passed Davis back to me.

Minns: Did the government subpoena you yesterday for this trial?

Davis: Yes, sir.

Minns: Did you cool your heels in the hall all day until they released you?

Davis: Yes, sir.

Minns: Is that part of your bill?

Davis: Yes, sir.

Minns: Is it fair to Geoffrey?

Davis: Not really, but the government won't pay it and I have to charge for my time just as you and Mr. Breinholdt do.

Minns: Did the government force you to attend a meeting for an audit?

Davis: Yes, sir.

Minns: Mr. Davis, did you also ask Mr. Alan to provide a lawyer for you to be present at the audit?

Davis: Yes, sir.

Minns: Why is that?

Davis: I understood that these were criminal proceedings that they were inquiring into. In addition to the years 1985, 1986, and 1987 they were asking about the years that I had prepared, 1990 and 1991. At that point, I thought it necessary to have an attorney there.

Minns: Did Mr. Alan have to pay for all of this?

Davis: Unfortunately, he had to.

On a scale of one to ten I would give Mike Davis a ten. He was honest, he was well prepared, and he was extremely effective. He had the statutes with him and the work product ready. Once, during the cross-examination, Judge Greene broke in and told him not to testify from certain of the notes that he had prepared. Without missing a beat, from his own personal knowledge of the law, he was still able to continue. A great deal of luck and good fortune was on Geoffrey Alan's side. With a tough case you need breaks. Sometimes I think God puts these breaks out there but requires us to find them; often finding them just means opening our eyes.

After having problems with accountants, Geoffrey had simply gone through the phone book looking for people to file his latest tax returns. He found Mike Davis in this way. A man with less skill and less presence in court might have lost his cool and lost Geoffrey Alan's freedom. Mike Davis and Riecke, two superb members of our team, had both been found through chance or divine guidance.

The government had made its point. Geoffrey Alan owed or paid

91

a total of five thousand dollars to Mike Davis. We made the point that Davis would have preferred to have been in his office working at the same hourly rate because tax season was approaching and he had more work than he could handle. Furthermore, the majority of the five thousand dollars was caused by the government's wasteful and inconsiderate use of Geoffrey Alan's resources during the trial.

I had to go out into the hall to find Davis and another witness while Mark finished examining a character witness. The final character witness threw us off a little bit. Although Mark knew him well from the phone, he had an unkempt appearance and Mark considered that his appearance in testimony could be negative. So we made the decision to cancel him. Fortunately, I had asked for Mike Davis to be at court half an hour early to anticipate any potential problem. While the last character witness was wrapping up, Davis appeared at the window by the courtroom door and I met him outside for any last minute information.

If you have no witness, you have to create one and put him on, or close your case, as the government had to do in the Hobbs case. We would call one fewer witness and I would have to get the rest ready a little faster. Mark finished the character witness and I put Davis on, leaving one or two more witnesses, depending on the big question.

Paul Des Fosses is a blockbuster witness and a taxpayer's best friend. He worked for the Internal Revenue Service for twenty years. After ten years he made the decision that the morals of the agency were in serious decline and he could no longer morally abide them. His wife, however, became ill with a fatal disease, and he was forced to remain for the medical insurance. When she died several years later, he stuck it out for a few more years in order to earn his pension. Immediately upon leaving the Internal Revenue Service he organized the Whistleblower's Association of former employees dedicated to cleaning up the rampant corruption in the Internal Revenue Service.

Paul has been called upon to testify about the Internal Revenue Service's abuses before Congress, has written several books and publications, and has dedicated a substantial amount of his time and life toward cleaning up abuses. Geoffrey Alan's trial would be finished with two witnesses, Paul Des Fosses and Geoffrey Alan himself, if we put him on the stand. Then would come the closing arguments of counsel.

Paul was our summary witness to counter the Internal Revenue Service's summary witness. Paul is nothing short of liquid dynamite: a gentleman, a scholar, and a gifted speaker.

Minns: Mr. Des Fosses, what do you conclude from listening to the evidence and evaluation of the trial?

Des Fosses: Mr. Alan simply put his figures on the wrong lines. He put what he believed to be the net figure on line 1A of the schedule C. He was supposed to put the gross figure. If he had done that we probably wouldn't be here today. The figure from Mr. Davis's testimony is essentially correct, it is just on the wrong line.

Paul showed these from the charts and from the blow-ups the Internal Revenue Service had prepared. They had tried to remove them the day before, but I asked the judge to let us use them too, and he agreed. Simply put, Geoffrey was entitled to over four hundred thousand dollars in deductions from his silver losses. Rather than put the four hundred thousand dollars on the return and subtract it, he just put down the lesser figure on the return. Civilly speaking, it was bad accounting, *but if in fact he was incorrect, and he did not have the right to deduct it, it was legally a civil error and not a criminal offense.* It was late and Breinholdt was tired. I turned Paul over to him for cross examination and, in what we think was an act of desperation, Breinholdt questioned Mr. Des Fosses on what he thought the Internal Revenue Service's motive was in bringing the case. Bad move.

Paul testified that from the Individual Master File he had learned that Monex had turned Geoffrey Alan in to the Internal Revenue Service. It was easy to speculate the reason why. Monex had gotten to him for four hundred thousand dollars and probably did not want him filing a churning suit against them. The tactic was certainly successful. Since Alan had spent the last five years in disputes with the Internal Revenue Service, he hardly had time to seek the help of a civil court against Monex. Finally, Breinholdt demanded of Mr. Des Fosses again,

Breinholdt: Why do you think the Internal Revenue Service brought this case?

In a very dignified and solemn manner looking him eye to eye Paul Des Fosses pointed to him a little bit sternly like the ex-school teacher he is.

Des Fosses: You *know* why, Mr. Breinholdt.

Breinholdt asked again and got the same answer. I could have objected, the question was repetitive, but Breinholdt was losing it and hammering in our point. He lost his temper and a cool, sincere former agent made it perfectly clear—there was *no* reason to have brought the case at all. Breinholdt sat down. Paul had knocked the wind right out of his sails. Our camp felt the case was won.

Nevertheless, the most important decision in the case had been made the night before. It was unrelated to Paul's powerhouse testimony. The big decision in any case in which a human being is charged with criminal conduct is whether or not to put the person on the stand. We all voted. Mike Davis abstained. Mark was opposed to Geoffrey taking the stand. He thought we were winning and it was too risky. Paul leaned in the middle, L. R. was strongly in favor of Geoffrey taking the stand. Frankly, I leaned slightly towards him not taking the stand. Geoffrey is not a professional witness. He is not accustomed to the courthouse. He is an honest, decent man who provided a lot of jobs for a lot of people, a lot of products, and a lot of pleasure for many hunters and antique collectors. You never know how someone will respond on the stand. The decision ultimately was Geoffrey's. It is not a democracy where everyone's vote counts. In the end, unless I am completely convinced his decision is wrong—we go with it.

Geoffrey was unyielding on the day before our ending of the case. He decided unequivocally that he would take the stand.

Of course, we had been working on his testimony between other witnesses and at the end of each day whenever we had a break, to consider how the jury would react to it. The rules are simple. The witness must tell the truth. That, however, still leaves a lot of possibilities. How is the truth told? Do you give long answers? Do you give short, succinct answers? Do you argue with the questioner, or answer politely? All of these decisions are extremely important, sometimes more important than the answers themselves.

We knew what our big problem was. How do we face Geoffrey's big lie? The false forms. We had already done a very good job of explaining them. Mike Davis had already testified that they were *not* income tax returns. The Internal Revenue Service agents had admitted this, and the court would give instructions to the jury on this. An income tax return is a piece of paper that is filed with the Internal Revenue Service. If it is not filed, it is not a return. Mike Davis had further testified that "dummy" forms are filled out constantly in preparation for the final correct one. While this sounds bad, in accounting there is nothing wrong with it. Geoffrey had tendered four false forms to the bank. How would we deal with it? We had truthful, legitimate explanations, but if Geoffrey took the stand he would simply have to own up to the fact he had deliberately misled the bank.

After a good night's sleep, Geoffrey, in his absent-minded professor suit, took the stand. The direct testimony was brief and to the point.

We hit the critical issue head on. I confronted Geoffrey.

Minns: Mr. Alan, I'm handing you four tax return forms which are already in evidence. The first two bear your signature and the second two bear only your name, which is typed in but no signature whatsoever. I am going to ask you questions about these documents. Mr. Alan, I want you to first look at these two signatures on these two returns bearing signatures. Are those your signatures?

Alan: Yes.

Minns: Is the material in these returns true and correct?

Alan: No.

Minns: Are you responsible for these false forms or representations?

Alan: Yes, I accept full and complete responsibility for everything in them.

Minns: Did you give these to the bank for them to rely on?

Alan: Yes, I did.

Minns: Was that honest?

Alan: No, it was not.

Minns: Why did you do it?

Alan: Unregulated foreign competition was basically putting me out of business. I could no longer compete on the device which I had designed and invented. I was losing a fortune in my commodities business and had been unable to open a new business and start selling. Finally, I had been under pressure for several years with audits and investigations from the Internal Revenue Service. I was losing my credit. I had already used up a great deal of my lines of credit. I was responsible for my mother and my sister and a number of employees whose livelihood was working for my factory. I lied to the bank in order to preserve my credit rating and stay open.

Minns: Are you proud of that?

Alan: No.

Minns: Are you responsible for those actions?

Alan: Yes, I am.

Minns: Mr. Alan, do you say this even knowing there is a possibility of criminal prosecution for filing false information to obtain loans from a bank?

Alan: I can't say anything about what the facts are, except that is the truth and whatever consequences there are, I will have to deal with them.

Minns: Now, Mr. Alan, I am handing you the two returns that do *not* bear your signature, just your typed-in name. Are you willing to accept responsibility for the two returns that you did not sign?

Alan: Yes. I accept full and complete responsibility for all four of those returns.

Minns: Do you remember when you filled them out or how you filled them out?

Alan: No. It has been quite some time, but I am fully and completely responsible for them.

Geoffrey's defense was basically a full confession regarding the bank. Next, he explained the problem with the social security number. The bank had converted it by inverting two of the digits. He had called them ten years ago and tried to have them straighten it out. They had failed to do so, and he had simply kept using it.

He had used it only when he was doing business with *that* bank. With any other organizations he used his regular social security number. The other false social security numbers were on the unofficial forms, which were never submitted to the Internal Revenue Service.

Testimony now got to the real point.

Minns: Mr. Alan have you ever told any lies to the Internal Revenue Service?

Alan: No.

Minns: Have you ever intentionally falsified information with the Internal Revenue Service?

Alan: No.

Minns: Has it ever been your intention to cheat on your income tax returns?

Alan: No.

97

Minns: Pass the witness.

The government, through Jeff Breinholdt, battered Geoffrey on one big issue for two and a half hours of bitter cross-examination: the inaccurate tax forms submitted to the bank. Over and over again, *ad nauseam*, Geoffrey admitted his wrongdoing regarding the bank. The weakness in our case had become a strength. The lie that Geoffrey had told the bank was being hammered almost to the exclusion of anything else in the case. We would come back the next day for closing arguments. Breinholdt had been unsuccessful in battering our last two witnesses. While he had an incredibly successful career prosecuting for the government, Breinholdt appeared to be beaten down. His younger colleague, the yuppie Lisann, took over. Lisann was smart and aggressive, but a bit too abrupt. His attitude would reinforce the abruptness of the social security agent, "Ms. Stone."

We entered the judge's chambers for the charge conference. The charge conference is an important part of the case. In it, decisions are made as to what instructions the judge will give to the jury and what the law is. In this regard, since a number of critical appellate cases involving jury instructions on criminal tax issues were *my* cases, there was an occasional humorous note when Lisann argued to the court that I was misinterpreting cases like *United States v. Buford* (see Chapter V) on the portion addressing court instructions, and *United States v. Powell* on those same instructions, cases I wrote the briefs on and gave the successful oral arguments on in Louisiana and California, respectively.

We were successful on some issues, and unsuccessful on others, but we succeeded in obtaining the primary instruction that we were after, that the government has the burden of proving that Geoffrey Alan knowingly violated the law. The charge conference went particularly well because I was well aided by L. R., my trusted legal assistant, and my extremely competent local counsel, Mark McLachlan. Breinholdt still seemed a bit battered from his cross-examination wars with Des Fosses, Davis, and Geoffrey Alan.

Closing arguments began the following day. Lisann opened and went through the fact history again so well that he reopened speculation that we could still lose. He began to read, and then, improving, extemporize from approximately twenty pages of typed speech. He had good eye contact with the jurors behind the podium and was extremely effective.

Lisann: Ladies and gentlemen of the jury. Geoffrey Alan, by using false social security numbers, giving the wrong birth date on his drivers license, using false assumed names, and ultimately not reporting his fair share of income taxes has cheated us all. He lives the lifestyle of a king. He believes himself to be a king and the rest of us just have to pick up his burden. I don't like filing returns and paying taxes any more than you do. I don't like the way that our government spends money, many times wasting it, any more than you do, but we all have to follow the law. Geoffrey Alan, in order to buy his precious Persian carpets, antiques, mansion, in order to gamble in the commodities market, simply decided he couldn't afford to pay his legitimate share of taxes. We have to pick that bill up for him. You saw the man on the stand, unsure of himself, awkward. Is that an honest demeanor?

Lisann eloquently went through the list of each of the government's witnesses and counterbalanced a great deal of the positive effect that we had gained throughout the week. The jurors listened to him for over an hour, which is an exceptional feat. Ordinarily fifteen minutes is about the longest that human beings will listen to another human being speak. He had done an excellent job: over an hour of spellbinding oratory to a jury that listened.

Mark and I had worked a significant amount of time together now and had agreed that he would speak for the first five to ten minutes. I would close out with as much time as the court would allow me. I ended up with an hour and fifteen minutes. Then the government would give its finale, which Lisann would do. Mark got up, he was seasoned and mature.

McLachlan: Ladies and gentlemen of the jury, one very important thing to focus on is that while Geoffrey Alan was on the stand, the government didn't ask him a single question about the returns he actually filed. They spent their entire argument going over the false forms filed with the bank. If this were a murder trial, you would expect them to discuss the murder, wouldn't you?

Mark then waxed eloquent as he went through the life history of Geoffrey Alan, his character witnesses, and his value and importance to the community. I knew that Mark, as Geoffrey's personal lawyer for over a decade, would have personal credibility vouching for his friend's character. The judge called a break.

It was time for my closing argument. I addressed the jurors.

Minns: Friends, we have been here for an entire week, and we have been here discussing the sins and crimes of Geoffrey Alan. The government has complained about his lying about his age. I hope that each and every one of you know from dealing with me throughout this trial that if I had known in advance that Geoffrey Alan had lied about his age—I never would have agreed to take his case. The government spent millions of your dollars investigating Mr. Alan. We all know about the horrible deficit problems. So I ask you, each and every one of you, while you are in that jury room, to perform another service. Write down the name and address and phone number of everybody you know who has been lying about their age so that we can hand them over to the government and save them all of the necessary research and time and save us the expense.

It was time to get serious, although even my humor had been intended as serious commentary.

Minns: When Mr. Lisann complains to us about the way in which we pay his salary, I am outraged. This public servant has gotten a little bit out of hand. He has been writing out checks in our name all week for foolish and ridiculous purposes. We have been insulted by the actions of the government. It was important for the government to try to make us jealous about Geoffrey Alan and his twelve Persian carpets, which testimony shows were paid for by borrowing against his home. The testimony shows that it was his intention to resell them for a profit. Even if he hadn't borrowed for the carpets, the ownership of Persian carpets is not a crime. We were supposed to hold it so and to be jealous of Geoffrey Alan because of his success that had allowed him to buy those carpets. The government showed us a check for sixty thousand dollars, and we acknowledged that in fact he had paid sixty thousand dollars for the Persian carpets. But our government didn't think we were smart enough to figure that out, so they spent the time and money to accumulate pictures of every room and invade the privacy of Geoffrey Alan's home. As they invaded the privacy of others by printing their names, addresses, and telephone numbers publicly in this courtroom to show us the Persian carpets. Still our government officials and our public servants didn't think we were smart enough to get the message even then. So they brought in a witness, a neighbor who testified that "Yeah, those look like carpets that I saw in Geoffrey Alan's home." Was this enough? Are we smart enough to get the message? No. Our government flew in Mr. Hassan who had left his sick son in California and asked him, "Did you sell Mr. Alan Persian carpets?" And, by golly, he had. Who knows how much of our money the government spent that Mr. Lisann complains is not wisely spent, proving what we knew anyway and what Geoffrey Alan admitted to? We heard from two other government witnesses. One was a professional witness whose job it is to testify for the IRS and who told us about preparing tax returns. We heard from another government agent. We know from that testimony these professionals can't properly apply the law Geoffrey is accused of violating because

101

they got their figures crossed. Perhaps Geoffrey isn't as eloquent or pretty as the professional witnesses, especially the one who admitted to taking government classes on how to testify.

I hope after getting to meet Geoffrey Alan that you like him as I do. That you have gotten to know him a little bit, the very fine and decent human being that he is. The good American citizen that he is. But perhaps you don't like Geoffrey Alan. If you were to find that Geoffrey Alan was a child abuser, rapist, or murderer, then you would certainly have the right to *not* like him. You could say to yourself or your family, "I don't want this person in my home for dinner. He is a bad person." But even so, even having determined that he was guilty of those crimes, you would not be legally allowed to convict him on mistakes on 1985, 1986, and 1987 tax returns, whether intentional or otherwise. Of course, he is *not* guilty of any of these crimes, or even of a parking offense. If he were, you would have heard about it like you heard of the discrepancy about his age.

This is, in fact, what he is being tried for by the government, but the state of their evidence on the actual years in question is so very weak that they want to try him for his false comments to the bank and lying about his age.

You've heard from the professionals who make a living preparing tax returns and who put their name on them, Davis and Des Fosses. You've heard from those who make a living judging rather than doing the work, the IRS expert witnesses. Geoffrey Alan doesn't owe any income taxes. Not because of cleverness or sophistication. He just simply doesn't owe any taxes. If you are convinced that he has committed a crime against the Social Security Administration and also that he is being cheated out of his social security monies, if you are convinced that he has committed a crime against the bank who he has never avoided paying at any time, you should not use that or weigh that against him in this case. He is on trial only for

1985, 1986, and 1987 and only for his reported tax returns. In order to convict him of that, you must find, beyond all reasonable doubt, that he understood the applicable sections of the Internal Revenue Service code and that he intentionally violated them. The only thing in that regard that the government has proved beyond a reasonable doubt is that *none of their agents* understood the applicable statute of the code. None of them could completely and fully comply with it. The dealing of commodities and distinctions between a business and an investment are so complicated that we must give the benefit of the doubt to citizens or we are all criminals.

Mr. Lisann appeared to be affected by my closing. His closing was not as effective as his opening had been. When I talked about overzealous government employees abusing the public trust and complaining about the way that we pay them, I had pointed to him and his co-counsel. His head dropped a millimeter and he looked away for a moment.

I left the case in Mr. McLachlan's competent hands. While L. R. and I were on the plane en route back to our office to prepare for our next trial in Detroit, Michigan, the jury deliberated. Their session began at noon and ended about 1:30 PM, including lunch break. On the first vote, the verdict was not guilty on all counts. We had not even gotten back to Houston before Geoffrey Alan had been acquitted on all counts.

While we could rejoice in the fact that Geoffrey Alan was acquitted, we still couldn't forget about the years of misery he had to endure just because he put the wrong numbers on the wrong line of his tax return. Furthermore, while Geoffrey bore the brunt of this IRS abuse, let us not forget about all those persons who were inconvenienced when they were forced by the government to testify against Geoffrey Alan. His case is not an isolated one and the abuses found in his case are multiplied throughout the system.

103

Chapter IV
The Coal Miner

"The life which is unexamined is not worth living."

—-Plato

LONDON, KENTUCKY

I could not have invented a more decent, honorable client. Tall, curly-headed, Boy Scout leader, devoted parent, coal mine engineer from the mountains of London, Kentucky, where men trust each other and forge powerful bonds arising from their shared risks in the mines. The mountain air seems to breed rugged, strong minded, clear thinking individuals who perceive and appreciate the same qualities when they occur in fellow human beings. Eric Laschon was a man of character, molded by his religious and scholarly upbringing, his engineering education, hard mental and physical work, and sincere devotion to his church and his kids. He had not filed his taxes in ten years. The IRS wanted to put him in jail for four years.

Eric was the veteran of two failed marriages. His first ex-wife, Mary, living in Pennsylvania, had long ceased being a part of his life. His daughter, who was attending college up north, was out on her own. His sixteen-year-old son, also from his first marriage, lived with him in Kentucky. Eric had still not completely recovered from the relatively recent break-up of his second marriage. *The IRS had caused this divorce*! Eric's second ex-wife, Yvonne, and their two elementary school-aged children were living in Houston, Texas. The IRS criminal investigation, which included threats of prosecution and imprisonment of his second wife, was directly responsible for the divorce and her decision to flee to Texas with the kids. In fact, right up until the day of trial, Yvonne Laschon remained under subpoena as a government witness. She tried to be excused because she could not afford to miss work and had no one to care for her young children or her ailing, elderly parents if she were forced to travel to Kentucky. She even sought help from our office to get the subpoena lifted. The IRS had left her with the impression that it was all Eric's fault she was on call. We assured her that we were not responsible for jeopardizing her loved ones' care, but that there was nothing we could do if the prosecutor was determined to enforce his subpoena. I also didn't want them to bring her to Kentucky, put her on the stand, and elicit testimony that Eric or I had tried to keep her away from the courthouse. My hands were tied.

It ended up as nothing more than a cruel ploy.

Her fear of the IRS was merely stoked until the end of the trial, leaving her in turmoil. Eric worried about the forced involvement of this woman he still loved. Was the threat an unethical trial tactic or merely some gratuitously evil deed designed to warm the heart of an IRS agent? We can only speculate, but the threat never materialized. She was never called. Unhappily she would be required to be on standby, waiting to fly to Kentucky without notice, until the trial was over.

Despite his personal tragedies, Eric remained a devout member of the local Roman Catholic Church. His parish priest, Father Arnsparger, could always count on his participation in any charitable endeavor. Eric was ecumenically minded and public-spirited. He assisted with Cub Scout Pack 488 in the Corbin Kentucky Presbyterian Church, even though his third grade son, a former member of the pack, was now living in Texas with his mother.[1] When Father Arnsbarger was unavailable to testify at trial because he had been called out of town to officiate at a funeral, the Reverend Steven Ashley, pastor of the Presbyterian Church, substitute as one of Eric's character witnesses. He was aware of Eric's good deeds. Eric also helped coach a little league baseball team.

Much of Eric's living in the last decade had come from reading and interpreting an intricate web of state and federal coal mining safety regulations and environmental protection guidelines. He assisted his clients in filling out complex forms to obtain the mining permits they needed for exploration or operation, and Eric instructed his clients on how to remain in compliance with the regulations. He would bill his clients by the hour for his services. He had a lot of work. He was known in the business as an honest and bright man, a man of principle who could back up his opinions with research. He was effective in getting the job done.

Eric learned that the government was not always truthful or honest. State and federal officials often refused to give permits that the coal miners were entitled to under law. They would back down when he faced them with the correct regulation or case citations to back up his opinion. He was in every sense of the word an "Underground Lawyer,"[2] learning how to do his own research and then making the case stick. One of his best methods was to throw the burden of proof back in the government's face. "Under what authority are you proceeding?" he would ask over and over again for his clients. If an agent could not answer, he would restate his position to a supervisor on the next level. Eric learned that dealing with the government took persistence and dogged determination. In the field of mining and environ-

---

1. This one would later request to live with his father. Both parents, though divorced, remained cooperative partners in the interest of their children.
2. I coined this term, with the help of friends, which connotes anyone trying to work within the system to achieve justice. It defines the attitude of many of my rugged, individualistic clients like Eric Laschon and Jim Hobbes.

mental regulations (unlike the tax code, as he later discovered) there was some sort of logic. In his profession, Eric's basic approach was effective: use logical arguments, be persistent, launch a determined quest for an answer, or at least the correct official who could explain the policy, and do not back down just because "they're the government" and "you're the individual." These attitudes that stood him in good stead in his profession contributed to his problems with the IRS.

State law required that Eric's work be performed under the supervision of a licensed engineer. However, it was very costly for clients to have a licensed professional engineer perform all aspects of the projects.[3] The mining community generally acknowledged that Eric did thorough, thoughtful research and was unequaled at getting government officials to back down from unreasonable positions. Consequently, the usual pattern was to retain Eric, who would then submit his work to the scrutiny of a professional engineer, who would stamp his seal of approval on it and add extra charges. The engineer with whom Eric worked most closely was Carlos Naranjo. Eric's life would have been less complicated if he had limited his association with Naranjo to professional projects. Unfortunately for both of them, Naranjo became interested in offshore trusts to try to cut his tax liability. He became a consumer of a mixed variety of "tax seminars" and started inviting Eric to join him in attending these popular lectures. Members of the audience were basically treated to the mind-boggling assertion that they were not "persons required to file income tax returns."

This information was not given out for free. Fees were charged for "attorney opinion letters," "trust packages," samples of "silver-bullet" type affidavits and other documents which, if filed, were guaranteed to put the signer in a non-taxpayer status. Many of these "remedies," touted by the purveyors of anti-IRS snake oil, were mutually exclusive. Their proponents often bitterly disagreed with one another, and tried to convince their desired customers that the other guys were doing it all wrong.

---

3. In some respects Eric was far more knowledgeable than many licensed engineers.

Eric's mother, an English teacher, had raised her son to have an inquiring mind and a thirst for knowledge. He was taught to question, question, question, a preoccupation that would serve his clients well when he was retained to research mining regulations. It also made him vulnerable to novel approaches to federal tax law. Eric fed his curiosity on the smorgasbord of tax theories that abounded in the mid 1980s.

He traveled to a seminar in Sewannee, Tennessee, to hear some alleged experts expound on their theories about the American tax system. Many of them, including licensed lawyers, espoused theories that the entire federal tax scheme was a scam. With proper coaching, a willing student could wade through the deception and not "volunteer" to be a taxpayer. One key was in the definition of what a taxpayer is.

Eric decided to do some studying for himself. He was familiar with mining and environmental codes. Why should the federal tax code remain a mystery? He plunged into Title 26 of the United States Code, the part of the code that discussed filing returns.

As regular as flowers that bloom in the spring each year, a new theory or two blossoms forth as to why you do not have to file and pay income taxes. In the early 1990s, one that got considerable attention was "The Pilot Connection." For several thousand dollars, the promoters guaranteed they would take you out of the system so that you would never have to file again. People all over the country called us to ask why these guys could get away with it if it was not legal. The leaders appeared on the talk show circuits like 20/20, expounded their theories to America, and signed up a lot of people. The questions remained. In 1993 a number of the program's founders were indicted. They were tried in San Francisco. The jury could not reach a decision, so they were re-tried and convicted.[4] Do not worry. There will soon be replacements.

Lest you be tempted to purchase some "snake oil," be aware of

4. The organizers had hired a young, green lawyer and blamed him for their troubles. I was hired by the lawyer's parents to keep him out of the organizers' problems.

this: while the requirements to file a tax return vary from year to year, essentially, if you earn $5,000 in a calendar year as an employee, or $500 through self-employment, you are required to file a 1040 form of some type. If you do not, and if you know you are supposed to file, you are guilty of a violation of 26 U.S.C. 7203. For each unfiled year you can be fined $25,000 and sentenced to one year in jail. If the government alleges that in addition to willfully failing to file, you have committed an overt act motivated by an intent to conceal the income you did not report, the charge against you can be boosted to a felony: income tax evasion, 26 U.S.C. 7201, the crime for which Leona Helmsley of New York and Marvin Mitchelson of California were convicted. An overt act can be something as simple as checking the box marked exempt on your W-4 form if you are not exempt, or as complex as setting up a lot of trusts to funnel secret money through. Often, the only difference between someone charged with a misdemeanor or a felony is the attitude of the special agent or his/her understanding (or lack thereof) of the criminal law. The government convicts 95 percent of the people who are charged with the crime of failure to file. Only the best cases (from the government's viewpoint) are brought to trial. The only other crime with a higher conviction rate is mass murder. Everyone who has ever been charged with mass murder has been convicted. Eric diligently pored over Title 26, just as he had studied the federal regulations he encountered in his regular profession. Eric could not find a section that specifically told him, in plain language, that he was required to file a tax return. He found a plethora of regulations describing the nuts and bolts of filing returns and taking deductions and exemptions, all of which applied to those "persons required to file." But where in the code were those "persons" defined?

How was Eric to know if he was or was not one of those "persons"? Were only government employees or corporate officers "persons required"? Were only dealers in alcohol, firearms or tobacco "persons required"? How did the IRS distinguish between a "person" and an "individual"? To someone who has not looked into the code

110

and struggled with its poorly drafted inconsistencies, these questions sound silly, but the profiteers of the "tax shelter" games sell them and lure in medical doctors, lawyers, and college professors. Most of us just accept certain things as facts, such as, "The government can not get by without an income tax." These persons ignore American history which, following the tax rebellion in the Boston Tea Party, had nearly two hundred years of prosperity without an income tax!

Most of us just accept as a matter of faith that we are legally required to file tax returns, because we have a nationally recognized tribute day when we formally make sacrifice, April 15. The Mayans had days when they sacrificed virgins to the gods and because of their tradition, they knew they were supposed to keep doing it. Both cultures required conformance or exacted punishment for disobedience. Obviously it was the virgin's family which faced the punishment.

Eric's usual information-seeking techniques, which had worked in his encounters with mining and environmental regulations, and even with the state of Kentucky taxing authorities, broke down when it came to the "public servants" of the IRS.

Eric would usually read the annotations to code sections he was trying to understand. Annotations are explanations, often articles, often actual cases. The annotations to Title 26 did not help him. They only further obscured the issue in a morass of gobbledygook. Eric also consulted experts in an attempt to understand. To get answers to his federal tax questions, he wrote to IRS employees, individual attorneys, accountants, professional associations, and even elected government officials. He rarely received a reply, and the answers he did get were too vague to be of any use. There was a notable exception. One lawyer wrote back that Eric was not a "person required to file." Out of about twenty of these guys and gals who will commit in writing for $100 or so that you don't have to file, only two that I am aware of are still licensed. Both have stopped selling the opinions. I'm sure more will open up to replace them. America does not have a shortage of lawyers who will sell bad legal advice.

111

When Eric wrote to the state of Kentucky with a question about a statute requiring him to pay certain state taxes, in contrast to the IRS, he received a prompt reply on government embossed letterhead, citing him to a particular statute and telling him he had to pay. This caused him to further distrust the feds. As a result, Eric continued complying with all Kentucky taxing laws. All of the forms Eric filled out for his clients in the mining business stated whether or not the law required them. If Eric was unsure whether or not a particular client was obligated to submit a certain form for a specific project, all he had to do was contact an official of the state agency and describe the situation to get an answer. But the IRS agents Eric talked to kept mumbling about "persons required to file" without citing any particular statutes and "voluntary compliance" without explaining that "voluntary" in their twisted view (as in Orwell's doublespeak or *Alice in Wonderland*) really means involuntary. This would be funny if it were not so tragic in terms of human suffering. When you start trying to read and analyze the tax code you find out that no one understands it. *No one.* Former Chief Justice Richard Neeley of the Virginia Supreme Court said it very well when he honestly shared with us, "The Internal Revenue Service lawyers responsible...confessed...they did not understand the Tax Reform Act ... they opined that the Congress which wrote it did not understand it ...the court would make it up as they went along and pretend to understand it." ("How Courts Govern America"—Richard Neeley, pg. 25 Yale University Press 1981.)

One root cause of the confusion is the fact that this complex code was written by politicians who steal from us to give themselves lifetime positions, larger-than-life pension funds, and the legendary, supposedly non-existent "free lunches." If professional writers or English teachers wrote the code, and if politicians were prevented from misusing words, fewer people would get into trouble. One of the most pernicious lies is that the Internal Revenue system is based on "voluntary compliance." It was probably intended to sugar coat the bitter medicine of taxation because we were "volunteering" to calculate the dose ourselves. It's true there is no such thing as a "free lunch." In reality, people are forced into picking up the bill by trickery and bullying. You can find tons of government printed literature and propaganda describing our wonderful "voluntary" tax system.

We volunteer as a nation to give billions of dollars and work hours to charitable organizations; we volunteer to put our kids through school, and we volunteer to feed them. Very few volunteer to pay taxes. We pay because we follow the law that we almost universally dislike and protest against. Every president elected in my lifetime got elected in part by complaining and protesting that the tax system was unfair and he would fix it. Only two presidents in my lifetime actually "fixed" part of it by making significant tax reductions: Kennedy[5] and Reagan. Each reduction was followed by a massive upsurge in production. Contrary to the assumptions of some denizens of Washington, D.C., we are not stupid. When they tax alcohol, we reduce consumption of it. If they tax cigarettes, our smokers cut down. If Nevada taxes prostitution, it declines. By the same token, if work is taxed, we get the message and cut down on it. If the tax on work is reduced, we work more. It is very easy for an intelligent person to figure out that taxing work is immoral and that the dumbest guy on the planet often spends his own money more intelligently than the best so-called public servants. At the very least, the average person on the street spends money on items he wants to spend it on, as opposed to watching the government indiscriminately fritter money away on outrageously wasteful projects no one really wants—not even the government. It's a big leap, though, to go from cherishing these widely held opinions to making the momentous decision of letting April 15th come and go without filing an income tax return. It's a decision no ethical lawyer or CPA would counsel a client to take because it is a blue print for personal punishment. If you don't file and are charged with a crime and are very fortunate (perhaps you are one of my clients) and win a "not guilty" verdict, you may still be

5. The reduction proposed by Kennedy was passed after his death.

attacked civilly. Civilly, there is no "state of mind" defense to not filing a return. That means that if you are required to file and you do not, you lose when you get to tax court to determine how much you will have to pay in taxes, interest and penalties. You do not get a jury, and the judge will probably rule against you before trial. It is a waste of time and money to proceed in tax court if you have not filed a return at all.

The Sixteenth Amendment, passed in 1913, is the one allowing income to be taxed. There are those who assert that the amendment was not properly passed. The most believable exposition of this theory was written by Bill Benson and "Red" Beckman, entitled *The Law That Never Was*. Benson, a former state tax collector, became convinced by his own research that he was not required to file a tax return. Benson and Beckman discovered that there were substantial irregularities in the ratification process of the Sixteenth Amendment. Some of the states counted as having endorsed the prospective amendment had not really done so, or had voted on a slightly different version. According to Benson, since the amendment was not properly enacted into law, in effect it "never was." Well-researched and documented, Benson's book was quite popular as a source of reliance for many people who claimed it as their reason for not filing tax returns. Federal courts did not share Benson's fans' enthusiasm. None reviewed the actual evidence produced by Benson. Unfortunately, we do not have the legal right to second-guess the courts except by appealing their decisions. The Supreme Court has never overturned the affirmations handed down by various circuit courts of appeals, upholding convictions of defendants whose reason for failing to file was based on their belief that the Sixteenth Amendment is not law.

Do the federal trial and appellate courts make mistakes? Yes and no. If they do something obviously wrong it may be a mistake, as the word is literally understood, but whatever ruling the Supreme Court decides is the last word on the subject until the justices change their minds. Logically, we do not have much of a choice other than reliance

114

on the finality of the rulings of our appellate courts. If every one of our more than 250 million citizens made his/her own independent decision on what the law was and felt free to ignore the courts, we would have anarchy. So, right or wrong, the court has ruled, and the Benson argument is "wrong." If I were on the court I would have been convinced, but I'm not, and Benson, honest as I believe he is, served time in a federal penitentiary. Lawyers who advise people, for money, that they don't have to file a tax return are stealing from the clients.

Compared to some of the theories that other non-filers espouse, Benson looks positively mainstream. There are those who argue that the presence of a flag with gold fringes around the edges invalidates the jurisdiction of a courtroom, because that flag indicates that "maritime law" is in force. Proponents of these various theories cling to them fiercely, and declare that the defendant or his lawyers just did not know how to plead the issues properly. Whenever someone pronounces the "magic words" just right, the judge will be "compelled" to let him go.

Some say that having a social security number places a citizen on a contract basis with the government, rather than under common law. They say that anyone can opt out by simply notifying the government that he has been deceived in the past, and he is now rescinding his social security number. Others allege that money not backed by gold is not legal tender and therefore money earned in Federal Reserve Notes does not give rise to a taxable debt. An old favorite argument is that wages are not income, because income means profit, not an even exchange. No employer would pay an employee more than he is worth. Therefore, what is commonly known as employment constitutes an even trade of labor for money. This is not a taxable exchange, and therefore no return is required. Warning: Some of these theories sound attractive, but believing them can be hazardous to your liberty! I am merely parroting numerous failed theories so you can get an idea what's going on. *None of them work.* All have been rejected!

The tax, allowed by the Sixteenth Amendment, had to be created by a statute. The politicians obliged immediately, creating the first post Sixteenth Amendment statute in the same year in 1913. It affected very few people. The income tax as we know it today began as a so-called "Victory Tax" to help finance the war effort during World War I. It was unpatriotic not to be part of the system. The use of the term "voluntary" to describe mandatory filing requirements crept into the language of American taxation. Another widespread myth is the "government need" argument, which most of us have bought these last fifty years: that the government has always needed and gotten an income tax and we all have to pay our fair share. The government relies on this "voluntary" effort to meet the "need" as a placebo to keep the populace from getting angry. The fact is that income taxation is a very poor method of raising money compared to other methods. The gasoline tax, the cigarette tax and excise taxes all raise lots of money, don't force us to do slave labor keeping records, and don't require keeping very personal and intrusive records for the benefit of government snoops. What is our fair share of costs incurred by the most wasteful government we can imagine? As much as they can take.

When someone who is required to file an income tax return does not do so, is he guilty or not guilty of a crime? The key distinction is found in the defendant's state of mind. Is the accused honestly trying to follow the law, or not? There were two theories as to how much evidence you needed to show your mistakes were not willful. One was that the evidence had to be objectively reasonable. If your excuse was not reasonable, then you were guilty even if you really thought you were doing what the law required. That's a tough two-pronged test. First you had to convince the judge. He had to let the jury decide because in the United States, without a plea of "guilty," no judge can order a defendant convicted, but he could tell the jury, "You may not consider the defendant's claim that he deducted his poodle as a guard dog as a defense. The court instructs you that is not objectively reasonable."

Now you may be saying, "So what? I do not think that is reasonable." If you are on the jury you can say, "I don't think that is reasonable and therefore I don't believe it. I think the defendant intended to commit a crime." The problem comes when the judge makes the decision for you or even changes the rule a little. You might say, "Hey, I think he actually believes he can deduct the poodle but I don't care—that's not reasonable. I will convict him." The other standard for instructions was subjective. No matter how unreasonable the reason for believing that the claim was legal, if the defendant sincerely believed it, that was a defense. The trouble was that different courts had different instructions and some demanded an objective test while others a subjective test.

In *U.S. v. Cheek*, Cheek was a pilot who thought he was not required to file his returns so he did not. He had a jury trial and was convicted. Then he appealed to the Court of Appeals in Chicago (Seventh Circuit) claiming that the instructions of the trial court, that his opinion had to be objectively reasonable, was unreasonable. The Seventh Circuit disagreed with him and he went up to the U.S. Supreme Court, which said that the standard must be subjective and Cheek must get a new trial with different instructions. A long story follows, which will not fit into this book.

While Cheek was on appeal, two other cases went to trial and resulted in convictions. One was Dixie Lee Powell, a sixty-year-old retired Mormon school teacher from Tucson, Arizona.

Each and every year the IRS would completely disallow Dixie's returns. Each year she would be audited and her deductions disallowed. Finally in desperation she began to do her own research. She found a statute, 6020b (which has since been repealed), which said: "If any person fails to make any return required by any internal revenue law or regulation—the Secretary shall make such return from his knowledge and from such information as he can obtain—" Consequently, she wrote the IRS and asked them to prepare her returns for her under the statute. She would no longer do so since she had the right to let the IRS do it for her. The problem was that the courts have said that with regard to 6020b "shall" means "may." The

IRS ignored her letter and charged her and her husband with failure to file.

Mrs. Powell represented herself at trial and her husband Roy followed. Roy, a seventy-year-old triple bypass survivor, said at trial, "What ever Dixie says, that's fine with me. After fifty years of marriage I can't go against her." Roy had no idea whether or not they had filed. Dixie had done all their financial planning and tax preparation for years. The judge gave the jury instructions on Objective Intent. Dixie wanted to show the jury the statue upon which she had relied. The judge said no. The jury asked to see a copy of the statute and the judge told them that it did not say what Dixie said it said. The judge was wrong. The jury returned a verdict of "guilty" and both Mr. and Mrs. Powell were sentenced to time in a Federal prison.

They were allowed out pending appeal. Mrs. Powell continued to do research and found the published case *U.S. v. Buford*, which had my name in it (next chapter), and she called me. She was interested in the IMF because she wanted to know what had caused her to be the subject of intense observation with the IRS. She read Buford, learned of the IMF, pulled her IMF, and discovered she was cross-referenced with an accused drug dealer who did not pay her taxes on the illegal drugs. Dixie's name was the same as a suspected drug dealer in Phoenix, Arizona. To this day the IRS claims it did not mix these two women up, but Mrs. Powell's IMF (Individual Master File) shows that it did.[6] Because the IRS agents confused her with the other woman, they disallowed all of Dixie's deductions, including her eleven children and her farm with her husband Roy.

She called me to handle her appeal. I did. I was very impressed with the way Mrs. Powell had protected the record, making all of the necessary objections at the trial. You can generally only appeal on things offered or kept out and objected to at trial. Lots of pretty good

6. See *U.S. v. Buford*, 889 F.2d 1406, and *U.S. v. Powell*, 995 F.2d 1206. For more information on the computer in Martinsburg, West Virginia, that has every American or legal immigrant listed under his/her social security number with a lot of private information, read the chapter on the Bufords.

trial lawyers are nevertheless bad appellate lawyers and do not set up things for appeal. In a tax case that is pretty important since there is a very good chance of a conviction no matter who is trying the case or what the facts are.

The Ninth Circuit Court of Appeals handed down an opinion reversing the conviction, ordering a new trial, and ordering the court to allow Dixie to read 6020b to the jury and to give subjective instructions to the jury instead of objective. Shortly thereafter the IRS office sent out interoffice memos saying that this case only affected the Ninth Circuit and that even there, it was not the law and that it would be reversed soon. In fact, a new Powell case was rendered, slightly changing the holding, but that's another story unrelated to this effort.

The third key contemporaneous willful case was the *Willie* case in the Tenth Circuit out of Denver. It was handed down within days of the *Powell* case. In fact, the government offered it to the panel in Powell to get them to change their mind, but it failed to offer *Powell* to the *Willie* panel. Willie was an American Indian who did not file. He had a treaty with the U.S. government saying that his tribe was exempt from income taxes. At trial he offered the treaty to the jury to prove what he had relied on. The judge said no. Willie could testify about the treaty but the jury would have to rely on his word. They could not see the treaty. I would have loved to argue the *Willie* case on appeal. Nevertheless, that is the law in the Tenth Circuit. Willie went to jail.

Whenever I have been faced with a fight between *Willie* and *Powell,* I have successfully persuaded the court to go with *Powell. Willie* is not only another of our country's sell-outs of Native Americans and the violation of another treaty, it is also a sell-out of our basic right to face a jury with the taxpayer's side of the story. So far *Powell* has won over *Willie* in every jurisdiction that I am aware of except, of course, the Tenth Circuit.

Laschon was the first case that I handled following *Powell* and would be the first case that any one in the country got to use the

Powell instructions. Actually it turned out not to be a significant issue. The prosecutor, a bully who used force over preparation, was not familiar with either case and had not done research on the issues before trial. He never offered the *Willie* instructions as an option. I found this to be curious since there had been a bunch of convictions recently in London, Kentucky. One of the reasons for the unusually high conviction rate is the fact that most people accused of tax crimes plead guilty. A lot of judges are extremely vindictive when lawyers defend these guys. Obviously I'm prejudiced, but I do not think that in a country where everyone is guaranteed a lawyer (perhaps not a competent one but a lawyer nonetheless) the person who takes the job should not be attacked for taking the job, and if there are those of us who have represented people accused of making mistakes on their returns (or even failure to file a return), we certainly should be given at least as much courtesy as the person who upholds the constitutional rights of people accused of murder or child abuse.

In order to convict a defendant of the crime of willful failure to file, the government must prove three elements:

1) The duty to file—The government must prove that the defendant had the threshold level of income to be required to file a tax return. This could be proven through the introduction of W-2 forms or 1099 forms, reconstruction of income through bank records, and the testimony of individuals.

2) Non-filing—The government must prove that the required tax return was not filed. Normally, the government has an IRS employee make a "diligent search" of the computer records and come up with a document that certifies that no return was found for that particular year.

3) Willfulness—Willfulness is defined as "... a voluntary intentional violation of a known legal duty ... and not because of mistake, accident or other innocent reason or motive." In other words, if you know you are supposed to file and you do not file; then you are guilty.

The government often uses a defendant's previous tax returns to show that the defendant was aware that he had a duty to file.

What criteria does the IRS use for selecting its "lucky three thousand" candidates for criminal prosecution each year? There are no absolute formulas, but certain generalizations can be made. The IRS wants to make an example out of public figures, and they want guaranteed convictions. They want to appear invincible. They are also rather lazy and would rather have a case handed to them on a silver platter than have to work hard to prove it up. That is why vocal opponents of the IRS are more vulnerable than hidden ones. The easiest target in the world is the so-called "tax protester," who identifies himself by writing letters to the government espousing any or all of the unusual theories discussed in this chapter. It is just like taping a "Kick Me" sign on your posterior. These people, often filers in the past, are on the national computer. The IRS keeps dossiers on all of these people for future possible criminal selection or civil audit. On the other hand, someone who has been out of the system for so long, that his social security number may never have been entered in the IRS computers is unlikely to be selected for prosecution because the IRS may not know he exists.[7] Someone who works for cash and never gets a 1099 or a W-2 form, especially if he moves frequently, is difficult to find and difficult to trap. A lot of the "snake oil" no-tax salesmen fit this category. Unfortunately, their customers are likely to be easy pickings for the IRS.

Sometimes a criminal indictment comes like a bolt from the blue, but generally a target is notified in many ways, sometimes subtle, sometimes not so subtle. There might be the armed special agents knocking at the door reading him his rights. The owner of a housecleaning service might find that an IRS special agent demanding copies of checks or records of cash payments made to the business has contacted her customers. An undercover agent, pretending to be a cus-

7. Less than a decade ago the IRS did not have the capacity to link up 1099s and W-2s/W-4s with social security numbers. Certainly most people remaining outside the system will be traceable by IRS computers in the foreseeable future.

tomer who wants "financial privacy," might visit the coin dealer.

The IRS also often cracks down on organizations promoting tax shelters, both legal and illegal, and then raids their main offices, seizing customer lists. Then, at their leisure, like Roman emperors reclining on couches and idly plucking grapes, the special agents can select some hapless soul to undergo criminal investigation or audit. There are two reasons why membership lists of tax shelter investment groups or organizations that advocate "tax protest" are prized. First, these lists offer ripe, easy targets. Second, destroying, impoverishing or just chasing away the clients of someone they want to take down is an effective way to hurt the major target economically. Often they will also seize the assets of someone they suspect of wrongdoing in advance to prevent him from using the assets to hire competent private counsel. Many wealthy people are reduced to using public defenders because their assets are seized pending further study, which sometimes may never take place.

Suppose the IRS has narrowed down its potential targets in an area to ten people. One is "poster potential," someone like the Mayor of Eric Laschon's town. This guy, if he can not pull strings and get out of it altogether, and if there is a good case, is going to be indicted. Another one is questionable: he may not even be guilty, but he can be shaken down to plead guilty to save his wife from indictment or merely for vague suggestions of leniency, which seem good against an invincible enemy. That leaves eight second-tier targets. One of them will be charged. If the target filed five years ago and then stopped, if the target then signed up with a group that advocated non-filing because of the tri-lateral commission, which was assaulting the national integrity of the United States, if the target sent in strange letters to the IRS threatening not to file ever again, if the target made an above average living, or better yet is a wealthy person or a small business owner, of whom the jurors may be induced to be jealous, all the better. These guys are easy to convict. Sometimes they are victims of con artists. Sometimes they are a little greedy, looking desperately for an answer that ordinarily would not make sense. Often they are people who had a run of bad luck and got behind for any one of a myriad of reasons: an illness, a bad year without enough money to cover the taxes, an accidental overlooking of a neglected return which everyone thought had been filed. People are so intimidated by the IRS that they often incorrectly assume that if they get outside of the system due to no intentional fault of their own, they are still at fault and are perpetual criminals.

There are a number of ways to handle the defense of this type of case. One is taking the posture that the law is wrong, the judge is wrong, and the defendant should walk because he alone is right. This is, in fact, the most common defense to a failure to file charge, and it is universally unsuccessful. Sometimes a lawyer handles it, but most lawyers who assert these types of defenses have been disbarred. Individuals raise their various theories on why they do not have to file. Even if they do a very good job, they still can not get their evidence in and figure out how to instruct the jury or get the judge to do so. They get convicted, go to jail, and contribute to the invincibility argument of the IRS.

Carlos Naranjo, Eric's boss who had first introduced him to the world of tax protesters, was indicted on three counts of income tax evasion. During Naranjo's investigation, Eric had accompanied him to some interviews and hearings with IRS agents.[8] Ultimately, Naranjo pleaded guilty and was publicly paraded as a tax cheat. One of the provisions of his plea agreement was that he would cooperate with the IRS in its further investigations. A number of other people were indicted including the mayor of Eric's home town. I thought the Mayor's counsel and I would work together to plan strategy. We didn't. The Mayor also pleaded guilty and was sentenced.

Eric had several face to face meetings with IRS agents where he literally begged to have his questions answered. He taped all of the

8. I generally forbid special agents from meeting with my clients. Their agenda is jail. In these one-sided meetings "confessions" are often listened to. Unfortunately these are confessions that clients frequently don't remember or didn't make.

interviews. These tapes later proved invaluable during the trial. He asked to be shown where in the code he could find a section specifically identifying "persons who are required to file" and how he could know whether or not he was one such "person." He asked repeatedly what the IRS meant by "voluntary compliance." The jurors were able to hear the rambling, insubstantial answers the IRS agents gave to plain questions asked in simple English.

In trial, the IRS agent was so embarrassed when questioned after listening to his inept sounding comments, he was ready to admit to anything on the stand rather than endure further playing of the tapes. Eric's case was one of two no-budget cases that I had for this time period. A no-budget case is usually a failure-to-file case, most of them have little money, and unlike the Simpson case, this dream team consists of just me and whoever else is interested and will come on board cheap. Jury consultant expert: Me. Graphic art expert: None. Local lawyer who is highly respected with the court and can tell you his idiosyncrasies: One who volunteered to work on the case with me for the experience. Accommodations: Holiday Inn was lucky. Expert witnesses: Try to make points cross examining the IRS expert. Just in case you are one of those people who are easily confused, do not be. All the money and assistance on a case with a high dollar budget does make a difference. In my career of twenty-four years I have only lost one case where the client could cover whatever I needed. Budget was our weak spot.

My case assistant was Wayne Bentson. Normally I like to have a trained legal assistant, and if the client can pay the freight and I am on board, I will supply one. In addition, I like to have an ex-IRS insider at the table to tell me when I miss the lies that so often accompany a tax prosecution. A private detective on top of that, great co-counsel, some human facts and witnesses, a good judge, and the 5 percent chance of winning jumps as high as 90 percent. With Eric, I had some of that. I did have a man with two priests ready to testify for him. I had a man with a son living at home who loved his dad. He was current on his child support, even the part he really did not owe, because one of the kids now lived with him, and a general all-around good guy. I also had big, intimidating Wayne Bentson.

Wayne Bentson is a leading non-lawyer expert who uses the Freedom of Information Act (FOIA) to get information out of the IRS. He also has dissected the IMF and can analyze it with often uncanny accuracy and then back up his interpretation with government documents. In my career, I have met only one IRS agent on the stand who answered questions on the IMF with any consistent, apparent accuracy and confidence.

Wayne is a big mountain of a man, about six feet tall and very stout. He brings to the case his own wooden case filled with papers collected through skillful use of the FOIA. Ask Wayne to answer any question on the IMF or the IRS and he will, with an incredible amount of confidence. Sometimes however, the answers are very strange. Sometimes Wayne comes up with theories that do not appear to be supported by research. When this happens, you can not argue with Wayne. In both cases Wayne "worked on" with me, *Buford* and *Laschon*, Wayne had come with the file. With Buford, the client had searched for lots of answers and found Wayne and found me. With Laschon I fear Wayne may have been part of the problem, convincing Eric not to file tax returns.

I have represented hard-core right wing and left wing tax fanatics. I have always preached that our freedom bird, the bald eagle, needs both wings to fly. I have defended people who felt compelled to shoot at IRS agents. I have represented some so-called protestors with few assets. Consequently I often take allies, whoever they are, unless they can not be controlled at all and will interfere with my defense. A low budget case requires sacrifices. Sometimes they just show up and there is nothing you can do about it.

I was able to show, with Eric's tape, that the revenue agent was lying. Then Wayne handed me some blockbuster forms to put on the overhead screen. One said Eric had lived in the Virgin Islands.

"Mr. Revenue Agent" I asked, "What does this code number mean?"

"I don't know."

"Doesn't it mean that Eric lives in the Virgin Islands?"

"Of course not."

Whereupon we put it on the screen and in English the government form says, "Virgin Islands."

"Are you sure?" I asked.

"Guess not," he admitted, looking at the floor.

"But you know Mr. Laschon lives in London, Kentucky don't you?"

"Yes."

Next Wayne tells me, blockbuster, the number on the IMF for Laschon says he is not required to file unless he lives in the Virgin Islands. Unbelievable!

I go with it, ask the question. The agent hesitates. I grab the slide from Wayne, confidently, get ready to put it on the slide machine, when I notice, glancing at it, that it says nothing of the kind. I am startled. If I put that on the screen we'll look like nuts. I am afraid that perhaps Wayne is not playing with a full deck. I look over at him big, confident. At the moment I am looking at the Duke, John Wayne himself, if he was an escapee from a mental ward. Big John smiles. It is intimidating to our agent, I smile back (inside my guts are churning... my client's acquittal is turning into a fruitcake defense where we just might piss the good judge off enough to get stacked sentences). I nod and wrap it up holding the paper in the air threatening to put it on the projector stand.

"Mr. Revenue Agent," I pause. "Are you really ready to swear under oath that the code doesn't say—"

He pauses again. Then barely audibly he says "No, I can't." I wave my hand and toss the slide on the desk toward Wayne who I know will pick up his treasure and file it before anyone reads it. Of course the truth did come out. The agent did not understand his own internal code. The fact that we didn't understand it either was beside the point. Of course Eric's lack of understanding was exculpatory.

However, I knew then and there I would not be sitting in a courtroom a third time with Big John. I later had to stop even taking referrals from Wayne when I received a call from *The Wall Street Journal* inquiring about a letter from Wayne, and a former governor of Arizona, Meacham, in which they claimed no one had to file income taxes unless they were born in Guam or the Virgin Islands, and that to support their legal opinion they had the backing of yours truly. The letter also claimed that I had used Wayne's theory to win several cases (including Laschon). Finally, to discourage follow up directly with me, Wayne told people that I was no longer available to do legal work, that I had retired, but Wayne had a new protégée who would be taking my place. Wayne also began to advertise that he had engineered victories on cases I had won where he had not even met the client.

The prosecutor against Eric Laschon, Tom Self, was a real "Rambo." We first met over the phone. He demanded that we sign a plea agreement that he had sent to me or else he would withdraw it and force us to trial. The plea agreement called for Eric to admit he was a criminal and then plead guilty to all four counts and throw himself on the mercy of the court. "Rambo" was abusive and rude. He refused to give us any discovery. The discovery process, which is not as extensive in a criminal trial as in civil trial, provides for a limited exchange of evidentiary material between counsel before trial.

In a failure-to-file criminal tax trial, the government first has to prove that the defendant earned enough to be required to file. This is usually a given. The second, more difficult, question is: Did he file? The government must prove beyond a reasonable doubt that the accused did not file. Generally they get to show this by offering what they call a certificate of account. This is a piece of paper saying that someone has looked at the official computer records and that according to these records, no return has been filed. This is pretty important because sometimes the certificate is not honest (see *U.S. v. Buford*). Sometimes the computer records show something different. For example, in 1983 IRS agents in Dallas deliberately destroyed a large number of tax returns that had been filed because they were behind on their collating. Had they been entered into the computer? Did the tax-

127

payer have any independent way of proving he/she had filed? Were all the checks cashed that were supposed to be cashed? There may never be answers to all of the potential questions that have not even been asked yet. In all probability most of those returns have been duplicated by requesting a new copy from the taxpayer, and sometimes no one cares. It is the job of the government to prove beyond a reasonable doubt every element of the case. If they can not prove that the taxpayer did not file, your client does not have to take the stand, and he may walk. The third element of a willful failure to file case and an important element of any criminal tax case is the issue of willfulness. "Willfulness in the context of criminal tax cases is defined as a voluntary intentional violation of a known legal duty" (see *U.S. v. Cheek*, 111S. Ct 604, 1991, and *U.S. v. Powell*, 955 F2nd 2206). The issue of willfulness is an intent and understanding issue. If the accused thought he was following the law, he is technically innocent of the commission of a tax crime. This one word is the most important defense word in the Internal Revenue Code. My job was to show Eric sincerely believed he was not required to file. We would concede two-thirds of the case.

Lawyers, who fight issues they have no chance of prevailing on, when there are better issues to fight, risk losing their credibility and the credibility of their clients.

Since "Rambo" would not give us the records we were entitled to by law, we had to file motions and I had to fly up to London, Kentucky, for a ruling by a judge.

Magistrate J. B. Johnson, Jr., who presided over the pre-trial motions hearing, ordered "Rambo" to obey the law and give us the IMF, the official computer form. The form indicated that Eric had not filed. Accordingly, we knew we would have a tough fight. The IMF would be important however in showing the investigative path the agents took against Eric. Did he owe a tax? Had the IRS sent out letters to Eric? We would use this information in trial.

Our trial judge was Magistrate James Cook, an extremely sharp man and a former prosecutor. He was determined to give Eric a fair trial. "Rambo" was mean and ornery each step of the way. He was determined to make a spectacle of the case and treated me like a criminal for having the audacity to represent such a low life as Eric. He was actually frustrated that Carlos Naranjo and the mayor had pleaded guilty, thus denying him the opportunity to humiliate them in trial and get more press. All that pent-up frustration came pouring out as he lit into Eric during cross-examination. The big "evasion" whale had beached itself, so "Rambo" could not thrust in his harpoon. Instead, "Rambo" was determined to use his harpoon to overkill the "failure-to-file" minnow.

My favorite type of opposition is the prosecutor who is so sure of himself that he does not even consider that we have a chance to win. He either does not take time to prepare properly or relies on canned, rote-memory preparation from other criminal tax cases delivered in a style of just rattling it off when the button is pushed. The over-confident prosecutor does not send out for expert back-up. If the prosecutor is meaner than a junkyard dog, and if we are fortunate to draw a jury that thinks public servants should at least be a little civil, we start to chip away at the enormous advantage that the government has in any case in a federal courthouse.

"Rambo" would not shake hands or be civil. Only when I extended mine in front of the judge did he reluctantly respond to it. No one wants to appear to be a "Rambo" in front of an experienced trial judge.

L.R. and I picked what we thought was a pretty good jury. We had coal miners and English teachers, mothers and dads, and lots of churchgoers who would relate to the two character witnesses I had lined up. I wondered, "Would the judge let me put on three character witnesses?" I wanted the jurors to meet Eric's sixteen-year-old son, so that they would realize that this single dad had a responsibility at home that would be impaired if he went to jail.

"Rambo" put his case on fast, furiously and with a vengeance. His prime witness was Carlos Naranjo, the now guilty boss who first had gotten Eric into this mess.

On Naranjo's re-cross, we made a lot of points. I asked him, "You are an honest man are you not?" Very few witnesses will fail, under oath, to admit that they are honest, even if they have been previously convicted of perjury. "When you told Eric about reasons why he was not required to file tax returns, did you believe what you were saying, or were you trying to con him?"

Naranjo affirmed that he believed these doctrines at the time. I then asked, "Is Eric an honest man?"

Naranjo's reply, "Yes."

Each customer who came on the stand to testify that Eric had billed him and collected money from him also testified that Eric was an honest man. The IRS agent was one of our best witnesses. After cross-examination he admitted that he did not know much about the code and could not really tell if Eric had committed a crime or not.

The Rev. Steven Ashley became the clergy spokesperson who testified about Eric's community spirit and volunteer work. Eric's sixteen-year-old son, Steven, was an extremely effective witness who tugged at everyone's heartstrings when he told the jury he had been taught to be honest by his dad and that his dad was an honest man.

The crux of the case was Eric's own testimony. "Rambo" grew steadily meaner during the course of cross-examination and finally turned the jury completely against himself and the IRS.

Closing argument was almost funny. Since the government bears the burden of proof in a criminal case, the prosecutor gets to go first and last. The one thing Eric was not was an actor. He was honest, and his sincerity shone through, but he fumbled and stumbled a lot under the angry attacks of "Rambo." When the prosecutor argued law with Eric, he was simply proving to the jury how complicated it was and helping us win our case. Judge Cook at one point politely interrupted with just a touch of cynicism, "Counselor, do you want to continue debating law with the witness?" He did, and while the jury may have agreed with some of "Rambo's" points and some of Eric's, the truth was winning the debate. The truth was that Eric believed that he had been following the law.

The night before closing argument, the over-confident government lawyer did some research on me to prepare for his closing. He should have done it before trial. Failure-to-file cases are so routinely won by the government that the prosecution does not prepare like they do on more complicated cases. He found some of my published criminal tax wins. He came up to me before closing argument and apologized. "I thought you were just one of those crazy protest lawyers. I really underestimated you."

I responded, "I *am* a protest lawyer. Every decent defense lawyer protests. That's our job. Protest is what we do." He looked at me again, reappraising his original thought.

He opened, "Mr. Minns will probably quote Shakespeare to you or other famous people to get your mind off of the facts here. He will probably tell you about his days as an English teacher or things like that to get your confidence, but what he won't do is give you any defense against the facts in this case. All right, Eric is a pretty nice guy, it seems, but remember about the nice guys who suddenly commit crimes of murder. No one thought they would, but they do. Eric Laschon is simply an actor who has memorized some lines. He is putting on a play within a play. In this inner play, he is a good guy. In reality, he is just a guy trying to fool you, trying to get away with not paying his taxes because he'd rather keep the money. Remember that you can fool all of the people some of the time, and you can fool some of the people all of the time, but you can not fool all of the people all of the time. Eric Laschon is trying to fool all of us all of the time. Will you let him get away with it? Of course not. All the nice things you have heard about him come to nothing when we remember that he did not file his tax returns. That is what this case is all about. Nothing more, nothing less. He broke the law and he is guilty."

That was essentially "Rambo's" argument, and he gave it in thirty minutes with gusto and rage, no compassion, lots of anger.

Here is a digest of my closing argument.

"Unlike Mr. Self, I believe in using the words of people who expressed themselves very well and crediting them with it. Self was too modest when he said that he would not use phrases from great writers and speakers, and then he went right ahead and did it anyway. The play within a play metaphor comes from *Hamlet.* Self didn't invent it. The two English teachers on the jury will support me on this." They did. They were already nodding. "The speech about fooling people was originally the wit of Abe Lincoln, but I don't think it is appropriate for Eric. Rather we might say, 'You can fool all of the people some of the time and some of the people all of the time... but you can *always* make a fool of yourself.' Eric got cheated by some authors, trust promoters and lawyers who are not here today to protect their theories. Eric got up on the stand and proved beyond any doubt that he is no actor. He and the government's witnesses and his character witnesses have proven one thing beyond any doubt: Eric Laschon is a good man, a man of love, honor and truth. The fruit of this tree is good fruit because he is a good man. The only one here today who lied to you was the prosecutor when he promised not to quote great men and use their ideas and then flooded you with them. The only person not sure of his convictions was the IRS agent who does not really know what he is doing here today and does not understand the code he works with every day. The government rushed into this 'crime scene' and beat up Eric Laschon, causing his divorce, wrecking his life, and failing to go after the real criminals: the guys who sold him the advice that got him here in the first place. The government is like the Keystone cops, jumping in at the sound of a problem but beating up the victim while the real criminal gets away."

It is very difficult to package an entire trial into a few pages, especially when living through a week of it feels like a lifetime spent in Hell. There is no way to adequately describe the feeling of the combined effects of the tightening stomach, the dry, scratchy throat, the increased heart rate, the tension in the courtroom. The only relief is immediate escape for lunch breaks and at the end of the trial day getting out. I can not share with you the mounting fatigue of all the out-of-court hours spent in hotel rooms in strange cities, interviewing witnesses, preparing the client, rehearsing closing arguments, all the

132

while trying to second-guess and pre-empt the government's strategy.

I have mixed feelings about going up against a Rambo-type prosecutor. The antagonistic human contact is very unpleasant. No one likes it. However, properly dealt with, having a Rambo opponent can increase your client's chances of acquittal, because, given enough time, he can make the jury hate him and throw more logs on your victory bonfire. Nevertheless, prosecutors are very powerful and often cruel people, especially those prosecuting alleged tax crimes. They are not saving little children from pedophiles, or protecting high school cheerleaders from the likes of rapists, or keeping drug dealers off junior high campus....*These* guys are beating up nice people.

Even when I am going through a trial, intently focused on the legal and factual issues, I cannot seal my heart inside a steel vault of professionalism. I find myself becoming emotionally invested in the personal concerns of the client and his loved ones. I wanted badly to win for Eric's son Steven Laschon, as well as for Eric and his mother. It is tough to worry about making a kid an orphan when he can not go back to Mom. She sent him to Dad in the first place because there were problems. A lot of problems can not be solved in one trial, and no story is completely over when the trial ends. Each story is a segment of someone's whole life that continues to unwind year after year. Litigation is an intense battle that has significance long after it is over. Among litigators and parties alike, victories can still be savored years later. Remembered defeats can be relived and feel just as devastating years later unless you can laugh at them. Sometimes you never can. The singular experience of defending yourself in the face of intense cross examination in front of strangers or listening to an impassioned closing argument tearing you apart in a public forum can have permanent effect on a person's psyche. One man I cross-examined had a heart attack and died. He was an evil man.

In Eric's case, the jurors found him "not guilty" on all four counts of failure-to-file income tax returns. The courtroom trial was over, but not the inner emotional trial to which Eric was still subjecting himself. At one point, he had felt secure that his opinions on the tax laws were correct. The counsel he had received from me had shaken him to the core. It was not easy for him to set aside the fruits of almost a decade of study and beliefs, which had cost him dearly in terms of time, money and human relationships. He still had deep concerns that volunteering information to the IRS would get him in a world of trouble. Eventually, we were able to persuade Eric to go ahead, file, and put this painful episode of his life behind him.

I have written about and spoken about people who do not file tax returns but are still unindicted in front of a jury. The vindication brings freedom from jail not collection. I have yet to handle a case where my client, even acquitted, wouldn't have been better off filing and not going through the trial at all.

Nevertheless, all that aside, those two words "not guilty" are worth an awful lot of sacrifice. Eric Laschon was "not guilty."

Chapter V
Targeted Tax Preparers

"The Fifth Amendment is an old and good friend. It is one of the great landmarks in men's struggle to be free of tyranny, to be decent, and civilized."

—William O. Douglas

Before he read a word, my surrogate father and best friend, former firefighter and Texas Middle-Weight Champion, Mickey Brown held an early version of this manuscript, judging its weight like a fisherman assessing a freshly caught river catfish. "What criteria determine which cases make it into your book?" he asked.

That was a good question.

At that point, the sole criterion was that I liked the case and felt I had accomplished something while trying it, but he made me think. Every lawyer, of course, would like to try a case that becomes a precedent, digging out obtuse applications of case law that will be quoted for generations to come. The single most important tax case of my career would be the appellate case, *U.S. v. Powell*, because it made it easier to win tax cases. Without *Buford*, there would have been no *Powell*. Without *Powell*, it is likely that Eric Laschon and the Absent

Minded Professor, and many clients of other lawyers would have been convicted instead of acquitted. If setting precedent *is* the criterion, then Stephen Buford's story, like the Persian poet Kahil Gibran, leads the rest.

Stephen's Story

Stephen Buford was born to Bob and Dorothy Buford in 1953 in Dallas. When he was eighteen, his mom died of cancer. Eventually his dad remarried. Peggy, Bob's second wife, helped raise Stephen's two younger brothers, Paul and Phillip, as well as her son Don. Bob Buford was not a spare-the-rod sort of guy. He was considered by the entire community to be a man of strict religious principles, a leader of various church youth groups, and a board member of Trinity Christian High School in Dallas, the private religious school his son graduated from in 1971. His minister and peers praised Bob as an honest man.

Stephen was raised in that strict Christian environment of discipline and work. Well-mannered and polite, Stephen adhered to a strict Christian code, and while some of his peers in the sixties experimented with drugs and sex, Stephen did neither, marrying his high school sweetheart, Linda, and shortly thereafter starting their family. At the time of Stephen's first criminal tax trial in 1988, his son, Zachary, was six years old and his daughter, Alicia, was nine years old.

In his freshman year at college, he had started to work with Jack A. Woodward and Company, at first as a warehouse man and later as a supervisor. His boss, proud of him, moved him rapidly up to management positions. Six years later Stephen was in charge of the office and a vice president, but he decided to go it alone. Jack Woodward was sorry when Stephen decided to leave and start his own business, but they parted on excellent terms.

Like many others who forego the completion of their college education, Stephen simply never got back into school. His dad and grandfather had both been tax preparers for many years, and Bob taught Stephen to prepare returns. With his close friend Charles Samuels, Stephen decided to open a tax preparation service. Through church and family referrals and quiet but aggressive salesmanship, Stephen prospered. Later he dabbled in oil and gas ventures. Like many others in the Texas boom years, Stephen's oil and gas investments turned him into a paper millionaire at the relatively young age of thirty. His tax practice was also booming. The neighbors trusted him, his partner, and his dad, and the men gave fast, efficient service.

Bob Buford's health forced him to take a decreasing role in the work. He had suffered from a heart attack and had a triple bypass operation. Shortly thereafter he was stricken with another heart attack. Dr. Jay Teng, who had saved Bob's life in the operating room, ordered him to slow down and later testified that stress, such as hard work (or facing years in prison) could kill him. Bob had saved a few dollars and could do a few simple returns for his son and partner, and so he got by on that with his wife, who still held down her job, and with it, the accompanying medical insurance.

As Stephen's prosperity grew, so did his ambition. He decided to start selling trusts to avoid the requirements of probate and to insure added tax benefits. By this time Stephen was not poor and he wasn't willing, ambition or not, to take any chances on behalf of his growing client list. He subscribed to several tax reporter services and hired Gary Joslin, who was alleged to be one of the top tax lawyers in the United States, as well as half a dozen other nationally prominent tax specialists. In the late seventies and early eighties the great tax experts all over the country were touting something called straddles and were paying handsome commissions to lawyers, stockbrokers, real estate brokers, and tax preparers all over the United States to sell these straddles. The basic purpose of this vehicle was to "straddle" two years or more with income and thereby avoid or delay a taxable event.

A taxable event is simply legal talk for something that occurs that makes you liable for taxes. When you get your paycheck from your employer, that is a taxable event. When you buy stock with your pay check, that is not a taxable event. It is simply a purchase. If you sell that stock and make a profit, that is a taxable event. The law is full of ways to make something that looks like a taxable event a non-taxable event. The advantage is, of course, that you do not pay taxes on a non-taxable event. If you buy bonds and a statute of the federal government says the interest is non-taxable, then the procurement of that interest is a non-taxable event. However, if you *sell* those non-taxable bonds for a profit, that may very well be a taxable event. The determination of a taxable event and a non-taxable event, compared to the study of straddles to deter taxes, is a very simple concept. Straddles were complicated shelter devices presumably understood only by the most advanced tax experts, nearly all of whose opinions turned out to be *wrong*.

Suddenly, in the mid-eighties the government decided that straddles were not legitimate ways of deferring income. Billions in deductions were disallowed. The tax court filled up with straddle litigation. On a $50,000 deduction taken in 1979, it was possible to owe several million dollars by 1989. The practice of straddling was widespread. All the big eight accounting firms were involved to one extent or another, and thousands of hitherto fairly wealthy or at least financially healthy middle-class citizens were ruined and forced into bankruptcy over innocent misinterpretations of the tax laws, even after relying on supposedly the finest tax minds in the country.

In addition to reliance on great tax minds, Stephen enlisted the assistance of veteran IRS agents. He would regularly call the IRS for advice and answers to his questions. He did this years before the *Money Magazine* surveys came out showing that you were as likely as not to get a wrong answer from your CPA, tax lawyer, or IRS agent, on a complex tax issue. Stephen, boy genius that he now appeared to be, was tackling some of the most difficult tax areas. In fact, until the late eighties when Stephen's first trial was over, many of the key questions answered in an earlier period of time were being re-examined and given new answers. It was a heady feeling to be hiring tax lawyers, information services, and discussing the most complex tax questions of the day with IRS agents. Stephen even represented attorneys and CPAs to set up trusts for them.

Both of Stephen's disasters hit at the same time, although he did not realize then that the more horrible one had hit at all. The more horrible one was the audit of his own 1982 return by IRS collection agent Phil Millian. The one that occurred later appeared to be worse at the time because the audit by agent Millian seemed to go all right.

Stephen had straddled (using the word as it comes from the dictionary and not the tax laws) two independent businesses. He was making money in oil, constantly letting it ride, and he was making money as an accountant and a salesman for oil rights and straddles. His million-dollar statement was pushing two million dollars when he was called in for an audit. No one likes going in for an audit. Yet Stephen and his partner Chuck were not new to the process. They had represented many clients in audits before the IRS, so Stephen felt comfortable representing himself in an audit of his own return. In fact, when the audit was over, agent Millian concurred and passed Stephen. No taxes were due, no interest, and certainly no penalties. It was doubly satisfying because many of the same deductions that his clients were taking with the approval of tax consultants who had been paid for with big dollars by Stephen and Chuck, were also taken on Stephen's return.

In 1984 the dam burst. Stephen, the boy genius, pride of his dad and step-mom, worshiped by his kids and adoring wife, fell victim with more than a hundred thousand other investors and speculators. Oil investments crashed lower than they had during the flood of new oil from the huge Spindletop Dome explosion before Stephen's lifetime. Oil died. Overnight Stephen's financial statement dropped from nearly two million dollars to a negative figure. His friends and clients who had bought oil rights from him were left holding empty bags. Stephen fell into a serious depression and could not face anyone. He could not work; he could not play; he could not cope. He simply gave up.

His wife and family helped get him back together again, but he still could not face his customers and friends, so he simply left Texas to start over in Florida. Years later he was living in a wonderful home and prosperity appeared right around the corner. He was re-established in his new community, and, in fact, was elected as a precinct chairman in his local Republican Party. Stephen was, in short, getting his life back in order and healing from the pains of his prior failure.

Then special agent Jager arrived. Jager would prove to be more difficult to get rid of than herpes.

Jager's arrival reminded me of the cartoon: "We're from the government and we're here to help you." The picture in the cartoon depicts the government agent has a bag labeled IRS on it, a gleam in his smile and horns on his head. Those of us accustomed to dealing with the government on a regular basis need no cartoon. Simply the allegation that the government is here to help you is funny all by itself.

Suffice it to say that the special agent is *never* there to help you. If he is interviewing, you or someone you know is likely to be in serious trouble. The arrival of the special agent at your doorstep should give rise to an internal voice screaming, "Fifth Amendment, Fifth Amendment," because special agents, unlike collection agents, are charged with the responsibility of putting people in jail. Generally they are charged, too, in the special agent's handbook, and often by law, with reading you your rights. Two special agents showed up at Stephen's home. Later, special agent James Jager would spy on Bob Buford and his wife and secure intimate pictures through his surveillance camera as he followed them to the restaurant, to their home, through their curtains, and in their front yard, in his quest to prove Bob and Stephen were dishonest tax cheats.

Stephen opened his door, listened to the agents read him his rights, shook their hands, and foolishly invited them in to talk. They talked about a lot of things while the agent took notes. When the agent talked to Stephen and Bob, he took notes without recording. When he talked to all of the witnesses in the upcoming trials, he recorded them, then reduced the recordings to paper, and then "misplaced" the tapes. At the trial, years later, he was able to remember many things that he had not put in his notes, but he would forget things that had happened recently. A psychiatrist I know calls it selective retention. Most of us untrained in psychology just call it lying.

One thing he remembered very well and, in fact, put into his notes was Stephen's answer to the question relating to his 1982 tax return, the one that had been audited and that had passed. He asked Stephen if he could copy his return. Stephen said sure and then could not find it. He "confessed" saying, "It's embarrassing, but I went out of business a few years ago and we made a sudden move. I guess I could not face up to my failure. My records have been turned around topsy-turvy and I can not find them all. The 1982 return is missing. It could turn up or we might never find it. Can't you just look up the one I filed?"

The agent nodded in a vague way without answering Stephen but giving him the implied assurance that it did not matter and went on questioning him. In fact, that innocent "confession" would later be used against Stephen and his father to secure a false conviction against each of them and nearly kill Stephen's dad—literally!

Our friendly gun-toting rights-reading special agent spent a lot of tax dollars over a year of intense investigation of Stephen Buford, Bob Buford, and Stephen's partner, Chuck Samuels. He may have interviewed every client Stephen ever had, and, in fact, as the calls came in from former clients to both Bob and later Stephen, they repeated the same advice they had already given their customers orally and in writing: "We have compiled careful records documenting all of your financial transactions for the very purpose of a possible government audit. That is one of the chief reasons the law requires the completion of records so that they may be reviewed." And reviewed they were.

On April 13, 1988, without prior warning, Stephen Buford and his ailing father Bob were charged by the grand jury with thirty felony counts, totaling a possible ninety-four years of jail time! After reviewing thousands of returns prepared by Stephen and his father Bob, and some returns that neither one had anything to do with, the government indicted based on several returns. Basically, Stephen was charged with fourteen counts of violating 26 U.S.C. (United States Code) 7206(2), which means intentionally filing false tax returns or assisting someone in the filing of tax returns that he knows are incorrectly put together. His father Bob Buford was charged with assisting on the same fourteen counts. Each of them was also charged with one count violating 18 U.S.C. 371, conspiracy to do what the other twenty-eight total counts accused them of doing. Each of the tax return counts was worth three years in jail and the conspiracy was worth five for a total of forty-seven years apiece.

So the Bufords hired a hotshot, never-lost-a-case tax specialist, gave him what turned out to be a non-refundable twenty-five thousand dollar initial retainer, and after letting them know he would probably amaze and surprise them once the check cleared, he did exactly that. He told them the case was hopeless and that he would represent them both. If each would plead guilty to two felony counts he could get them off with whatever the judge agreed to give them. Probably less than ten years apiece. He also told the prosecutor that he was throwing in the towel because the case was too tough. This he did very quickly and used up the retainer overnight. What a guy! If they still wanted a trial, another $100,000 would get the hero started. Stephen, not feeling quite as happy as he was at the time he parted with his first check, broke down and told his new hero, who had indeed surprised him, that he was innocent and so was his father. If there were any mistakes in the returns, of which the Bufords were unconvinced, they were honest mistakes. If a tax preparer could go to prison for making mistakes, it was a tougher profession than they had bargained for. The hero calmly told them of the wonderful deal he had worked out. Stephen had one question: "Guilty or innocent, what kind of deal can I make to keep my dad out of prison?"

"None," was the hero's reply.

A prominent underground advisor, and a fighter, then met

Stephen and suggested that he fire the hero and hire one of several lawyers who had actually won a case against the IRS. His list, made up from people all over the country, had five names on it. Stephen went cross-country interviewing the four men and one woman on the list. I try to make my services as expensive as the next person because this kind of work is very taxing (no pun, of course). Most of my clients are innocent even under the government's twisted version of an innocent person. However, it's tougher to keep an innocent taxpayer out of prison, once indicted, than a guilty child abuser. More heroes promised Stephen victory. I could not match those promises. I recommended he get a warranty in writing. If the lawyer had a fat malpractice policy and would give him a written guarantee, I would be happy to take the malpractice suit if he still ended up in jail.

Stephen confided that none of the five who had records of verifiable wins were willing to guarantee victory, although he had secured a few guarantees with other lawyers. He then showed me a brochure from his number one choice demonstrating an impressive list of wins with the names of the clients on them. It was a full color printed brochure with lots of testimonials. It was impressive. What was even more impressive was the history behind the actual cases.

One of them was a very famous case out of the Ninth Circuit Court of Appeals in 1983 that had been won by my former partner, known by many as "The Great Izen." Apparently this hero had tried the case in court, lost, and gotten fired. Izen had taken over on appeal and then Izen had won. Bill Cohen out of California had actually won another one of the hero's cases on appeal. The hero had lost the case in trial. These unimportant details were left out of the handsome advertisement. I pulled the published cases with Izen's and Cohen's names listed out of the reporters and showed them to Stephen. For some reason (perhaps his non-involvement at the winning stage) the hero's name was missing. Prior to Buford, I had usually declined to give newspaper interviews. They were usually inaccurate, seemed to be mostly steered against the side of truth and justice, and were very time consuming. After Buford I changed this policy because I realized how this type of stuff seemingly swayed intelligent people like Stephen. (I also had a book to sell about a year and a half after Buford began which required a compromise. Publicity sells books. It can also turn public opinion in your client's favor or against him.)

Stephen took the information and left. He told me he would decide shortly. When he returned he hired me with a couple of provisos. In turn I asked him why he chose me over the others on the list. I have seldom seen people make rational decisions about hiring legal counsel. They hire because John Doe, who may know little or nothing about the lawyer, regularly had drinks with him or because he vaguely remembered Doe's name from a newspaper article, although it is possible that he is confusing Doe with another Doe, or worse, because Doe is the head of some exclusive sounding bar organization or listed in the Best Lawyer in the Universe poll or who's who in outer Mongolia. I think that the best scorecard is simply that, a scorecard, but again I am prejudiced—I have a scorecard. Nevertheless, I always want to know what brings in the business. Stephen's reasons were instructive.

I really was not in first place. I was tied for second with two others (apparently only the brochure exaggerator was taken off the list). Choice number one wanted a huge fee. Stephen was fortunate that, while he was well off, he did not have that kind of money. I was elected because I lived in Houston, and therefore it would cost less to fly me back and forth to Dallas for trial. What a vote of confidence!

Stephen asked that I put a team together for him and his father and make his interest subservient to that of his dad. Stephen was willing to make a deal in which he would plead guilty to a crime he had not committed if the prosecution would guarantee in writing that his dad would not serve any time in prison. What a sweetheart deal. In my opinion it was a very workable deal. In fact, it is the type of deal that is very often made. I have seen quite a number of husband/wife, father/son, partner/partner deals made where one pleads guilty so that the other can walk.

A deal to hire me was struck and I was put in charge of the defense for both Stephen and his dad. I was given what I felt was a pretty good budget, and I got a friend on the phone from Fort Worth, Texas, Mike Ware. From personal experience, I knew Mike to be a first rate criminal trial lawyer. First we had tried *United States v. Joe Oliver* in Ft. Worth together. Oliver was charged with not filing his tax returns. Aside from the one big weakness in the case, that Oliver had not filed his tax returns, Ware and I won acquittals on all four counts. Most tax lawyers won't do criminal law, they don't even like to go into a real courtroom with real jurors, and most criminal lawyers don't like to defend people on tax cases. I had two reasons for bringing in Ware: First, he was one of the best lawyers I'd ever had the privilege to work with (I had entrusted a relative of mine into his care and he had done an excellent job for him) and I knew from experience he was a tough, honest team player. Second, I have a personal goal, along with two people who recruited me over a decade ago, to get some top flight lawyers into the criminal tax defense field. If the list could be raised from five to ten, we could start our own bar organization and have deductible business meetings in Honolulu. Mike was also the only criminal tax defense lawyer I knew who could boast of a better win/loss ratio than I had. He had tried one tax case, *Oliver*, and won. Hard to beat a 100 percent win ratio. I hoped to let him keep it.

We reviewed the copious indictment, which informed me that it looked like the same charge photocopied over and over again. Stephen and his dad were charged with one count for preparing a trust return for a client for a certain year. Then they were charged with another count for using the information on that trust return when preparing the tax return for the same client for the same year. Then, of course, since they were alleged to have done it together they were both charged for conspiring to create the two incorrect returns. The penalties for the tax statute were relatively clear, if not the rules for compliance, because of case law.

You could lose your shirt, home, car, underwear, and escrow funds for your home real estate taxes if you made a mistake on your return and got caught within the three-year statute of limitations from the date of filing. However, if it was an honest mistake you weren't guilty of a crime and should not be indicted or go to jail. The criminal statute required willful conduct. Willful meant the intention to violate the law. A very important distinction in tax law, which is so complex that the best erred daily and the worst, well, who could guess?

One of the returns that Stephen and his dad were charged with falsifying was for an individual return they had not prepared. A competitor prepared it. Another client's returns, both trust and individual, had been prepared without following Buford's or Samuel's directions. One client didn't even think that Stephen worked on his return. The open and shut case that the hero had decided was not winnable by the defense looked pretty ridiculous to me, but I counseled Stephen that the federal pens were filled with people charged with ridiculous crimes. With all that in mind, Stephen gave me orders to settle if the government would take the deal they usually suggested: one good guy for another good guy, or as they interpret their offer, one bad guy for the other. The United States assistant attorney, John Repsis, turned me down flat. The hero had already agreed to plead guilty for both clients. Why should he now take only one? Stephen had paid $25,000 to make his case more difficult. Frankly, Repsis was astounded with my "dishonesty" insisting on a trial and even considering the possibility of innocence. Didn't I know with whom I was dealing and in whose court I was?

Stephen was in Judge A. Joe Fish's court. Judge Fish had just sentenced a person convicted on a white-collar crime, stacking the sentences. (This is according to a press account, which may be unreliable). Stacking the sentences is a trade term of judges and lawyers and criminals. It simply means that the convicted really has to do a lot of the time that the media and the government suggested was possible in various interviews. It scares accused and counsel when a judge has a reputation for doing this. It means potential death in

146

prison. My actual experience with Judge Fish, while not always pleasant, was that he was a very intelligent and decent man.

I walk a line here. I do not believe in imprisonment for non-victim crimes. From my personal perspective all incarcerations for taxes are unjust. By just or unjust in this context I mean without justification. Fish is a moral man. He will not imprison an accused for purely vindictive reasons or to exercise his federal power. A defendant in front of him has the potential of receiving mercy. I believe when Fish hits someone with a sentence, he does so with difficulty, fulfilling what he believes is his obligation as a judge. He would prefer not to, but the defendant has to give him a good reason not to. After trying three cases in his courtroom, I am convinced that the people who got their sentences stacked in his court (if in fact this happened) must have been drug dealers or bankers, i.e., criminals who needed to do serious time for the benefit of society.

Nevertheless, initially, the prospect of potential conviction in his court was frightening and plea-bargaining began immediately. I am seldom the attorney of choice for initial plea bargaining, although I often get much better deals than lawyers the government knows never win, or even worse, never even go to bat. Many lawyers take large up-front fees, never even considering the possibility of going to trial—they seldom share that bit of strategy with the client before separating them from some savings. If the case must go to trial, they dump it. These villains should not be confused with the lawyer who withdraws because the client does not honor the fee agreement or some other legitimate reason, such as authorizing the lawyer to make a deal and then backing out, making the lawyer look like a liar.

BUFORD ONE — The Jury Trial

We went to trial in August 1988, just a little over three months after the indictment, a significant fast track from the government. It was clear from the beginning that the IRS attorneys expected Stephen to roll over and play dead.

Stephen took the stand and admitted that he had made some mistakes on the returns but that he relied on information from nationally prominent experts as well as IRS phone calls and his own research. His dad did not take the stand. Stephen spoke for him. Stephen accepted all responsibility for every return filed by his organization including some returns filed by his dad that Stephen had never even seen. The plan was to win it all, but if we couldn't, Stephen would do the time for his father. Ware and I worked like a well-oiled gun shooting holes through the irrational theory of the government, and frankly the trial might have been enjoyable if we hadn't known that no trial is guaranteed and any case can be lost with the wrong moves or bad luck. Couple that with the horror of sitting at the table with a ghastly gray Bob Buford who seemed closer and closer to dying on us in the middle of the trial. He was a very sick man, and it was obvious that the trial was, at the least, not medically helpful for him.

Stephen, on the stand, went through his history and then into his own audit on his 1982 return in which agent Phil Millian had reviewed his return and with similar deductions had passed him. Is it any wonder that he thought the deductions were permissible? Even an IRS agent had passed on it. Mike and I are both veterans of many battles in these pits, and we both felt very good about our case and the warm looks we were getting from the jurors, and, more importantly, the hostile looks they were giving the IRS agents at the other table. Jager, the IRS special agent, had stepped on his tongue so many times it looked as though he wouldn't be able to put it back in his mouth. The government rested. The defense rested. And then the surprise happened.

Marsha Boatright, an IRS technician who had no personal knowledge, got up for rebuttal testimony. Rebuttal means the government needs more witnesses to refute what the defendant said. It is relatively rare, most trials have no rebuttal witnesses. She was a professional witness for the IRS. She was paid to testify and was in fact so good that she was used to teach other witnesses to testify. What was she

148

there for? Of what could her rebuttal possibly consist? We were about to find out.

Ms. Boatright testified under oath that she had reviewed the official records of the IRS and that Stephen had lied about his 1982 tax return, that in fact the records showed he had not even filed his 1982 tax return! The IRS auditor Stephen had met with, according to IRS records, didn't exist! We were stunned. We had on several occasions demanded the official records on both Stephen and his dad, and the audit report, but the request had been refused. We were required to take the word of Marsha Boatright, who sounded very good, that the official records stated that Stephen had not filed his 1982 returns. (In the third trial, this return would magically appear and the non-existent auditor would "come back to life." Makes you wonder why federal perjurers are not in jail. The IRS actually encourages such perjury. Agents lose coveted overtime bonus awards if they lose a case in court.)

The IRS pro had told the jurors in her very well-rehearsed, well-delivered tone that Stephen had lied about the audit, that not only had he not been audited for 1982, but he had not even filed. The jurors looked over at me and Mike and Stephen and his dad with pure disgust. "We had apparently misled them," their looks scowled at us. Who would believe anything that a tax preparer said if he didn't even file his own return? The answer to that question, which the jury would soon share, was: "No one in his right mind." The only way to bring this case back for the good guys was to show the jury what we believed to be true, that Ms. Boatright was either mistaken in her reading of the official record or for some other reason was not being completely frank with us. The following is an edited excerpt from Stephen Buford's first appellate brief.

On cross-examination, after the assessments were improperly admitted without the transcript (i.e., the Individual Master File), the defendant attempted to clear up the issue.

Minns: These three exhibits were prepared only for trial, correct?

Boatright: Yes, as far as the certificate of the assessments and payments.

Minns: What is the procedure?

Boatright: There is a group and when they...gather information they...transfer the information from the computer transcript (IMF) over to the Certificate of Assessments. Then it is forwarded, both things, both the certificate and transcript to this person that signs the blue sheet and she is responsible for making sure that both things correspond.

Minns: Are there ever mistakes in taking from the computer ... transcript to the Certificate? Does the IRS ever make a mistake?

Boatright: I have never seen it.

Minns: Does the programmer ever make a mistake when they look at the computer transcript?

Boatright: You mean interpreting the transcript?

Minns: Yes.

Boatright: Again, I wouldn't be able to answer that.

Our paralegal had been trying, through FOIA (The Freedom of Information Act), before and during the trial to get what the judge would not give us. The same day that Ms. Boatright took the stand, during a break, a small piece of the official record arrived that showed that Stephen *had* been audited for that year. The record was faxed to us and on cross-examination I was able to ask Ms. Boatright a few questions.

Minns: What is Exhibit 5?

Boatright: That is a computer transcript...a summary...AMIDSA.

The Court: Is this a record that emanates from the Internal Revenue Service?

Boatright: Yes sir.

Minns: Would you tell the jury what the Individual Master File is?

Boatright: The Individual Master File is a computer system where individual income tax returns—and it is nationwide. It is the database of the information from tax returns.

Minns: It sits in the largest computer in the world in West Virginia, correct?

Boatright: Yes, it does.

Minns: And just certain, select people have access to that computer?

Boatright: That is correct.

Minns: Do you have access to the computer without going through someone else?

Boatright: Not the computer in West Virginia.

Minns: Do you know what a Dif score is?

Boatright: I know where it is located, yes.

Minns: Are you aware that there are things on Exhibit 5 showing years 1980 and 1981 that can't be on this exhibit unless there is a tax return filed for those years?

Boatright: That is correct.

After a short break, not reflected in the record, the witness on redirect was vague about her prior answer that Defendant's Exhibit 5 showed a return *had* been filed.

Boatright: At this point right now it appears that somewhere in the examination or (later) on the reporter someone has created a database for this individual. It is not as clear but there is an indication that it is not indefinite.

The Certificate of Assessments comes from a group in Criminal Investigation that is preparing the Certificate for Trial purposes.

Repsis: And was this information on Government's Exhibit 16, 17 and 18 retrieved from the computer database?

Boatright: Yes, it was.

Repsis: Where did the records come from in the database ma'am?

Boatright: It comes from the Master File.

Minns on re-cross, Boatright answering:

Minns: Where it says "No record of return filed?"

Boatright: That is correct.

Minns: That wasn't printed by the computer?

Boatright: No, sir.

Minns: Someone saw the computer printout and then filled this out for trial?

Boatright: That is correct.

Minns: And you weren't the person that did that?

Boatright: No, I am not.

Minns: Exhibit 5, that is...directly from the computer.

Boatright: Yes, but that is a local format. It is not a Master File.

Minns: It is directly from the computer though?

Boatright: From our computer, yes.

Minns: And you're saying it might not be the same as what is in the Master File?

Boatright: Exactly.

Minns: Did you say that indicated a return was filed?

Boatright: No, sir, I stated that there is an indication that there was a return because there is a database but that does not mean it...is a fact.

Minns: There is no Dif score unless a return is filed... and we have a Dif score.

Ms. Boatright was also asked about the freeze code. If a freeze code were placed on the IMF, it is possible that a return filed would be rejected and, therefore, show no return filed even though one had been filed. Ms. Boatright confirmed this. This was another reason to actually examine the official record.

I made another request for the Individual Master File and in the alternative re-urged the request for an *in-camera* review. (This means the judge should examine it privately in his office in his chambers and decide if we should see it.)

The Court: I have not seen that.

The Court still didn't have the IMF.

Minns: It (the Dif score) is formulated from the tax return filed by the taxpayer?

Boatright: Yes, sir.

Minns: Does Exhibit 6 have a Dif score on it?

Boatright: It shows an area where the Dif score would be.

Minns: And is it blackened out?

Boatright: It is blackened out.

Minns: Why?

Boatright: I have no idea.

Our expert later explained there had to be a tax return filed to have a Dif score.

Minns: Now, if you had...the national computer transcript (NCC or IMF) is it possible that you would be able to tell this jury the exact date...the return was filed if it so reflected?

Normally, the transcript of accounts is used in trial.

153

Boatright: This is the first trial that I have ever had to work with AMDISA only.

To make matters worse the court then instructed the jury as follows: "Unless and until outweighed by evidence in this case to the contrary, the presumption is that every person knows what the law forbids and what the law requires to be done."

We were being hit from both sides. First, the chief issue in the trial was the state of mind of Stephen Buford when he made errors. Stephen had taken the stand and given a good account of himself until he faced the charges of the United States attorney that he had not filed his own tax returns. A tax preparer who does not file his own tax returns has no credibility. Buford's personal copies of his returns had been lost. He could only support his version by swearing he had filed the returns or by showing that the official record agreed with him. (Of course, since he had not sent them by registered mail, even the copies would not be great evidence.)

Even worse, as if the jury needed an excuse to convict him after he had been branded a liar by the federal government's professional witness, the court was telling the jury that they couldn't even presume that Stephen had made a mistake, which is constitutionally required, and that they must presume that he knew the correct application of the law and intentionally violated it.

These two rulings, if left standing, would be enough for the government to convict any individual in the country who prepared tax returns for others for a living unless they never made a mistake. Little wonder that lots of tax preparers were very interested in the ultimate decision. In some ways the dishonesty of the IRS in claiming that Stephen had not filed his own returns was a less frightening issue than one of the instructions that the court, at the request of the government, gave to the jury: *Ignorance of the law was no excuse.* It is one of those very dangerous sayings, a common cliche that we unwittingly repeat over and over for decades and start to believe. Historically, ignorance of the law has been defense. If the law was so complex that you could not understand it, you should not be forced to go to jail over

154

the mistake. I felt that was an erroneous instruction for the judge to give the jury, that it was contrary to the spirit of the law in criminal tax cases and in Buford's case. On that day, in that court (prior to appeal), I was wrong. I made my argument for the record and would later reargue it before an appellate panel.

In his closing argument Repsis told the jury that Stephen was a liar. He told the jurors that there was no agent Millian to whom Stephen had gone for an audit and that Stephen had never filed his 1982 return because he was a liar and a tax cheat. The jury bought it. Both Bufords bit the dust.

The jury convicted Stephen on all fifteen counts and convicted his father of conspiring with him to break the law fourteen times. Stephen was sentenced to five years in a federal prison and probation for a long time thereafter. The rumors about our judge, that he would stack the sentences, were untrue with regard to the Bufords. However the IRS professional witness had not just convinced the jury, she had convinced the judge too. Bob Buford was given probation for his conviction on conspiracy. Strangely enough the government had gotten what the defense had offered in the beginning. Stephen was going to jail and his dad would stay out. Unfortunately the trial proved too much for Bob and immediately thereafter he was hospitalized. When Bob got out alive, Stephen was revitalized. Judge Fish allowed Stephen to stay out of jail pending his appeal and his dad, although not sentenced to any custody, decided to appeal only for his good name. Stephen now informed me that he was ready to start a real legal battle. He was certain that he would win on appeal. I was certain that he should win on appeal but that is a function of the right judges and the right decision. Stephen was a little right and a little wrong.

BUFORD TWO — The Appeal

This is the only case in the book that deals heavily with appeals. So, following is a short explanation of the appeals process.

If you don't like what happens to you in a Federal District Court (trial court) you appeal to the circuit court. The United States has twelve circuit courts. Number One is in Boston, Number Five is in Louisiana and covers Texas and Louisiana, Number Nine is in Los Angeles, and Number Eleven is in Atlanta, Georgia (it was formerly part of the Fifth Circuit, which was divided by Congress).

The Fifth Circuit has about twenty judges. They hear appeals from the lower circuit (trial court) in random three judge panels. In New Orleans, the three random judges sit on a tall wooden bench that includes majestic wooden podiums as conference desks. There is no jury.

Lawyers sit in the back except for those arguing the case. Those arguing sit as tables in front of the bench. Each side gets about twenty minutes; the judges ask questions that come out of your time.

You have no witnesses. You argue the facts as they are typed by the trial court reporter and the law from the statutes, as well as the cases previously ruled on by the appellate judges themselves.

Clients usually do not attend, but Stephen always attended. I enjoy the process and find it a lot less pressure than the trial. Some lawyers don't. If you lose, you can appeal to the entire panel (all twenty), who almost never agree to hear you, and then to the U.S. Supreme Court.

The judges may pepper one or both sides with questions. They do this sometimes for answers, sometimes to stimulate each other. They may add to your time if they choose to do so, or cut you off without explanation. A two-to-one majority rules.

Stephen was a new man now that his father was not facing imprisonment. No reasonable government would try him again if his case were reversed, and even in that unlikely event (that the government tried either of them again if there was a reversal), the general rule of law is that absent new compelling evidence, a sentence cannot be increased in federal courts. Bob would not take the stand in a new trial. Stephen was insistent on that, even if Bob were needed to help Stephen. Mike Ware and I were both retained to handle the appeal.

We submitted the briefs and the court notified us that the case had been accepted for review and oral argument. This is important because the court rejects many appellate briefs outright and does not ask for oral argument. The State of Texas is in the Fifth Circuit Court of Appeals, which sits in several states but has its main office in the city of New Orleans. The Bufords' appeal was set to be heard in Houston.

The appellate court sits with three randomly selected judges. Our random panel was Judge Gee, Judge Smith, and Judge Jones. Gee had been on many Democratic presidential short lists for the Supreme Court (the eleven circuit courts plus the circuit of the District of Columbia are subservient only to the United States Supreme Court) but never selected. He was unquestionably one of the greatest living scholars of the law. He was also very forthright in his opinions. Unlike many appellate judges, he would often let you know where you stood at oral argument. The opinions of the circuit courts are important, not just for the people whose lives are judged by them, but also because if they order an opinion published, then that opinion becomes part of the new law throughout the United States. It is absolutely binding on every federal court within its jurisdiction (one out of about eleven, a little more than four average states to a circuit) and influential in all of the other circuits. If two circuits disagree on the law, the United States Supreme Court is supposed to step in and make the final decision. Sometimes it does; more often, it seems, it does not.

If Judge Gee sits on your panel and is dealing with a bit of law important to you or others for lasting use, you are blessed if he rules in your favor and cursed doubly if he rules against you. Especially if he writes the opinion, because he is one of the best writers on the bench. His style is crisp, well reasoned, and very persuasive with other circuits.

He was joined on the bench by Edith Jones, the conservative Republican on Reagan's and then Bush's short list for a seat on the Supreme Court. The panel's decision would hold a lot of weight. The third member of the panel was Steven Smith, a recent Republican selection. If I had my "druthers" I would pick two Democrats and one Republican, but perhaps it was fair play for Stephen's lifetime of Republicanism. The judge with the most seniority, except for the chief judge, who votes in the majority (a panel can vote unanimously or two to one) gets to assign the writing of the decision. Occasionally all three will simply say *per curiam* which means they all wrote it and then you have to try to guess who wrote it in an original identifiable state. Some judges are only politicians and rely completely on their clerks, often not even understanding the opinions they "author." Some of the judges have their clerks write the decisions under specific guidlines. Some do not write very well. From experience and reading the decisions and speeches of many of the judges, I presumed that if Jones or Gee wrote the decision, it would likely be their own work. I knew very little of Smith other than his relatively recent appointment.

All three judges seemed very receptive. Why weren't we allowed to see the official record, Judge Gee asked? Didn't the presumption require the government to prove that Buford knew he was violating the law? Each side was allotted twenty minutes, but, frankly, I felt as though we had said it all. The court was centering on what I regarded as the two essential issues. The secret Individual Master File was supposed to be in an envelope, which Judge Gee held up playfully and looked at, pretending to peer inside. Did it agree with Marsha Boatright and the special agent, or did it say Stephen had filed?

At trial I had asked to see the IMF for Stephen. The IRS objected, and so I asked for it to be given under seal to the court for first, the court's review, and if the trial court ruled I couldn't see it, for the Fifth Circuit's review.

What does this mean? "Under seal" means the IRS hands the paper to Judge Fish and he puts it in a secret envelope and seals it. I know what's in there, the secret IMF, but I can't read it unless the court says it's OK.

When we got to the appellate court Judge Gee said, "Let's see what's under seal," and he opened the sealed envelope. The IMF wasn't in there. The pre-sentence report was in there.

The pre-sentence report is created after the trial is over by the probation department to the federal government. It is supposed to be used to guide the court on sentencing. Theoretically, it is a summary of the convicted defendant's life history and criminal record, among other things.

Apparently, the IRS never gave Judge Fish the IMF and the contents in the envelope weren't put in there during the trial—they weren't even created until after the trial.

Evidently the IRS never expected the appellate court judge to open the sealed envelope and review it, and they surely didn't expect it to happen publicly, in the appellate courtroom.

There was no doubt Judge Gee was not impressed with the state of the unsealed record. His eyebrows went up half an inch and he looked over at the perplexed government appellate lawyer as if to say, "Can you explain this?" To her credit, Debra Watson, the appellate lawyer for the government, made no effort to do so.

The government attorney elected to use all of the time allotment. I sat down with half my time left over. A great part of good advocacy is simply figuring out when to shut up. I shut up. The judges discussed our argument with interest. If it had been a jury reacting that way, I would have felt very sure of the result but with the judges I had to wait. Stephen was certain. He had no fear whatsoever.

The decision came out on November 29, 1989 and was published. Judge Gee authored the unanimous decision. The decision in every law library in the United States (889 F.2d 1406) reads in the relevant part, "The government then called Marsha Boatright, an IRS records custodian, who testified that there was no record of a return filed for Stephen Buford. Ms. Boatright based her testimony on Certificates of Assessments and payments, which were admitted into evidence...in the meantime, repeated requests by Buford's attorney for an *in camera* review of the IMF apparently fell on deaf ears. The district court abused its discretion in denying Stephen Buford's request...."

The circuit court panel also examined the equally critical charge to the jury (the charge simply means the instructions that the trial court gives the jury concerning their deliberations).

Judge Gee wrote, "The court charged the jury as follows: 'It is not necessary for the government to prove that either defendant knew that particular act or failure to act is a violation of law. Unless and until outweighed by evidence in the case to the contrary, the presumption is that every person knows what the law forbids, and what the law requires to be done.' The court's charge was erroneous. The trial court, when instructing that specific intent is required, may not instruct that ignorance of the law is no excuse, because ignorance of the law goes to the heart of the defendant's denial of specific intent."

The conviction was reversed and the case ordered, if the government wanted to proceed, to a new trial. The part on the IMF received some international press. The clarifying instructions would add some measure of safety for tax preparers against an increasingly brutal and immoral government branch. We thought the case was over. Shortly thereafter the mayor of Washington, D.C., was given a mistrial on several drug charges. If they would not retry him on drug charges, was it even remotely possible that they would go after Stephen and his dad again? Of course not, but then you never know. We were doubly sure that his dad could say goodbye to any future prosecution. We were wrong.

BUFORD THREE — The Second Trial

The United States of America declared that it would try both Stephen and his dad again. This time their Exhibit A would provide a new twist, which the discovery of the IMF had told us existed, the government produced the 1982 tax return of Stephen Buford that they had previously sworn did not exist!

Apparently, Stephen had left his copy by mistake with the "non-existent" agent Millian. The government, after the revelation of the IMF that a return had been filed, conceded that they had made an error and produced the return. If Stephen had never talked to agent Jager, both he and his father would have been acquitted in the first trial, or probably not even been indicted in the first place. These are the lessons you learn in the sewers with the IRS. We had more lessons to learn. In *Buford Three* we would face in the IRS's carnival another "coincidence."

What do you do if you are in a debate contest and the winning fact you utilized turns out to be false beyond argument, if in fact a high court judge has ruled that it is false? If you are not playing a game, and if you have any character, you should simply say you made a mistake and that perhaps you were wrong in the first place. Unfortunately the IRS plays criminal games with people's lives and has no integrity.

The exhibit that they had originally said did not exist, the 1982 tax return Stephen had filed for himself, which had then been audited, was produced. It was now their position that, although it did exist, they had not needed it before. They had beaten Stephen in round one by telling the jury that here was a tax preparer who did not even file his own tax returns, ergo he was dishonest. Now we had the IMF, which showed conclusively that in fact he had filed. What was their position? Simply this: "Sure, he had filed, but he had filed a patently fraudulent return." How can that happen, you ask? It's really quite simple. Trust law is complicated and often two different preparers make mistakes or come to different conclusions with the same information. Stephen had, relying on lawyers and CPAs, the IRS, and handbooks, made serious mistakes, but now under the guidelines of *U.S. v. Buford*, he was entitled to the benefit of a doubt. Was it intentional or was it a mistake?

If this were all we faced on our first day of round three, it would have been plenty. Our new opponent was a little more honest than the last U.S. attorney but no less frightening. He was weed tall and lanky with stringy wavy hair and a long beady nose. His companion and co-

161

counsel was a young, shapely blond woman upon that caused the male jurors and our male judge to have trouble focusing during the trial. The lead counsel's shrill voice and emaciated look earned him the name "Icahbod" with us. His striking co-counsel had never tried a tax case before. I surmised that she had been brought in as a diversion. Mike and I called her "Marilyn" after America's favorite sex symbol.

If terror and sex were not enough to win the hearts of the jurors and judge, another more obvious ploy was put into effect, which was the subject of articles that literally made papers all over the world. The IRS held its first and so far, only *annual* "Tax Fair" in the lobby of the federal courthouse beginning on the first day of the Buford's second trial. In the lobby, IRS clowns with painted smiles handed out balloons with an IRS logo on them filled with IRS hot air, and gave out "free" (free meaning, of course, free to them, we the taxpayers were certainly billed for this abuse) IRS pizza to everyone in the courthouse who was willing to eat it.

As we entered the federal building, unaware that the IRS was engaged in this goodwill gesture, the Buford family walked past an IRS clown. On the first day the senior Mrs. Buford, who was watching the kids, came to the courthouse. She generally kept the kids at home, but she was so afraid that Bob Buford would have a heart attack right at the courthouse that she came for the second trial. An IRS clown handed nine-year-old Zachary Buford a piece of IRS pizza and a pretty floating red balloon. The young man grabbed the string with delight and pulled it down with one hand while he stuffed a piece of pizza into his mouth with the other. As he pulled the balloon down and read the words on it, he was shocked. The gift he had just taken came from the organization that had been spying on him and his family and his grandparents half his life, had almost put his dad and granddad in jail, and was now trying again. Tears filled his eyes and he politely returned the balloon to the not so funny IRS clown and then went into the bathroom and threw up the IRS pizza. Child abuse may wear many different costumes.

It was an outrage the young Buford would survive, but it was an outrage that Stephen's and Bob's constitutional rights could not abide. A trial was going on in which Stephen faced jail time in a federal penitentiary. What would the government do if Stephen, Mike, or I offered free tax preparer's pizza, or lawyer's pizza, or defendant's pizza to the prospective jurors? We would all have ended up in jail, and rightfully so. This unfortunate incident was chalked up to an oversight. The trial would proceed and no one was allowed to even ask the IRS to give away their pizza in another location. The only good thing to come out of the event was that at the end of the day most of the free IRS balloons and pizza had gone unclaimed. Apparently even the street people, who gathered around the courthouse, failed to come in and take advantage of the IRS's generosity with our money.

So, the IRS, led by "Icahbod," "Marilyn," and the IRS clowns, began to launch World War III to prove that Stephen and Bob Buford were evil people and that the real good guys, the misunderstood IRS, deep down inside were really a bunch of clowns. To a limited extent they succeeded.

During the first Buford trial, Stephen, to refresh his memory and motives regarding trust documents, relied primarily on a scrapbook that he had compiled over a decade full of case law, articles, library pieces, and other information he had relied on to form his opinions on the tax rules. He used the original from which to testify. Fifteen copies were made for the twelve jurors and the two alternates and me. The government asked to borrow my copy and so I stayed next to Stephen while asking him questions. After the trial *the government mysteriously lost my copy*, never returning it, and then *the bailiff threw away all the jurors' copies. The court misplaced Stephen's original* and it was not found or available for the second trial.

Stephen was charged with falsifying the trust returns and actual returns of a client, Mr. Flores. Mr. Flores did not follow the terms of the trust nor the instructions Stephen gave him. Specifically he was supposed to put his home into the trust and then depreciate it as rental property. He did not put the home in the trust, but he depreciated it anyway. (Putting the home in a trust would not have legally allowed him the deduction, that tax theory was wrong, but at least he would have acted in good faith.) Jamie Flores deducted his personal expenses on his tax return although he testified under oath that Stephen had told him not to do so.

There is no question whatsoever that Mr. Flores intentionally included false statements in his income tax return. There is also no question whatsoever that he did not follow either the oral or written instructions given to him by Stephen Buford. Flores claimed that his trust had property, which he had never conveyed to it and apparently had no intention of conveying to it. He let the trust take the depreciation deductions for the property and he transferred those deductions over to his personal return. In other words, right or wrong, Flores did not want to listen to Stephen, did not file the way he was instructed to, and took inappropriate steps to file a false return on his own; yet Stephen was indicted for it.

Another client, Robert Deming, stated that he and his wife had gone to the IRS and requested an interview with a special agent on the advice of their attorney after it became apparent that the Demings needed to make a deal with the IRS to help catch the people who got them into their situation. Why would a CPA tell someone to turn himself in? Why not wait the three years for the audit time to pass? Is it possible Deming was the victim of a consultant more interested in helping the IRS than his client, or was the consultant simply trading him for a favor? Mr. Deming stated that the trust he purchased came from a Mr. Wozencraft, and that Bob Buford, not Stephen, actually prepared the trust returns. The signature at the bottom of the return was illegible.

So here we have an indictment against Stephen Buford for a client he never met, whose return was first prepared by Bob Buford but was eventually re-done and filed by another accountant unrelated to the Bufords. The other clients seemed to be honest taxpayers; they followed the rules and attempted to get legitimate deductions. They were told to keep minutes of every meeting, and according to the trust, that's what they did. Stephen Buford never told them to hide any figures and, in fact, had them create records from which it was extremely easy to document where every penny went. When the IRS came and asked questions, they handed them the records that Stephen Buford had specifically asked them to create for the IRS. Stephen Buford never told them to tell lies to the IRS.

The testimony of Mr. Deming showed that Stephen Buford had nothing to do with the preparation of his return. He stated that Bob Buford prepared his returns. Mr. Deming stated that he had not even met Stephen Buford until the spring of 1983, at which time they had a conversation—nothing more. Judge Fish later wrote in an opinion that Deming deducted pet expenses, veterinarian bills, and kennel costs even though the dogs were not retained for any use related to business and that the trust never operated as a business. Deming's testimony shows that Mr. Wozencraft is the person who informed him that pet expenses were deductible. Nothing in Mr. Deming's testimony connects Stephen Buford with any wrongdoing. I asked Deming:

Minns: I want to be absolutely certain about this. Mr. Buford told you to turn this property over to the trust, to deed it over?

Deming: He suggested it, yes.

Minns: And you didn't do it?

Deming: No.

Minns: Did you have two dogs at the time you deducted a guard dog?

Deming: Yes.

Minns: Neither of them had any guard dog training, did they?

Deming: No.

Minns: Did you go to an IRS criminal agent and try to make a deal?

Deming: No.

On the conclusion of the case, I asked the court to give us an instructed verdict on counts eight through eleven of the indictment for Stephen. There was no evidence against him on these charges. The judge disagreed. One of the biggest problems we had with the second trial was the "Marilyn" prosecutor. Whenever she made an objection it seemed as though she was destined to win no matter how unreasonable it was. The judge apparently found her logic to be practically indisputable. On the other hand, "Icahbod" seemed to rub the judge the wrong way, so his rulings appeared more neutral.

Objections are made for several reasons. Maybe you want to tell the jury what they need to hear, to know what is going on, and you do not want unfair evidence to be admitted. An example of unfair evidence is hearsay. The legal definition of hearsay is an out-of-court statement offered in court for the purpose of proving the matter asserted therein. An example of hearsay was the statement of the two agents who testified that the computer said Stephen Buford never filed his returns. How can you cross-examine something like that? You cannot. It is unfair. You have to object. You should have, at the least, the computer statement in front of you. You want to keep your objections to a minimum because the judge does not like it, and if he rules against you an emphasis is put on the evidence. The jury often becomes suspicious of a lawyer who does not want them to hear anything.

Ideally (an ideal that is seldom reached in real courtrooms) the jury would get to hear the objection and understand the reason for it. Most jurors, if they understood that the government lies a lot and that the records can be falsified, would listen attentively, but if they are given no explanation at all, they tend to see a cover-up. Another reason to object is that in federal court you are going to lose some cases. You need to object to make a record for the appellate court for possible review. Of course you must strike a reasonable balance. You cannot try your case only to the appellate court or you will lose every jury trial. Finally, you may convince the court to keep the evidence out. In the first trial, I was very much opposed to letting the jury hear that the allegedly infallible IRS computer had determined Stephen was guilty. This was hearsay on top of hearsay. We wouldn't get to see exactly what the computer "said." We saw only what the expert said she saw when she looked at the computer printout. The original computer printout was the IMF. We had to take her word for what it said.

After nearly two days of deliberation, the jury came back with full final acquittals of Bob Buford and hung eight-to-four on the counts against Stephen. We would have preferred straight acquittals on every count, but we were pleased. The majority, who now had heard the facts, believed that Stephen was innocent, even without his critical evidence, the scrapbook, and they had unanimously acquitted his dad. Even our judge seemed convinced that the government could not make a legitimate case against Stephen. We were certain that it was all over this time, but we were wrong again!

"Ichabod" was furious. He vowed to fight to the death. I will never forget his statement, "We've got a blank check to go after him. This case will never be over until Buford goes to jail." In that regard, he was at least half-wrong the moment he said it. Bob Buford had now been found not guilty on all fifteen counts. He could not be tried again, and I felt that it was unlikely that the IRS wanted any more of Stephen, but I was wrong.

The jury foreman was a successful construction engineer. Alice had predicted correctly; he would be on our side and be the foreman. I knew we had him. He hadn't hidden his feelings throughout the trial. A strong man, I felt he would pull all the jurors together. I was wrong. One young man, who wore a leather jacket to court each day, had been eyeing and smiling at "Marilyn" the whole trial. I figured he would start off subconsciously planning to date "Marilyn" but give up and let our contractor do the right thing. We had another juror, a young blonde, who seemed shy but angry. I thought she was an abuse victim. Alice Weiser, my favorite jury consultant and handwriting analyst, reviewing her handwriting, confirmed that she was beaten down physically and mentally by a spouse or boyfriend. We guessed, incorrectly, she'd just go along. She did not. A coalition of eight for not guilty led by our contractor, versus four for guilty led by the "Leather Jacket" and the young blonde hung the jury.

Judge Fish graciously suspended the local rule and allowed us to visit with the jurors. The blonde had bonded with "Ichabod" and "Leather Jacket" had gallantly stood up for her against the other majority jurors who thought the whole case was a bunch of muck. The contractor was able to get the panel to let Bob off because of his bad heart. Of course we wanted a clean win for both Bufords, but no one in his right mind expected a third trial (a fourth round).

"Ichabod's" angry promise to fight to the death lasted a couple of weeks. After getting a new setting for trial he resigned, and Jager, the revenue agent on the case who had just graduated from law school, took it over.

BUFORD FOUR — The Third Trial

When we began the third Buford trial, Stephen and Bob Buford had more trial experience than half the lawyers in the United States. Stephen took an active role, sitting at the defense table even during appeals. Most clients do not even show up for these. He pointed out that he got a "law degree" the hard way. Stephen said, "I paid more than a Harvard tuition with more at risk! If a Harvard student screws up, he can come back next year. If I had screwed up, I would have gotten twenty years!"

Bob was out. Stephen was still in.

Stephen had run out of money during Buford Three. If I was to stay, it would be on the house. Stephen was completely broke and had exhausted all possible funds from relatives. He refused to apply for government assistance and told me that if I would not extend him credit he would represent himself. Judge Fish did not want this case to be tried again. Jager shook every time I got near him. Frankly, I was more afraid of the revenue agent turned trial lawyer than the first two lawyers. This guy had the file memorized. The third actual trial would be without co-counsel, without experts, without funds.

Judge Fish remarked that if he had decided the evidence based on the second trial he would have leaned toward acquitting Stephen. For the first time in my career I regretted not going before the bench instead of a jury. There hasn't been a second time.

The revenue agent asked me if I minded using only typed testimony to "recall" his witness. Of course he could do this without my permission, but I could recall them for the third cross-examination and put my witnesses on live.

We came up with a happy compromise. Since there was no longer an alleged co-conspirator, only Stephen, the government would drop the conspiracy count, leaving fourteen counts. I was glad to leave in the ones that could not vaguely be considered; I thought it would enrage Fish, but I was wrong. The government would submit half the witnesses on paper only. I could put on a rebuttal testimony. My plan was to let Stephen wrap it up as the only witness. We would then give closing arguments.

We did. Stephen, however, still did not have his scrapbook and felt unable to testify about his past state of mind, which with two trials and a third paper trial with open arguments had left him very confused. So we rested after arguing to the judge. Judge Fish did not rule that day.

His ruling came down in writing two months later. He found Stephen guilty on all fourteen counts! I was shocked. Perhaps he had forgotten what he originally said. Perhaps he had changed his mind after re-reading the transcript. Nevertheless, Stephen was convicted. At sentencing I informed the court we would appeal. Judge Fish's response was, "I know you know where the Fifth Circuit is."

Judge Fish this time graciously allowed Stephen to be under home detention (he had moved to Oklahoma) with a leg monitor, as long as he did not fill out any tax returns, pending his appeal. I know he still thought Stephen was guilty but I believe he agreed that the trials had been punishment enough.

BUFORD FIVE — The Second Appeal

This time the court set oral argument in New Orleans. This was an unusual case. It was an appeal of Stephen Buford's third trial. This court reversed the first trial; a second jury trial failed to reach a verdict. The third case was submitted to the bench based on limited testimony resubmitted by agreement. The court had found Stephen Buford guilty on all fourteen counts, even though there was no evidence on several of the indictment counts.

We argued in New Orleans, and then, as always after appellate argument, we waited for the results. This time our panel consisted of two democrats; Judge Politz, a strong defender of the Constitution, Judge Garza, a critic of government overreaching, and Judge Wiener, a new Republican judge. I had been before Judge Wiener recently on the Doyle appeal and he had voted with the other judges to reverse the conviction. (Emmet Doyle was an electrician from Ireland convicted of income tax evasion and sentenced to ten years imprisonment. It was the longest sentence a judge had ever imposed on a client of mine and it was a great relief to have it thrown out by the appellate court.) I felt I had a good panel.

It should have been undisputed that there was serious misconduct in the first trial by the government. In the second and third trial the defendant had been deprived of his evidence provided in the first trial due to government error. In my brief, along with much of the argument you have already seen, I again discussed Jager's convenient memory. On his written report he had claimed that Bob Buford had blamed the clients, saying: "Bob Buford admitted that it was wrong to list personal living expenses as deductions on trust or fiduciary income tax returns, but states that he did so at the insistence of the taxpayer/client."

In trial four years later he remembered it was Bob's son Stephen, not the clients, who had insisted. This sworn statement by Jager that he remembered Stephen Buford saying that this was listed in the written report, made four years earlier by reviewing his memorandum,

170

was erroneous. The IRS also perpetuated a lie in the first trial, through the testimony of Ms. Marsha Boatwright under the control of agent Jager, that Stephen Buford had not filed his 1982 tax return.

The charges with regard to another client, Mr. O.K. Deming, were patently absurd. Of course some of the returns had been filed by Stephen and some of those returns were incorrectly completed, but that is not unheard of in the tax preparation business. In fact, the IRS has a special form, the 1040X, which has no other purpose except to correct previous errors made. It is assumed that errors will be made.

I also argued, without much on point law, on the double jeopardy part of the Fifth Amendment. The Fifth Amendment, in addition to the right to remain silent, guarantees protection from multiple trials. Stephen Buford was tried three times for the same offenses. While we were not successful in getting Fifth Amendment relief, the argument definitely got Judge Politz's attention and thus may have contributed to our conclusion.

Although there was no such thing as a foregone conclusion, the justices were not shy about their disappointment with the government's conduct in the case. Judge Politz gave the government a strong reprimand for trying the case three times: "Maybe the law allows this," he said "but shouldn't there be an end to trying someone over and over again somewhere? Doesn't the spirit of the double jeopardy clause require this?" He added, pointing his finger at the government attorney, "I know this wasn't your decision, but would you please see that my feelings reach the proper ears!" Both Garza and Politz wanted to know about the irregularities of the government. Garza seemed to be on the government side at first but turned when he found out that the IRS was charging Buford with returns prepared by someone else. Wiener seemed unimpressed. He chastised me for calling the government witnesses perjurers. I replied that perhaps they were merely mistaken, but, frankly, I am not that charitable. I think the IRS agents were lying. My guess was that we were one to one with Wiener, the tiebreaker, leaning toward the government. I was wrong.

171

Stephen had prayed about it and told me confidently that we would win all three judges.

On March 30, 1992, I received a call from Oklahoma. The IRS had raided Stephen Buford's home, taken both of his cars and their home computer. The Buford's teenage daughter was in the shower at the time, and a federal agent barged in and prevented her from dressing and moving about while the search of the Buford home was conducted. It seems that there were tax returns on his computer. Was there a violation of the probation order? The judge would decide. He was not required to find a violation beyond a reasonable doubt. Parole revocations are pretty mean and fast affairs. I sent a letter to the authorities condemning their actions and waited for a decision to come down. Why take the Buford autos? Why search the entire home? If the judge believed that Stephen was still preparing returns, he would surely put Stephen in jail even though all of the information had been compiled according to the law. His condition of probation was not that he not fill in returns incorrectly but that he not fill them in at all. It seemed that after everything, Stephen would still end up doing time. His parole revocation hearing was set for May 1992.

In April 1992, the Fifth Circuit opinion came down. Stephen was right. It was a unanimous opinion. This time the charges were reversed and the court ordered the IRS not to go after him again. Having all charges against him dismissed, Stephen was now safe from incarceration. There would be no parole revocation hearing because he was no longer on parole. His name was cleared. While I was on the phone explaining the terms of the reversal, Stephen let me know that the government had already arrived at his house and was at that moment taking the home detention shackles off of his leg. Buford's case was over. A few weeks later the IRS returned his two cars. To this day they still have his computer. I don't think I need to reiterate the fact that Stephen went through years of sheer hell, but lest anyone forget, he did. Stephen does not prepare tax returns anymore for anyone. He even hires outside help to prepare his own.

Chapter VI
The Milkman

"When a man points a finger at someone else he should
remember that four of his fingers are pointing at himself."
— Louis Nizer
My Life in Court

In Camden, New Jersey, at a pre-trial motion hearing, my client, Harry Williams, faced a criminal trial on two counts of willful failure to file income tax returns. Assistant U.S. Attorney Tom Brown seemed inclined to work a deal that would let the criminal charges go away and just monitor Harry for eighteen months or so. Brown was a nice guy and a good public servant who honestly conceded that he would rather go after drug dealers and bank robbers than clean cut guys like Harry. Harry was unique among my "alleged tax protester, non-filing" clients. Unlike the last two, which were knockdown, drag-out wars, that I expected to lose but nevertheless won, Harry had filed his returns before he was charged with a crime. Basically Harry filed late, very late, but he had not failed to file. Did the IRS really want to go after someone who had given up and filed even though he still didn't think the law required it?

I had brought dozens of people back into the system by retaining a CPA and sending a power of attorney to the IRS letting them know that the client was under my protection and was coming in from out of the "underground." It wouldn't surprise me if a billion dollars or more a year comes in like this plus a lot in penalties that would make Mafia loan sharks blush. For over a decade, the IRS knew that I was one of a handful who had won cases in which the client hadn't even filed a return. Were they now going to go against people who actually filed—for *failure to file*? I didn't think so and neither did Tom Brown, so he made me an offer of deferred adjudication. This means a temporary finding of guilt. After a probationary period the conviction is thrown out. He said he'd get back with me when the IRS approved it. They didn't. It surprised Tom more than it surprised me, so after a brief round of discovery, Tom filed a motion to tell the jury what he wanted them to hear and suppress the rest. Funny, in a drug trial the defendant is always trying to hide things and the government always tries to get them in, but in a typical tax case, it is the IRS that wants to suppress evidence. Is there a parallel between the IRS and drug dealers? At least in their effort to *lie* there is. On September 13, 1992, L. R. and I were on our way to the nearby Philadephia airport. We were ready to see if our judge would let in the truth. The government wanted to convict Harry Williams for not filing his tax returns and they wanted the jury not to be told that he had filed them—cute. The Internal Revenue Service had instituted an amnesty program with their fingers crossed behind their tax collecting backs. "If you have committed a tax crime," they advertised, "come on in and let's talk about it. We may just let you off." The fact is the new program, launched in 1989 and again in 1992, was the same as the old one. You could always come in, always negotiate, and they could always decide what to do. Each year about three hundred actual criminal tax cases will take place. Deals are made with many who "volunteer" to come in, but many are also charged—amnesty or no amnesty.

Harry hadn't filed in years. He came in and admitted it. It looked like a good case, so they took his late filed returns, took his payments, and then backstabbed him, charging him with the crime of willful failure to file—nice program, this "amnesty." The citizen comes in, usually without a CPA or a lawyer, spills his guts, and then the IRS decides what to do with him. In this sadistic lottery the majority "win"—no criminal charges are filed, just penalty charges out the wazoo. The same number of people are still charged with crimes. It is just easier to find them and easier to develop a case. Harry was scammed. He showed clean hands, came in, asked for amnesty, but got charged with a crime.

Harry and Charlotte had been married for twenty-eight years. Their beautiful blond daughter Donna was married to Jeff Toton, a clean-cut handsome young man. They were two beautiful head-turn-ing people who had given birth to two beautiful healthy children, Amanda, age three-and-a half, and Stephanie Lynn, age one. Jeff, with the help of Harry, whom he considered his best friend, had got-ten started in his own business and was now president of Del Val Foods. Harry and Charlotte had mortgaged their home to lend Jeff the money. A witness at the trial was Harry's brother-in-law, James Kline, who was married to Charlotte's sister. James was a civilian employed on a military base as an air-crash rescue worker. His job description involved going aboard flaming plane wrecks and saving lives.

My personal favorite in this healthy loving successful American family was Grandma Emma MacDowell, Charlotte's mother, born in 1919, who could remember when her husband made fifteen dollars a week and got to keep it all. There were no deductions taken out for IRS or social security. The beautiful gray haired matriarch of the entire family was a picture of calm repose in the sea of troubles the IRS had created with the help of their so-called "voluntary tax."

Harry met Charlotte MacDowell in 1958 when he was fifteen and she was twelve. Her mother, the elegant Mrs. MacDowell, remembers what a young gentleman Harry was. He became another son to her, and in 1964 Harry and Charlotte became man and wife. Harry's relationship with his own mom was equally strong. In fact, the entire family was loving and close knit.

Harry worked as a milkman, the guy who used to come to your house and leave bottles of milk, a trade that no longer exists in the United States. One of his customers was Ron McBurnie, a man who had made an excellent living with the Instant Whip Company selling dairy products wholesale. He would later tell the jury that he had to hire Harry to keep him from selling dairy products to his wife and filling up the refrigerator. Harry was, in Ron's words, an honest and likeable man with a gift for friendly relationships and goodwill towards others, who couldn't help succeeding in the wholesale distribution business. He hired young Harry and Harry fulfilled the promise of hard work he seemed to emit. Harry's wages rose from about fifteen thousand dollars a year as a milkman to thirty-six thousand dollars a year as a distributor. He became the top independent distributor for the entire company. He led a normal life, if you consider being extremely happy, earning above-average monetary rewards, and weekly church attendance with his wife and daughters normal. His customers, men like Chris George, a baker who purchased from Harry while he worked for Instant Whip and who remained his customer when Harry began to sell his own line, testified to the high level of integrity of the man in his business life and in his personal life. There was literally no one to speak out against Harry's good name—no one except, ultimately, the Internal Revenue Service after the series of events that would begin in April of 1979.

In 1979, after hearing the author Irwin Schiff on the Irv Homer Show (a well-known New Jersey radio talk show), Harry decided to check out the teachings of Irwin Schiff. Schiff was the author of several best selling books, including *The Great Income Tax Hoax* and *How Anyone Can Stop Paying Income Taxes*. He also lectured all over the country that the income tax was voluntary (using the same word that the IRS used in calling compliance voluntary) and that it had been declared unconstitutional in the 1895 case of *Pollock v. Farmers* (ignoring the passage, whether legal or not, of the Sixteenth Amendment to the Constitution in 1913 allowing income taxation). He further discussed, in great depth, the ambiguities in the Internal Revenue Code (which everyone agrees is a disaster). According to Schiff's theory the Code did not specify where most ordinary wage-earning individuals were required to file. Schiff sells kits and books at his lectures, and on television and radio for cash but fails to tell people they could end up in jail and fails to tell them he's done plenty of time practicing his "fail proof" theories. He also fails to tell unsuspecting followers that he has been to jail on more than one occasion for following his own theory. Whether you like the theory or not, since the 1956 code was passed there have been a number of circuit and Supreme Court cases that disagree with Schiff. Anyone who studies the cases and says that they currently let you avoid filing is either incompetent or, if they have the ability to understand the cases, more likely lying. When the *Cheek* case came out, for example, in 1991, the Supreme Court made it easier for someone who honestly believed he was not required to file to avoid a criminal conviction. It had no bearing on civil penalties or obligations but still unequivocally reiterated the long-standing position of the courts that if you make a certain amount of income, you must file a return.

After attending several meetings in which lawyers, CPAs, and doctors numbered among those who contended that the income tax regulations were not mandatory but were voluntary, Harry began to buy written legal opinions, books, articles, and tapes and to explore for himself the legitimacy or lack thereof of the income taxation process. In 1980 he came to the conclusion that the whole thing was a hoax and in 1983, for the first time in his life, he failed to file an income tax return. Charlotte was not in agreement with Harry's new fiscal principles. Her folks had always paid (once it was required), and she and Harry had always paid, and she wanted to continue to

177

pay. This was the one and only big area of dispute between the two throughout their marriage.

In 1989 Harry finally gave in. While he was afraid that he could not file without simultaneously paying all the back taxes he owed, he decided upon a course of interim coping. He would begin to withhold again, at more than his legally required amount. He would pay extra each year and then he would file when he was caught up. He was not aware of one big problem that rendered his course of action impractical: If you don't file on time, the penalty is 5 percent per month plus interest. If you don't pay on time, it's one-half percent per month plus interest. You are much better off filing and not paying than paying and not filing.

Also, the IRS had problems with Harry that went beyond his lack of filing and paying. Over the years, on advice of numerous gurus, Harry had sent the IRS a number of strange letters asking them where to file, why he should have to file, and where it said in the code he was a person required to file. He never got any answers, except from Senator Bradley, who told him he couldn't answer his question about whether or not he had to file and forwarded Harry's letter to the treasury, who promptly advised him to seek legal counsel. Harry already had written opinions from Guy G. Curtis of Nebraska, implying that it was acceptable not to file and one from a CPA confirming this theory. In 1991 Harry, pressured by his wife, decided to take up the offer of the IRS and meet with them to file and pay whatever they wanted under the amnesty program. The special agent took it all in and then filed criminal charges against Harry!

There are similarities and differences in each tax case, and in each sub category. Harry was a forty-eight-year-old married monogamous man, who was loved by his son-in-law and mother-in-law, who sold American milk, who was a nice clean-cut family man, and on top of that he had actually filed and actually paid a bunch of money. In our practice, on a scale of one to ten for winability, I gave Harry's case a nine, a rating not given to any other of my cases. If the client has filed returns, paid some taxes, and even after shooting at IRS agents, has not actually hit his target, we consider it an above average case. (I actually handled a case like this in New York.) The special agent in Harry's case may have been sleazy, but she wasn't stupid. Balancing it all out, I expected to win the case.

When I flew up in August, 1992, for a pre-trial hearing, I stayed at the Ritz Carlton, which is actually much closer than the hotel where we stayed during the trial. The Ritz was only a ten-minute drive over the Walt Whitman bridge. For the trial, L. R. and I stayed at the Holiday Inn, thirty minutes away, to save funds for Harry. We conducted the trial with no local counsel.and no expert witness. There was no money for it. We had no assistance from a psychologist, a sociologist, or a handwriting expert. Again, there was no money for it.

The Internal Revenue Service has its national office in Washington, D.C., and its main headquarters for computers in Martinsburg, West Virginia. It also has tax-specialty attorneys to draft briefs. For its criminal-trial law firm, it turns to the United States Attorney General's office, the largest law firm in the world. Harry had L. R. and me. That was all he could afford, even at severely reduced rates. The difficulty of handling a case where the government traditionally wins 95 percent of the time is compounded greatly when you have no resources with which to compete. Leona Helmsley was reputed to have spent several million dollars and she had reported to prison for a four year term on April 15 of 1992, the month Harry was charged with criminally failing to file his income tax returns for the years 1985 and 1986.

Harry finally got around to filing his returns in July of 1991, just slightly over six years late, unless you include 1983 and 1984, which were also filed in 1991. The government couldn't charge for those years because of the criminal six-year statute of limitations.

Tom Brown, my opposing counsel, was a very decent person. He was a good family man, tall, thin, black, and conservative. Tom was an honest and straightforward nice guy. The jury would like him.

Unlike "Rambo," in Eric Laschon's case, Brown did not have an abrasive personality. We would not have a win-at-all-costs prosecutor who could be exposed as intellectually dishonest. Judge Rosen was competent and neutral. Camden was not a new courthouse to me. I had been in trial there two years earlier on an income tax evasion case and made some friends.

Another rough part in Harry's case was jury selection. It seemed that southwestern New Jersey had more then its share of current or former government employees. We got down to two strikes and knocked off a man who had recently retired from the federal government after a twenty-five year career. The judge graciously allowed me to ask questions, but it did no good.

> Minns: Don't you think you are pre-disposed after twenty years with the government to give them the benefit of the doubt?
>
> Juror: I don't think so.
>
> Minns: Would you want to be judged by yourself on a case like this if you had not filed your tax returns?
>
> Juror: It wouldn't bother me.
>
> Minns: Don't you really believe that if Mr. Williams owes a tax but didn't file he's probably guilty?
>
> Juror: I have no preconceived opinion.

This guy was so prejudiced he'd convict his mother if she didn't file, but he knew all the answers to the questions, and we had to use up a valuable strike. The same seat was then filled by the lottery with a second government employee, and, of course, he too knew how to force me to use up a strike. We had no strikes left. That seat in the jury box would be filled with whoever the lottery ball picked. She would be our last juror.

She was a prim and proper forty-something black woman who had never held a job in the private sector in all of her life. A pure bureaucrat of eighteen years, she had two years left until retirement. She beamed over at handsome Tom and then smiled courteously at me and I knew our case was over before we started. The only question would be whether or not I could win over the other eleven and get them to push her into a fair verdict. It was a long shot. One bad juror can turn a nine case into a zero. Of course one great juror can turn a one into a ten.

So many lawyers want to stereotype jurors by race and religion. The common thought is black jurors are defense oriented. "Rambo" would have kicked my black bureaucrat off the jury under the misguided opinion that blacks are always antigovernment (unless he had to use his strike on a nongovernment black). Tom Brown, an African-American himself, was too smart for that.

A black juror means that you won't have racist jokes going on in the jury room if your client or a key witness is black. Jurors, whether blacks, Hispanics, Anglos, or Jews tend to vote based on many factors: personal experiences, employment or socio-economic status, the evidence, and often education, which could be formal or informal.

All things considered, if you pick your jury solely based on race, you will probably lose your case. Maybe in the fifties or sixties there was such a phenomenon as a "black jury vote," but in the seventies, eighties, and nineties, while I've been practicing law, it has been primarily a fiction. That does not mean race is not a factor. It is. We all tend to identify and like people similar to ourselves, and we will give ourselves the benefit of the doubt. Race is almost always an important factor to consider — it is just not the be-all factor.

A common hardship or success can make two human beings closer brothers than a common skin color. One blockbuster witness was radio personality Irv Homer. He testified that he didn't believe you had to file tax returns. He filed them out of an abundance of caution, fear, and his lawyer's advice.

It was 10:45 PM "Philly time." The week was more than half over. We had been through three days of trial and then a full day of arguing on the jury charge, arguing to the jury, concluding by 12:00 PM and then the hell of waiting. We waited until 4:00 PM when the jury asked for a re-reading of the crucial instructions, the definition of criminal intent and willfulness. Obviously someone on the panel was on our side pulling for an acquittal and needed those instructions read back. An argument ensued as to what instructions should be read back. The court made a ruling and the jury came back into the courtroom and heard the instructions for the second time. They continued to deliberate until 5:00 PM when they were told to continue tomorrow. One of the jurors, a reverend, shyly raised his hand a little, but no one noticed him—no one except me. As the jurors began to file out I brought it to the court's attention and we (the lawyers and the minister) were brought to the side bar (this simply means out of the presence of the other jurors with the judge) to see what he wanted. Judge Rosen, when he realized which juror had asked, immediately figured out that the minister had to attend a funeral. I volunteered that we would have to accommodate him. My mission was twofold: first, life and death simply must take priority over mundane matters no matter how serious (unless they jeopardized the rights of my client, in which case I would reconsider) and secondly, the gesture may have had a slight effect on the reverend's vote. I had hoped that he was in our corner anyway but I simply could not tell. It never hurts to get points with any juror. We left the building. Deliberations would start again after the funeral.

After the four hours of deliberation it became time to start thinking about a motion for mistrial. Sometimes a jury will not make up its mind and sometimes it will. In any event, a mistrial starts everything over. Usually that's the end of it. In the case of off-and-on Washington, D.C., Mayor Barry, charged with drug use, there was no new trial on the charges that ended in his mistrial. Of course in the case of Steven Buford, the government put on three trials.

As we left the building Mrs. Lillian Ulinecz, Sr., Harry Williams' aged, frail, and anxious mother, who had been under a heavy stress all day, fainted in front of the courthouse. Harry and his daughter,

Donna, caught her. They helped her into the parking lot where she stood in front of Donna's stick-shift sports car. Donna picked up her car keys from across the street. She got behind the wheel and started the car, not realizing the attendant who moved it had left it in gear. The car moved forward only a notch less than an inch before bumping Mrs. Ulinecz, causing her to fall to the ground. A university student and a lawyer who came by both called the Camden emergency services and offered assistance. Help arrived fast. Grandma Ulinecz was all right. I put my coat under her head and kept her from moving.

Her main concern was not for herself. She kept saying, "I'm all right." Her concern was for Donna, who was now nearly hysterical after a day of constant stress over her father's dilemma, her grandma's previous fainting episode, and now this. Judge Rosen came out of the courthouse to see if he could help and remarked, "When it rains, it pours."

The paramedics arrived but Grandma couldn't stand on the leg that had been bumped, so the ambulance took her away while she protested that she was fine. Harry took Donna's car and handed me the keys to his vehicle to drive back to our room at the Holiday Inn. It turned out that Mrs. Ulinecz's ankle was broken. How unfortunate that yet another misfortune had beset this beautiful family.

After the next day's deliberation, our panel came back hopelessly deadlocked. The judge declared a mistrial and released the jury. Mr. Brown, prodded by the IRS agent prosecuting Harry, told the judge the IRS would pursue the case again.

Harry's family was shattered. I asked to poll the jury but my request was denied. We could only ask if they were deadlocked. It is not a science, but I think from the tears and weakened looks on most jurors' faces, with our bureaucrat's arms folded in front of her triumphantly, we had an eleven-to-one hung jury in our favor.

If we had been able to use a few more dollars to hire an expert to help on jury selection or hire local counsel, we might have gotten one more strike and had twelve free citizens on the panel, instead of one with a government employee.

Judge Rosen brought us back in chambers to talk. He said these kind of cases shouldn't result in jail time and he gave us the biggest hint he could legally give that a plea to one count would probably result in probation. He couldn't promise probation. The law requires a plea first then the sentencing, but good judges often let you know the likely outcome, and if the judge is honest, you can go with the unpromised implication. The unpromised implication was no jail time. After being in his courtroom for a week, I trusted Judge Rosen and advised Harry I believed he would probably get probation at this point.

Harry decided to take it, not for himself but for his family. He pleaded guilty, telling the court he knew he should have filed but broke the law anyway. I don't think anyone in the courtroom believed him. It is the only thing I ever heard Harry say that I didn't believe. It put the prospect of jail behind him and ended the case.

I had second thoughts about representing him for the plea. I don't like to let a client I believe is innocent plead guilty. Harry had been conned by tax scam artists and the IRS. However, if I refused, he would have to wait for other counsel, let the wonderful character evidence and the feelings of love in the courtroom dissipate, and then come back so he could plead. Things could change. The bailiff and I and all the women in Harry's family were crying. Only the IRS agent had a smile on her face.

Judge Rosen agreed to sentence Harry right then and there: probation, no jail time, and no fines. The criminal trial was over. Harry would do no time, but I left with an empty feeling that justice had not prevailed, that an innocent man had taken a guilty verdict to save his family from the hardship and expense of another trial.

The horrible backstabbing blow of the IRS in its unjust administration of its bastardized amnesty program had succeeded in a way. When the sentence was read the IRS agent stopped smiling. No jail? No fines? I thought she was going to snap at us as we trudged out of the courthouse.

Every federal tax case is a three fold process: First, you try to the jury; second, you try to the judge to help with the jury, and if you lose, to help with the sentencing; and third, you try for the appellate court. If all else has failed you want a record available to attempt a reversal on appeal.

Too many lawyers try mainly for the appellate court. Unfortunately, they risk losing the jury, their best bet, and the judge, their second best bet, as they aim for the long shot, the circuit court or the Supreme Court. These lawyers usually lose.

A plea bargain is a sort of a tie. A plea bargain ending without a fine or imprisonment is the best sort of tie available. For an idealist, which I am and which Harry is, it is not nearly as satisfying as an acquittal or dismissal.

Harry had compromised himself for his family. It was probably the right thing to do. At least he knew he would be available for his highly anticipated weekly outings with his granddaughters. However, he certainly never received "amnesty."

Chapter VII
Dentist, Yo-Yo Champion and Gambler

In 1915 Hugo Black, perhaps the greatest trial lawyer ever to sit on the Supreme Court, was still a trial lawyer, and he won a jury trial acquittal for a Klan member, Chum Smelly, (his real name) who had shot a black man in the back of the head. After the verdict Smelly said, "Thank God, Hugo. You got me off." Hugo replied, "Don't thank him. Thank me. God knows you're guilty."

—Hugo Black

If I were to decide to take down my "shingle" and join confreres John Grisham, Richard Patterson, Robert Tanenbaum, et. al. in writing a novel based on my legal practice experience, I could easily fictionalize the wild case of the dentist who loved to gamble: Dr. William Allen Bussey. If anything, I would probably have to tame it down to make it believable!

When we first met, he was fifty-six and had dark hair with shocks of gray. He was tall, stout, and healthy. He always wore a suit, conservative gray or black, leather or ostrich-hide cowboy boots, and thick glasses, indicating strong nearsightedness. While he was dignified, he was extremely hyperactive.

My family and co-workers will tell you I pace a lot, a trait I inherited from my father and apparently passed on to my daughter—a form of nervous energy. But I am calm compared to Dr. Bussey. Watching the two of us in a meeting, racing around the conference room, must have been an interesting experience. We were a sort of carousel that stops every now and then and reverses direction.

Dr. Bussey was fascinating. He collected exotic animals on his ranch where he and his wife lived and, as we shall see, he was an inveterate, but professional and generally successful, gambler. Perhaps his most unique claim to fame was as a yo-yo champion, and, indeed, he was listed as such in the *Guinness Book of World Records*. Yet he also prized his privacy and secrecy.

On May 10, 1991, Dr. Bussey was placed in federal custody, charged in a thirteen-count indictment, including conspiracy to commit an offense against the United States in violation of 18 U.S.C. 371, structuring transactions to evade reporting requirements, filing false income tax returns, and attempting to defraud a federally insured institution (a bank). Dr. Bussey's wife, Eugenia Ann Bussey, was charged as co-defendant, on counts 8 through 13, including the bank-fraud count.

A lot of the most interesting facts in this case came not from my client, but from the government reports. Probation officer Carolyn Clark determined that, "The criminal investigation began as a result of the Internal Revenue Service, criminal investigation division, Las Vegas office, being contacted by a local bank reporting suspicious currency transactions being conducted by Dr. William Bussey. It was determined that Dr. Bussey was making multiple currency deposits of $9,900 in several area banks." Does this sound sinister?

The special agent report created by Internal Revenue special agents Bonnie Vannett and Van Carlton at Dr. Bussey's home in Austin, Texas, on January 11, 1989, fills in a lot of the additional blanks. They determined that he was born December 12, 1935 and thus was fifty-four at the time of the interview, that he was married in

188

1990 in Waco, Texas to Eugenia Ann Bussey, formerly Pooley, now Schumann.

Vannett advised Dr. Bussey of his constitutional rights as required by existing instructions read from the Department of Treasury, IRS Document 5661 (as revised 8/82). Bussey stated that he understood his rights and "wished to talk".

When a special agent introduces himself to a man and wife and tells them they are under criminal investigation and reads them their rights, and the man and wife say, "Fine. We understand our rights, we would like to talk to you," the first thing I know about them is that they do not understand their rights. If they did, they would not be talking to the special agent!

There are inaccuracies throughout the memorandum of the interview. Dr. Bussey is referred to as *Mr.* Bussey. The names of his wives seem to be confused and dates are strange.

"Mr. Bussey has been married twice previously. Carol Schumann was Bussey's second wife. They were divorced in January 1979, in Tarrant County, Texas. She was living in Arlington, Texas. Mr. Bussey's first wife was Virginia Bussey. They were divorced in 1978 in Waco, Texas. Mr. Bussey has three children from his first marriage: William Allen Bussey, Jr., age thirty-one; Nan Copeland Braley, age thirty, an attorney in Dallas; and Mary Kathleen Bussey, age twenty-one.

"Mrs. [Eugenia Ann] Bussey has two children by a previous marriage, a teacher and a veterinarian. Bussey stated he was a retired dentist. He closed his office at 2121 Park Lake Drive, Waco, Texas, in April 1988. He stated that he presently considers himself an investor. He draws interest on his bank account and also invests in Las Vegas. Mr. Bussey plays blackjack in Vegas but does not like to be called a gambler. He considers his wagers investments. Mr. Bussey stated that in 1988, he made over $1,000,000 playing blackjack in at least twelve different casinos in Las Vegas and the Bahamas. Bussey has been gambling since the fall of 1985. He retired from his dental practice to see if he could be successful at his 'card counting.' ["Card counting" is a system of card playing in which a skilled practitioner can keep track of the high and low cards played. In blackjack, he can then predict with a fair chance of success whether the house or the player can win a particular hand. The more cards that have been dealt the better he can "predict" what will come up. He can figure the odds—or even know with certainty that, for example, all the aces have been played so, he doesn't have to worry about the house drawing an ace to match up with a face card.]

"Casinos know the regular counters and cut them off. Bussey admitted that for this reason he might give the casinos a different name to play, but he always gave them his correct name and social security number for currency transaction reports [CTRs]. Bussey always takes his winnings in cash. He wants the cash to deposit in his bank accounts to draw interest. He draws extra interest by transferring the funds from one bank to another. During the time it takes the second bank to clear the check through the first bank, he is drawing interest from both banks on the same money. Bussey plays in Las Vegas by using markers (credit at the casino). When he wins in blackjack, he takes his winnings in cash and deposits it in the bank to draw interest. He repays the markers every thirty days. There is no interest charged by the casinos. This is like a thirty-day interest-free loan. Bussey keeps meticulous records of every day's gambling. Bussey stated that he goes to many banks and deposits his funds in amounts less than $10,000 to avoid banks filing currency reports, because he doesn't want the IRS to take an interest in his cash. It is a private matter. Bussey is afraid of the IRS and is just keeping a low profile on CTRs. Bussey explained that banks had to send CTR's to the IRS and that this law was enacted by Congress to catch drug traffickers. 'I am not a criminal,' Bussey told us. When (the IRS agents) read subpart (b), Bussey said, 'I am aware of the purpose of the law.' Bussey felt safe in what he was doing since he had researched the law. He said the purpose of his 'surfing' was to protect his privacy. Bussey provided Special Agent Vannett with a photocopy of 31 CTR 103 that he stated he made at a local library.

"Bussey made his first trip to Las Vegas in 1985. At that time he read a book about gambling. Having established himself as a high roller, his business is sought after by the casinos. He incurs no expense for traveling and lodging while in Vegas. Everything except a rent car and side trips are provided complimentary to him by the casinos. An individual named Jack Strause from Dallas, Texas books his junkets. Bussey plays the tables with a $500 minimum bet. He usually plays the entire table, three hands at $10,000 per hand and bets $30,000 a hand. He usually plays ten to twelve casinos on a junket, usually the big casinos on the Strip or downtown. When playing, he will make some dumb bets on purpose to leave the appearance of not knowing what he is doing. This is the way he gets to continue playing at the casinos. In addition to the complimentary gambling junkets, Bussey has been given complimentary fishing trips to Alaska and Mexico and complimentary seats at the fights, etc. by the casinos. In 1988 he traveled to Vegas about twice a month. During 1986 through 1988, he has also gambled in the Bahamas, Australia, and St. Martin. Bussey claimed that he never took more than $10,000 in currency out of the country; [It is illegal to take over $10,000 cash out of our country without filling out a Federal report.] However, he did take cashier's checks made payable to himself to Australia for deposit. Mr. Bussey was shown his federal income tax returns for the years 1981 through 1985. He was also shown copies of 1986 and 1987. He stated that the returns were true and correct as filed. He stated all income was reported and deductible expenses were claimed.

"Mrs. Bussey was shown the same returns. She identified her signature on the return but would not comment on the accuracy of the returns, stating that she never looks at the returns, she just signs the returns. Allen Bussey prepares the tax returns and keeps all the records. Mr. Bussey declined to give his cash on hand for any years except 1984 and 1985. Bussey has bank accounts at sixteen institutions in Austin, Waco, and Las Vegas. Bussey was wearing a Rolex watch he obtained through Bouger and Weaver Jewelry in Waco. The watch would have cost $7,000; however he traded gold Kruggerands for it.

"Bussey stated that he deliberately deposited amounts less than $10,000 at each institution to prevent the filing of CTRs. He structured his deposits in this manner to avoid the CTRs to maintain his privacy and to prevent the IRS being alerted to his transactions. According to Bussey, his actions were not illegal because the law had been passed to catch drug dealers and his money was from gambling."

Bonnie Vannett, special agent, signed the report. There is also a memo dated October 24, 1990, taken by Van Carlton of the IRS, regarding a telephone conversation which it states started at 9:10 PM and ended at 9:15 PM. The typewritten transcript of this five-minute telephone conversation is two pages long.

Here are a few of the excerpts from the IRS record of that visit leading up to and including some of the phone conversation:

"After entry was made into the Bussey residence and the location was secured, I (Van Carlton) explained to Mrs. Bussey the purpose of our visit and stated that we would also be searching the contents of any safes located within the house. I asked her that if she could unlock any safes on the premises, it would preclude us from having to drill into the safes to get them open.

"After conversing a few minutes, Mrs. Bussey then said that her husband Allen wanted to talk with me. I then picked up the phone and introduced myself and advised Bussey of the purpose of our visit. I also stated that I was one of the special agents who interviewed him previously. Our conversation was a general conversation about the two search warrants, and I told Bussey that I did not want to ask him any questions or interview him at the present time. I told him that if he wished to talk, he should contact his attorney to arrange a meeting.

"Bussey then volunteered statements. Someone had opened a can of peanuts at his house and ate some peanuts. I told Bussey that I observed hundreds of cans of peanuts scattered throughout the house, some open, some not, and I asked how he drew that conclusion. Bussey said the length of the investigation was creating a strain on his life and he wanted us to realize he wasn't a drug dealer. Bussey said that the IRS had used dogs to sniff his personal car for the scent of drugs and had diverted airplanes he was flying on so that dog searches could be arranged. Bussey said that he was declaring bankruptcy and owed $1,750,000 to casinos for gambling debts. He said his lawyers were costing him a fortune and he wanted to end the misery of the investigation. Bussey said he stopped making cash deposits of $9,900 and now deposits the entire amount of gambling winnings, thereby permitting the proper reports to be filed. I asked Bussey if he knew how to park the hard disk on his computer. I explained that we were seizing his personal computer and did not want to damage it in the move. Bussey said he did not know how to park it but asked us to be careful with it. This concluded our conversation, and then I gave the phone to Mrs. Bussey."

Dr. Bussey had been utilizing the services of Fulbright and Jaworski, a very prestigious Texas and international law firm, to assist him in his defense with the IRS. His lawyer had apparently not stressed to him that he should not be helping the prosecution put him in jail. The firm generally does high quality legal work, and I have used them before but only when I know the specific lawyer in charge. They may not be equipped to handle criminal investigations and, with about five hundred lawyers plus support staff, the firm is a small city. Some of the lawyers are top-flight and some aren't.

It is extremely difficult to take over a case which has been handled by an attorney who has not properly protected the client, or a client who, like many of my clients, presumes that he is not guilty of wrongdoing and, therefore, convicts himself. That is not to say that I am picking on this particular law firm or the unnamed lawyer at the firm, but in this case, a large part of the case had been given away before I came to the table. No one wants to come to a poker table and take over a hand when the player has tossed his cards on the table, showing all.

Contrary to Dr. Bussey's self-researched opinion of the law involved, the crime of money laundering has absolutely nothing to do with drugs per se, although it is a tool in that war. Whatever your business, you have to file a currency transaction report if you receive $10,000 or more in cash (or now even money orders). It used to be that it was only cash. If you told someone that he or she could pay you in money orders so you wouldn't have to file the report, that used to be okay. The law was then amended so that if you told someone that he or she could give you money orders instead of cash, you were assisting him or her in the violation of money laundering and you were also guilty.

I had an interesting conversation with an assistant United States attorney at a seminar in New York. He told us that we were not allowed to tell our clients the correct law. He told us that if we did, we would be assisting them in the violation of the currency transaction reporting requirements and we would have committed a felony. I raised my hand and pointed out that he had just told two hundred lawyers what the currency transaction reporting requirements were and how to get around them. We could now go out and tell our clients what the law was. I asked him if I could indict him or arrest him on a citizen's arrest since he had started a national conspiracy that would undoubtedly lead to the violation of the law many times over. He told me that I was blowing it out of proportion.

I think that a lawyer ought to be able to discuss *any* aspect of the law with a client without fear of being prosecuted for telling the client what the law is and that a public speaker should be able to discuss the law and what it is under the First Amendment without any fear of retribution.

Almost all of the tax laws in the United States require that word "willful." There are statutes that don't and one of those statutes is giving false information to a lending institution that is federally insured.

You don't have to do it with any intent to defraud the lending institution. In fact, even if the debt is repaid early, without any late payments, if you lied on the application, you can be charged with the crime.

I represented an individual in Dallas where the judge told us that we would not be allowed to tell the jury that my client had paid everything on time and, in fact, had paid off the debt early, and that the bank had *no complaint against him.* The client had been indicted for other unrelated crimes in another case and courtroom, which another lawyer was handling, and could not afford to have a conviction during the trial of that unrelated crime, in which another attorney was representing him. Accordingly, we worked out a plea agreement. He would plead guilty but be given the right to appeal the judge's refusal to let him use the evidence on appeal. He would get probation. We would then appeal to the Fifth Circuit, so he would not have a final judgment against him. *We did this with the court's approval and permission.* If the Fifth Circuit decided he was entitled to tell a jury that he had paid all the money back on time and that the bank was not unhappy with him, we would get a reversal and a new trial but only on the one charge he had pled to. Four other counts were dismissed. He also got to drop several other charges which were pending against him as part of the plea agreement.

The case went on appeal. The client went to the other court with other counsel and was convicted. The client went to jail on that case, but the conviction in our case could not be used against him to add to his time, and he did no time on our case. Since then, in 1987, the Supreme Court has ruled that even an acquittal might be used against someone during sentencing on another crime.

The Fifth Circuit Court of Appeals unfortunately ruled that we could not have a reversal because the trial court followed the law correctly. They ruled we should not have been allowed to tell the jury that my client had done nothing wrong except make inaccurate statements on his loan application. Nor could we tell the jury that he had

195

paid the bank back in full early. My argument was that the jury would believe he had cheated the bank and not paid the money back. No one would believe us, unless we told him with evidence, that someone was being falsely charged with bank fraud when the bank had not been cheated out of one penny. It was a very bad decision on the part of the Fifth Circuit and bad law. Nevertheless, in loan applications, the individual borrowing money from a bank has a very poor status while, on the other hand, there are a lot of very good laws protecting the bankers from criminal prosecution. Bad law or not, in Texas and Louisiana, it's the federal law we have to live with.

Dr. Bussey had confessed to two IRS agents that he had intentionally put only $9,900 in a bank account on a single transaction for the specific purpose of avoiding the currency transaction report requirements. That was an intentional knowing violation of the statute and it had absolutely nothing to do with drugs. It is a stupid law. It makes me sick. This would be a very tough case to defend. The next part of the case that was also very tough to defend was an allegation of "false reports to a bank" signed by Dr. Bussey and his wife, Eugenia Ann Bussey.

Dr. Bussey had originally contacted me, telling me that he thought he was under constant observation and, in fact, had a large amount of cash stored at a friend's place that had been stolen. His wife thought that the friend had stolen the money. Dr. Bussey felt the federal government had stolen it. I have no way of determining how the money was taken.

Dr. Bussey interviewed me on the telephone and then had me investigated to determine whether or not he wanted to hire me. He agreed to retain me with a $50,000 retainer and explained to me that the money would be delivered to me. It wasn't.

Dr. Bussey called several more times and we had a few more telephone conversations, but I indicated that I would not be available again until the money came in. If I have agreed to a fee and the client eventually comes up with it, and I still have the time to take the case,

196

then I take it. Sometimes the client will come up with the money later, and I will have become completely booked. With Dr. Bussey, I began to suspect that the money was not coming and that I was just getting the run-around. I told him that the few hours I had spent with him would be written off, but I could not take the case. He told me that the money had been delivered and that he needed to find out what had happened.

About two weeks passed and I noticed in our cluttered library a small brown box, which did not seem to have any specific purpose for being there. My first thought was that it might be some sort of a bug or transmittal device planted by the IRS. That seems silly, but I can still recall a telephone conversation with Lorna Kahl, the daughter of the alleged tax protester and alleged murderer of the federal marshals, when I was discussing the case of the *United States v. Udey* (748 F.2d 1231) with her over the telephone. We could actually hear some people talking in a faint voice in the background and saying, "She's talking to the lawyer now." I asked Lorna what that was all about and she told me it was the bug, everybody had caught it.

Well, I picked up the box and opened it up. It was filled with hundred-dollar bills. Approximately $70,000 in hundred-dollar bills. My next concern was to figure out where it had come from. We had three clients at the time who were about to retain me with fairly significant sums of money, and Dr. Bussey was not the only one who might be paying in cash at that time. I did not want to credit it to the wrong client, and I certainly did not want to leave it in the office overnight. The security at my office was not the greatest at that time. We found out later that an employee had been stealing from us. There is no doubt in my mind that if she had known about the cash, she would have stolen it and I would not have believed it had ever been delivered. I had to fill out a CTR (cash transaction) form. I filled out the CTR form and in the place where an individual name had to go, I put "Fifth Amendment." The purpose was to follow the CTR requirement but not to give the name of the client who had given me the money. In a tax case, where the government has the burden of proof, one of the ways they can prove income is to show net assets and then let the taxpayer prove where he or she got the money. It can be detrimental to the tax case for the government to know that the client had $70,000 in cash, and, unfortunately, the government can often make the mere collection of cash look suspicious. (Under one of the doctrines in *U.S. v. Nunan*, this violates the law, but the IRS does it anyway.)

You no doubt remember O. J. Simpson's famous car chase scene and the fact that when he ended it, he had several thousand dollars in cash on him. America was told that this was very suspicious. If I had O. J. Simpson's money, I, too, would keep several thousand dollars in cash on me. People love cash. You get better service with cash. It's a shame that we have become so suspicious of each other that we think something is wrong when someone carries cash. In fact, the United States government used to print a thousand-dollar bill, a five-thousand-dollar bill and a ten-thousand-dollar bill. Not too long ago there was even a one-hundred-thousand-dollar bill with Woodrow Wilson's picture on it—but these were limited to transactions between the Treasury Department and the Federal Reserve system. In those days, pulling out a hundred-dollar bill would shock people. Often a restaurant wouldn't have change to break a hundred-dollar bill. Of course, then there were no VISA, MasterCard, or American Express cards. Nevertheless, private citizens could easily carry much larger sums of cash on their person, usually because many business transactions, even large real estate deals, were handled in cash. Lately, the highest denomination that you can carry on your person that is still printed by the United States Treasury Department is the hundred-dollar bill. Why? The less cash you can carry, the more easily you can be controlled and watched, the very thing that Dr. Bussey was worried about. You'd think that with inflation the denominations would get higher, not lower.

Of course, a lot of higher denomination bills are still in circulation, but as they reach the Federal Reserve banks they are removed.

Generally the IRS knows immediately where those bills came from!

It was about 3:30 or 4:00 in the afternoon when I discovered the money, and so I handed it to my wife, Michelle, to deposit in our trust account. My first thought was that it was a client out of Chicago, because the sum of money was in line with the fee that was being charged. Dr. Bussey was overpaying approximately $20,000, so I didn't think it was his. When the other client finally called, I determined that it couldn't be anybody else's except Dr. Bussey's. There was one other problem: when I asked him how much money he had sent me, he couldn't tell me. He knew it was at least as much as the retainer fee, but he couldn't tell me if it was more or how much more. I am fairly certain that the funds came from Dr. Bussey, but this just goes to show his eccentricity even more. If they didn't come from Dr. Bussey, then he had a guardian angel willing to cover his fees for him.

My wife took the cash to the bank. She had instructions to call as soon as she had made the deposit. I was a bit concerned because Bussey had said he had been followed constantly and he was worried that the money might have been seized en route to my office. A similar sum had been stolen from another source of his, and so I wanted to proceed cautiously. At first I had not believed him, but cash has credibility and with its arrival it seemed possible his first stash had been stolen. "The check is in the mail" is a cliche most business people learn to ignore. Cash is on its way means nothing unless it arrives.

Michelle left for the bank and did not call in. I went home at about 7:00 PM and got more concerned. About 8:00 PM, I was extremely concerned and by 10:00 PM, I called the police.

The police arrived at the house about 10:30 and wanted to know what had happened. I explained that my wife had deposited a large sum of cash in the bank and was supposed to call back in. Meanwhile, our son Jourdan suddenly remembered that he had received a call around 6:00 PM from someone identifying themselves as a banker who told us that the deposit had been made. This didn't make me feel better. This made me feel worse. If someone had been following Michelle and had done something with her and the cash, it would be smart to call the house and tell us there was nothing wrong. It wasn't Michelle who had made the call, and it was now 10:30 PM. The same people who were following Bussey might well have followed Michelle.

At about 11:45, Michelle drove up in the van wondering what all the excitement was about. There were three police cars in the driveway. She had deposited the money in the bank and had then decided to go grocery shopping. The van was stocked to the brim from the front to the back. It would have taken anyone quite some time to fill it. Michelle was surprised that anyone was concerned, because she had told the bank teller to call the house and say the deposit had been made.

I needed to meet with Dr. Bussey, transfer my fee from the trust account, and then get Dr. Bussey to allow me to return the extra to him. I would bill him for any amount over and above the retainer for out-of-pocket expenses. It was not safe for money to be sitting in one place that belonged to Dr. Bussey. It was not safe, because the IRS had seized everything else that Dr. Bussey owned because of the money laundering charges against him. To make matters worse, an article was printed in an Austin paper that implied that Dr. Bussey was involved with drugs. (The government often starts trying cases in the press and then complains when you respond to the press. Leona Helmsley, a millionaire beauty queen before she married her billionaire husband, was trashed in the press by the government and never properly publically defended.)

Dr. Bussey was an amazing man, and in his own way a meticulously honest man, but a man who definitely marched to a different drummer. The casinos would woo him with free air travel and rooms. He took it even further. He would get several different Vegas promoters to pay for his plane ticket to Vegas, give him a room, and give him some free chips to gamble. He would then use only one ticket, cash in the rest of the tickets, and stay at all the rooms at all the different hotels. There was nothing illegal in this and his actions were no more dishonest than the casinos that were trying to part him from his money. He was a master "card counter" and in 1988, won $1,000,000 playing blackjack.

It got to the point that he was blacklisted in the casinos. When they discovered him, they would throw him out. Bussey would use different names and different disguises to get into the casino and gamble. Gambling is supposed to be a gamble for the *patrons*, who nine times out of ten lose money, and that one time out of ten go back and lose their winnings. It is not supposed to be a scientific adventure as it was with someone like Dr. Bussey.

One of the things that the Vegas promoters have learned to do to beat "counters" like Bussey is to pad the deck. Put lots of decks of cards in and then change them out before running through a complete deck. Bussey's mind, however, was so sharp, he could still count the cards and calculate the odds, even when they were using multiple decks!

In 1989 and 1990 Bussey became convinced that he was being followed by government agents and gaming agents. He started to lose, and to lose substantial amounts.

The IRS has interesting tax rulings for gamblers. If you win $1,000,000, but lose $900,000 on the trip, then you only have to pay taxes on the $100,000. You are, of course, required to keep complete and full tax records. Does this mean you had to keep track of each hand winning and losing each time at a blackjack game? Does it mean each time you got up and left the table? Does it mean at the end of each day of gambling? Does it mean at the end of each gambling junket? I think just about any gambler can have his or her feet put to the fire with the appropriately offensive IRS audit and might fail to meet the requirements of the agent.

Shortly after Dr. Bussey's IRS indictment, the Vegas and Atlantic City people began to flood him with lawsuits to cover markers.

In the criminal case, the IRS was represented by Assistant United States Attorney Greg Lehman. Mr. Lehman is one of the few people working for the Feds who I believe is honest. Everything he told us throughout this case was true, and he attempted to back up not just the letter of his word, but the *spirit* of his word.

Greg was the spitting image of Opie from Mayberry and appeared as decent, honorable, and simple. He was decent and honorable, but he wasn't simple. He was an intelligent guy with integrity, and it came across. I knew that he would be very difficult in court. I knew the jurors would like him and respect him.

We were in Judge Nowlin's court in Austin. Judge Nowlin had recently come under fire because his telephone was linked to other telephones where, circumstantially, he may have been talking to some of the parties involved in a redistricting case pending in his court. I have no idea whether the judge did anything inappropriate or, from memory now, going back over five years, whether it affected him. It was a factor that we had to consider. If the judge has a fight with his or her spouse the night before, it can affect the way he reacts in the courtroom the next day. Even the best judges have bad days when they act unreasonable. We are all human beings. The big difference between a good judge and a bad judge is that the bad judge wants to blame his shortcomings on his minions, the subjects who are forced to come into his courtroom every day, whereas the good judge, when he makes a mistake, will usually apologize. I think that Judge Nowlin was under a great deal of stress during these proceedings.

The IRS seized Dr. and Mrs. Bussey's home and ranch. Every six months the property was re-evaluated by appraisers, and a security guard was hired to protect it. All of these expenses were to be charged against Dr. and Mrs. Bussey. The reason for the seizure? Dr. Bussey had used cash to purchase the property, cash to make improvements on the property, and cash with which to gamble.

He and his wife had borrowed money from a bank using statements that were different from the statements that had been used on their tax returns. I am an equal opportunity attorney. I take people of all races, colors, creeds, and political affiliation and because of that policy, I have represented a large number of Republicans. With all of the Whitewater scandal about banking going on as I write this book, it is interesting for me to reflect that it is common for the Republicans that I have known (and I presume a lot of other people) to inflate financial and income statements for banks. It is now practically a national pasttime.

I have had to sit down with my children, who were offered credit card applications by the thousands while they were in high school and college, and counsel them not to exaggerate income when there were periods of time that they were not working but living on allowances, and where the income that they made was fairly small. A large number of their friends file false reports of their income to the lenders. There is no possible way that the lenders cannot know that this is happening when they solicit the business of college students. Dishonesty is encouraged. Little do these students know that it is a potential felony to make a dishonest representation to a bank insured by the federal government.

I was retained to represent Dr. Bussey in his case and, as a sideline effort, Dr. Bussey wanted me to try to get back the real estate and property that the government had seized. None of the seized money had been reported seized by the government. However, the Bussey's ranch was seized. Part of the negotiations consisted of an effort to save some of the proceeds for Dr. Bussey and Mrs. Bussey.

Mrs. Bussey had been a schoolteacher before she married Dr. Bussey and retired. She was an attractive middle-aged woman who was now scared to death. She retained a top criminal defense lawyer, an attorney I have tried cases with in the past, Mike Ware, a cowboy out of Fort Worth, Texas. Mike Ware was a good associate to have because the rules on this case were similar to the rules in the Buford case: no matter what else we did, we had to keep Mrs. Bussey out of jail.

The banking charge was the most difficult. We would not be allowed to put on any case at all. There was another pending problem

203

throughout the discussion on this case: Dr. Bussey was being sued by half the casinos in Las Vegas, Nevada, and Atlantic City, New Jersey. The sum total of the claims exceeded $1,000,000. If the Bussey's homestead ranch was sold through forfeiture, even if we were able to get some of the money back, would these casinos intervene and tie up all the money?

Money laundering charges are among the most vicious of charges that a human being can face in America today. Prison time is very substantial and there are minimum sentencing guidelines. That means that almost everyone convicted of a money crime will do some time in jail, even if the judge doesn't want to sentence him. The mandatory minimum sentencing guidelines now in effect generally will force some jail time. Of course, the judge could say, "I'm not going to give jail time, I disagree with the sentencing guidelines," and the government could say, "I agree not to appeal," and that would be the end of it.

I can foresee certain situations where such pleas might be possible, but this was not one of them. "Opie"—as I still think of him today—was an honorable man who preferred to put drug dealers in jail and not eccentric people like Dr. Bussey, who was literally playing with statutes, trying to have some fun with them and at the same time keep his privacy, in which he took great pride. There is no question in my mind that the judge didn't want Dr. Bussey to spend time in jail and didn't think it was necessary. However, the government was not willing to drop the charge to a misdemeanor.

Dr. Bussey wanted to go to trial. It would have been a very tough trial, but I get hired for tough trials and was committed to it.

The prime factors in the case were many. Each of the Busseys was facing fifteen to thirty years. Under the minimum standards of the guidelines, complete and full convictions would have guaranteed several years in prison.

Opie wanted to get a conviction, had a lot of time invested in the case, and felt that the government needed a conviction. He was, however, willing to do whatever could be done by mutual agreement to minimize jail time and drop the charges against Mrs. Bussey, if Dr. Bussey would bite the bullet. Another problem was that the special agent had spent a lot of time and money on the case and needed to justify the seizures.

The bottom line was that Dr. Bussey agreed to one charge of not reporting everything properly on the 1985 income tax return in order to protect his wife. My job was to minimize the damage. The government agreed to drop all other charges, including charges unknown, which could be filed in the future. This was important because charges had been added in addition to those in the original indictment. The government agreed to drop all charges against Mrs. Bussey. Opie agreed not to fight me on the issue of jail time; I trusted him and he maintained that position with integrity. I can recall several times when government officials have not.

Dr. Bussey, however, was facing a fair judge *and* a fair prosecutor, an unusual and fortunate situation. Unfortunately he faced them with a horrible case made worse by his voluntary statements. We entered an agreement regarding the ranch. The ranch would be sold. I did not want Dr. Bussey to face the money laundering charges. The statements he made to the IRS agents on the phone at his house would have been very difficult to overcome. Most of us do not know there are laws requiring us to make these type of disclosures to our government. We are wrong. I hope that someday these laws will be repealed.

Even though his preference was to fight to the death, Dr. Bussey was willing to go to jail in order to put his wife at ease and make certain she would never go to jail. Also, he wanted to be certain that he would not leave jail broke. That was a tough one.

The ranch was worth somewhere in the neighborhood of $350,000. Even with an agreement from Opie, an honorable man, once it was signed it would be out of his hands completely. My experience with the federal government in getting them to pay money back had not been happy. I was also aware of a case in Colorado where my friend Bill Cohen had won an appellate victory against the IRS, ordering them to return over $1,000,000 to his client, and ten years later the IRS had still not obeyed the order!

All I could do was negotiate an agreement. Dr. Bussey wanted me to negotiate the agreement on a contingency basis, meaning I would get a percentage of the money that I collected. I told him I was unwilling to do that as the risk involved in collection was too great. I would enter into a negotiation, make a few calls, send out a few letters, and hope for the best. If we had a good negotiated settlement and the check came in, fine. If it didn't, he would have to hire someone else to chase down the money.

Once there is a plea agreement, your client has to plead guilty and then be sentenced. There is more risk involved. The court does not have to accept the deal. Generally you can take the plea back, but your previous sworn statements accepting guilt may be used against you.

Dr. Bussey pleaded guilty before Judge Nowlin and was convicted. The next step was for the government to prepare a report on the defendant, and then for the defendant to come back for sentencing. Judge Nowlin said that Dr. Bussey would not have to be in prison until the sentencing and even then, he could report in at a convenient time.

The pre-trial sentencing report created by the government made Dr. Bussey out to be a nut. L. R. and I did our job. We learned by asking that the judge did not like to hear a lot of testimony at sentencing, but what he did like was to receive letters from interested friends and would read them. Dr. Bussey didn't want us to solicit letters because it was embarrassing to him. We solicited them anyway. Dr. Bussey shouldn't have to spend an extra year in jail simply because he didn't want people to know what had happened.

The letters that we got were very good. Since his wife had been a co-defendant, we did not want to put her on the stand and incur potential jeopardy, so we simply asked her to send a short letter. She did to-wit:

July 29, 1992

Judge James Nowlin:

William Allen Bussey is my husband. He is soft-spoken, well-mannered, even-tempered, kind, and considerate. In the four-teen years that I have known him, I have found him to be a sensitive, caring, and many-faceted man. His human frailties and imperfections are far outweighed by his goodness.

Ann Bussey

A sweet and endearing letter, perhaps a little brief, but we were unwilling to let her commit to any of the specifics of the allegations themselves. It also seemed a touch condescending. Her remarks about his "frailties and imperfections" ironically seemed to be targeted at his "crime," the same one with which she had been charged.

Dr. Bussey sent letters directly to the court. This is something that I don't encourage and try to control because I want to know what the court (or the jury) sees. It is very hard to argue about it, for or against, if you haven't seen it in advance. That doesn't mean I didn't like Dr. Bussey. I loved the man. He was an individual. He was unique, but he was always a bull in a china shop. I have won difficult cases before with difficult clients; it just makes for a tougher fight. I have also had a lot of unique individuals who work with me on a team effort basis, like Stephen Buford and the Absent-Minded Professor. Even though they were used to controlling all facets of their life normally, at trial they let me call the shots with their substantial input. What Bussey pleaded to was filing an incomplete return. That is, leaving off income. As a matter of fact, he specifically stated that in a letter to the judge, which I did not authorize:

I did not file a false return, nor is that what I am pleading. The return was true. It was incomplete, not false. What was omitted was any reference to gambling winnings, because they were offset by losses. It was true, but it was not correct, because of the omission, there-

207

fore, it was not true and correct. This may seem trivial to you, but it is an important distinction to me, otherwise I could not have pleaded guilty to it. For me to say that I filed a false return would have been a lie. I filed an incorrect return and incomplete return. What was false about anything that I did with respect to that return, was to sign the statement at the bottom claiming that to the best of my knowledge and belief, it is true, correct, and complete. I did think about putting it all down, but decided not to because I expected it might be a red flag that would kick out my return for audit. No one wants to be audited no matter how true and correct the return might be.

Dr. Bussey decided to take it upon himself to write Judge Nowlin directly with his personal observations and opinions regarding sentencing and the federal government and everyone else. The general rule of thumb, however, is that the defendant needs to "kiss up" to the judge. The defendant needs to show his abject humility and the judge will lower the sentence.

The sentencing guidelines allow the judge to adjust the sentence downward for "acceptance of responsibility." You have a very fine juggling act with these silly rules. The way acceptance of responsibility goes in the United States today is a humiliating, undesirable, and unnecessary ceremony. The defense counsel and defendant get up and beg the judge for leniency and tell the judge that they are bad and ready for punishment. The judge is then supposed to say, "Okay, you are bad, but since you have admitted it, I will shave several months off your sentence." The opposite is also true. The judge finds that the defendant is unrepentant. Many judges interpret that to mean not humble or servile enough, although someone like Dr. Bussey is incapable of servility; then they add to the sentence.

Opie kept his word and took no stand on this. The full time would have been nine to twelve months. A downward adjustment for acceptance of responsibility would give Dr. Bussey six months. Refusal to accept responsibility and a tough calculation on the amount owed the government could push the sentence up to two years.

The pre-sentence report by the probation officer of the court said that Dr. Bussey, due to statements similar to the ones that you have now read, was unrepentant and should not receive a downward departure.

I disagreed. I spoke up for Dr. Bussey as was my job under the law and the Constitution, told the court that he had accepted responsibility for his actions completely, and was entitled to the downward departure. I was also worried. We didn't have as many letters as we could have had because Dr. Bussey didn't want people sending them in.

Judge Nowlin made it absolutely clear that he thought that Dr. Bussey had satisfied all of the requirements necessary to obtain a downward departure. The government attorney behaved admirably. The judge was a strong man who was not challenged by Dr. Bussey's strength. Dr. Bussey was sentenced to the six months, and Judge Nowlin wished him well. I appreciated that and have been a fan of Judge Nowlin ever since.

I am in the risk business just like a gambler. When I am hired on a criminal tax case it's usually for a fight and not a surrender, but the decision belongs to clients like Cookie Hobbs and Steven Buford and Dr. Bussey. If a great injustice is weighed against a smaller one or if a sacrifice is a choice in the equation, my job is to counsel the client so he can make the decision. Dr. Bussey went to jail and I closed my file.

I received two collect telephone calls while he was in jail. He told me that he regretted not having his day in court and not going to trial, even if he would have lost and spent more time in prison, but he would do the same thing, if given the opportunity to do it over again, because the ranch would be sold, the money would go to him and his wife, and they would have a chance to start over. He had saved Ann Bussey from prison. I never heard from Dr. Bussey again.

The civil settlement was complicated. The agreement was that one-half of the sale of the ranch would go to the government and one-half to Dr. and Mrs. Bussey. However, we didn't want it to go directly

209

to Dr. Bussey. It needed to go to Mrs. Bussey personally, as her separate property, so that none of the casino judgments could ever be issued against the money. Dr. Bussey asked me to pursue this matter and, I agreed to do so for a limited period of time, by the hour, and then quit. I spent $1,000 worth of time working on the agreement, following up with some phone calls and some letters. At that point in time, I was off the case. My refusal to take the case on a contingency fee turned out to be bad financial judgment.

In late November of 1993, I received a check with my name and Eugenia Ann Bussey's name on it. It was in the amount of $157,330.30. I was excited for Dr. and Mrs. Bussey and immediately attempted to get hold of Dr. Bussey. I presumed he was out of prison by now. I was right. Dr. Bussey was out of prison but there was more news, bad news.

While he was in prison, Mrs. Bussey had filed for divorce against Dr. Bussey. The divorce decree was about to become final, and she was living with a boyfriend.

Dr. Bussey had gone to jail and given up his day in court in order to keep her out of jail. Dr. Bussey was released from prison and then filed a motion in his divorce for a new trial preventing the judgment from becoming final. He then went to talk to Mrs. Bussey, entered the property where Mrs. Bussey and her boyfriend were staying. The boyfriend, William Walding, was armed. Dr. Bussey was killed. The boyfriend was charged with killing Dr. Bussey.

I didn't know any of this at the time. I was trying to find Dr. Bussey, or any other relative of Dr. Bussey, who could tell me where he was. I sent letters out to Dr. Bussey and to Mrs. Bussey that went unanswered.

Finally, I asked Otis Owens, my private investigator, to go find them. By the strangest of coincidences, on the same day Otis was in my office going through the Bussey file in preparation to set out to find Dr. Bussey, I received a phone call from Dr. Bussey's daughter. She told me the entire story and I told her about the check.

I learned of most of these facts from Dr. Bussey's daughter, and even though she knew that the widow Bussey would be making a claim for the money, she gave me the phone number and address of the widow Bussey's attorney so I could contact them.

I told Dr. Bussey's daughter that I would prefer that she, her brother and sister get the money rather than the widow Bussey, but it was not my choice to make. I also told her that I was the only one besides Mrs. Bussey, Opie, and Mike Ware, (who probably would not be permitted to testify since he had been Mrs. Bussey's lawyer), who knew the intentions of Dr. and Mrs. Bussey. The intention at the time that the agreement was drawn up was to make certain that the casinos couldn't get the money. It was intended to be utilized as a new life for Dr. Bussey and his wife.

Shortly after that, I received a phone call from James Hull, representing Aladdin Hotel and Casino, d/b/a Golden Nugget, with a judgment of $119,000. He asked that I recognize his claim to the money.

I also received a letter on March 11, 1994, from Richard C. Mosty claiming to represent Ann Schumann (formerly Ann Bussey) making a claim for the money. Shortly thereafter, the heirs of Dr. Bussey requested that the money be held for them. Thomas Terrell represented them. Mr. Terrell stated in his letter, "Please be aware that this money is the community property of the parties and any agreement to the contrary is void as being in fraud of Dr. Bussey and, in addition, being a transfer in fraud of creditors." Mr. Terrell also suggested, "Ann Schumann is being represented by Mr. Mosty of Kerrville. ... Mr. Mosty may, however, demand that the check be turned over to Ann Schumann. If you were to do so, after having knowledge of the above claims, then you may be personally liable to the estate and to the creditors." Our office had sent out a letter on November 16, 1993, the day we got the check, drafted and signed by L. R. Robertson. By far the most interesting of the letters and claims made came on April 7, 1994, from Attorney Jim Tatum. Tatum wrote,

211

Mr. Minns:

I am representing William Walding in the death of Dr. Bussey. Ann Schumann has asked me to represent her in the matter of the Internal Revenue Service check, which she says you are refusing to turn over to her. ... Ms. Schumann has been advised that if she owes you money pursuant to an agreement between you and Ms. Schumann, that you should be paid. ... If you are refusing to turn over the check because of some claim or out-standing bill against Dr. Bussey, or some contemplated legal action against Ms. Schumann, the State Bar will not hesitate to sanction a lawyer in such a case and/or the courts will act quickly to correct this situation, along with appropriate damages and sanctions. ... I will insist that my client honor any agreement she has to pay you. If there is no legal basis to withhold her check, I will expect the check delivered to my Houston office...by 3:00 PM on Friday, April 8, 1994. Failing the above, a suit will be filed immediately as well as a grievance alleging theft and conversion of Ms. Schumann's property.

The man alleged to have killed my client, Dr. Bussey, was being represented by Mr. Tatum, who was also collecting money for the widow Bussey, if, in fact, she was a widow, which was a disputed fact. Some were saying the divorce was not final, some were saying the divorce was final. The only fact everyone agreed on was that Dr. Bussey was dead. There also appeared to be a not-very-subtle suggestion that I might receive a contingency fee, presumably between one-third and forty percent of the $157,000, if I would merely realize that I had been working on a contingency fee agreement with Mrs. Bussey.

There were a lot of problems with that. There was no contingency agreement. It would have been unethical of me to change it in order to change a fee from $1,000 to over $50,000.

There were now two lawyers asking me to deliver money to them on behalf of Ms. Schumann, one of them representing the person who had been indicted for killing Dr. Bussey, and a third, with a different standing, whatever that was, representing a gambling casino, and finally fourth, the legitimate legal heirs of Dr. Bussey.

There was another problem. Aside from being offended by being offered what I took to be a bribe in writing, by being unethically threatened with a grievance (the check wasn't turned over the next day and Mr. Tatum didn't file suit the next day), but even in addition to my legal responsibility (which was to hold the check until a court decided to whom the money belonged), there was no way in hell that I was going to hand over $157,000 voluntarily to the lawyer who represented the man who had killed my client.

There was still another problem. The check would expire one year after it was dated. While all of these people were fighting over the money and some of these people were threatening me personally, I knew that if the check was not negotiated and became void, it would become difficult for anybody to get the money back.

I really do hate the IRS and the taxing codes of the United States of America. If you had asked me before this case to think of a person or entity I would rather give money to than the IRS, it probably would have been *anyone*. Of course, I had never been tested to this extent. I am also not a fan of organized crime or gambling, and if you had asked me who should get the money, the gambling casinos would not have been very high up on my list. My list of personal preferences, which I can reveal now that the case is completely over is, first, the heirs of Dr. Bussey, second, the gambling casinos, third, back to the IRS, and only fourth, and last, to the law office of the person defending the accused murderer of Dr. Bussey.

I hired my former law partner to file an interpleader for me. An interpleader is a cause of action whereby money is put into the registry of a court and then the court decides who gets the money. Generally, the person or entity, often an insurance company, who files the interpleader, has its legal fees paid out of the funds in the court.

This is for a rational person, a good argument to not fight and to try to settle. The interpleader's attorney can eat up all of the funds and then no one gets anything.

I drafted the motion, signed my lawyer's name to it with his permission, and filed it. I then drafted a motion asking the court to accept the check and to deposit it in the registry of the court. I couldn't get my lawyer for nine months to do anything on it, so I contacted Mr. Terrell. He filed his own motion and set it before the court. The court granted it, ordering the money deposited in the registry of the court. This was important because no one else was rationally cooperating. If the check was not negotiated before the year was up, it might never be available again. I was not willing to sign the check with all the different parties claiming it, and I was not willing to turn it over to Mrs. Bussey for fear that she just might sign it, forge my signature and negotiate it, ignoring the court system. I did not want Dr. Bussey's estate to pay for the defense of his executioner. The money was cashed about two weeks before the expiration date.

Of all the lawyers on the case, I think the one who did the best on the interpleader was Mr. Terrell. I was certainly cheering for him. The final disposition was $10,150 to pay for the interpleader legal fees, $40,000 to John C. Adams, Trustee, which went to the gambling casinos that had filed interventions in the case, a third of which went to their lawyer as a contingency fee, whose name was also John C. Adams. The balance of the funds, including all interest, went to Thomas S. Terrell, Trustee.

Mr. Terrell entered into a confidential settlement agreement with the former Mrs. Bussey. I hope none of it ended up in Tatum's hands. That's all I know about the case.

Chapter VIII
Pilot: Retirement
Savings Seized

The physical power to get the money does not seem to me a
test of the right to tax.

—Robert Jackson, Supreme Court Justice

Writing in language that people cannot understand is one of
the judicial sins of our times.

—Hugo Black, Supreme Court Justice

When I met him, Captain Clyde Orr was a pilot with Delta
Airlines. During the Cold War, he flew jets for Pan
American Airlines in and out of Berlin, helping to keep capitalism alive, since German airlines, like Lufthansa, were not allowed
to fly into the city of Berlin. In fact, Captain Orr, on several occasions,
actually flew Chancellor Helmut Kohl from Hamburg into Berlin.
Clyde went to Berlin in 1986 and came back to the United States in
April 1991. While a resident in Germany, Captain Orr paid taxes to
the German government. He didn't know that as an American citizen,
he also had to file with the IRS. His story is essentially one of a taxpayer making an honest mistake and then suffering severe retaliation
and trauma inflicted by the IRS for no reasonable explanation.

215

Clyde Orr, because of mistakes in interpreting the IRS Code, owed approximately seventeen thousand dollars in taxes. Seventeen thousand dollars is a substantial sum, so Captain Orr hired a CPA, Thomas Snell, to straighten out the mistake and negotiate a settlement with the IRS. The government, while negotiating on this with Captain Orr's CPA, unilaterally decided to end the negotiations and *seized all of his retirement funds of over four hundred thousand dollars.* They also charged him the statutory 10 percent early withdrawal penalty and then taxes on the over four hundred thousand dollars! Clyde Orr had to sue if he was to get his retirement savings back.

Clyde W. Orr was born December 22, 1938. He is divorced and the father of three children. Orr is a Marine Corps veteran and served as a pilot with top-secret clearance in the Vietnam War. He was decorated for the missions he flew during the Vietnam War. After he left the Armed Services, he was a pilot with Pan American Airlines from February 14, 1966, until November 1991, when it was acquired by Delta Airlines, his employer at the time of the deposition and trial. At that time, June 1995, Clyde was based in Dallas/Ft. Worth.

Since Berlin was an occupied city, Orr was given Federal Military I.D.'s and had PX privileges at the Berlin Army Air Base. He was required to report to the Berlin base. He served all internal German cities as Berlin's connection to West German cities. Between 1986 and 1991, while he was based in Berlin he had no regular flights to the United States except three or four to New York to service the planes. When Berlin was united, Pan Am sold its internal routes to Lufthansa.

In 1986, he leased an apartment in Germany on the corner of Lietzenburger Strasse and Kudom on the fourteenth floor. He shared the lease with another Pan Am pilot, Claude Hudspeth. It was his intention to make Germany his domicile while there, but it was always his plan to return to the United States. A couple of years later, he moved to another apartment. He had to register with the German police as a resident and had a residency stamp placed on his pass-

216

port. He was subject to German taxes. Orr's paychecks were deposited in the Berliner Bank at Tegel Airport. He also had a doctor in Germany, Dr. Winter.

Most of these facts were obviously known to the United States Government or available with a minimum amount of investigation, before Clyde Orr was even forced to file suit. All were firmly re-established in evidence after Orr's deposition on June 16, 1995.

This case involved an involuntary seizure by the federal government without cause. The history of the case was one of frivolous positions, bad faith, and the type of subtle machinations by the government counsel one would expect of a card shark or shell-game master. It included specific and deliberate violations of settlement agreements; efforts by the government counsel to blame Congress and his superiors; trying to imply unilateral influence with the court; disobeying discovery rules by refusing to make admissions; refusing to mediate; and failing to abide by final written settlement agreements in a timely fashion.

In 1994, Orr requested that the court strike the pleadings of the government and award attorney's fees, or in the alternative, enter the specific judgment already agreed on (in 1993 by the IRS accountant) and order attorney's fees. One of the arguments maintained by Clyde Orr was that there never was a position for the government to assert. Nearly two years of litigation from July 20, 1994, until the date of the second Motion, March 15, 1996, plus a year of pre-litigation negotiations, were unnecessary. The court had isolated the key contested issues after reviewing Clyde Orr's Motion for Summary Judgment and the government's response, saying in its order of April 27, 1995, "...it appears that at least two issues are relevant to Orr's federal tax liability, to-wit: his residence for tax purposes for the tax years in question and whether Orr paid German income taxes for the tax years in question that were not refunded."

The court's analysis was correct. Unfortunately, with inaccurate information supplied by the government the two issues would have

217

been decided incorrectly, preventing Orr from getting his $70,000 a year off-shore deduction and credit for all of the taxes paid to Germany. What the court did not know at the time of its ruling was that the government had no evidence to support its positions and no reason to suspect the positions were valid, which they were not. They did not prove my client did not pay German income taxes and was a not resident of Germany beyond any doubt, reasonable or otherwise, and despite the fact that their positions were invalid, they continued to negotiate and delay in bad faith. Even after "settling"(which they did only because of the influence of the court through its mandatory Mediation Order), they would continue to delay and renegotiate in bad faith.

It is undisputed and has always been indisputable that Clyde Orr lived in Germany from 1986 until 1991. No reasonable person could doubt that. No reasonable person could have raised the issue based on the evidence.

Estimates have been made that as many as 90 percent of American citizens who live abroad do not file federal income tax returns. Many people who do not owe a tax mistakenly believe they are not required to file a federal income tax return, even though they may have earned the requisite minimum amounts requiring them to file. Clyde Orr also believed that, living abroad, he was not required to file a federal income tax return. This "case" began as a result of an honest patriotic American who simply did not fully understand a complex area of tax law or the international understanding between Germany and our government about taxing resident non-citizens. In fact the government counsel, Andy Sobotka, also labored under many misconceptions regarding this difficult area of tax law and obtained instruction, direction, and advice from Clyde Orr's CPA, Thomas Snell.

We had stated that during the years that he lived in Germany, Orr did not file federal income tax returns. Upon his return to the United States, Captain Orr retained an American CPA, Thomas Snell, to prepare his federal income tax returns. The CPA informed him that he would also be required to file returns for the previous years that he had not filed; and that there would be some tax debt. He was retained by Orr to achieve full compliance.

An Internal Revenue Service agent and Orr's CPA began negotiations and number crunching. "Number crunching" is a term used for calculating all taxes due, interest received, penalties, and credits. A "numbers cruncher" is any person, such as a CPA, trained in doing these calculations. In math calculations, two mathematicians will inevitably reach the same conclusions. In tax calculations, some of the decisions are subjective and the numbers usually will differ. In this case, the two crunchers (one from the plaintiff, one from the government) were always very close. These two tried to determine what amount, if any, Clyde Orr owed from his previous negligence in not filing while living abroad.

In 1993, an agreement and final resolution was about to be entered into when, without warning, without justification, and without timely notice (notice of seizure is required by federal law unless there is a jeopardy assessment or unless an outstanding warrant has been entered against the taxpayer), Orr was deprived of his life savings, when his retirement fund was seized.

Clyde Orr had a venture annuity account with North American Security Life Insurance Company. On October 29, 1993, the Commissioner of Internal Revenue Service levied the sum of $426,418 from his account and claimed that it was all due the federal government for delinquent taxes! Orr's CPA and the Internal Revenue Service had already come to an understanding about the amount of money, which totaled $17,157, that was due from Clyde Orr to the Internal Revenue Service. The figures were broken down as follows:

Tax Year	Amount Owed According To Tax Return	Amount Seized in IRS Levy
1985	$2,006	$14,897
1986	$7,214	$44,623
1987	$ (501)	$92,955

1988	$5,603	$88,075
1989	$1,527	$95,352
1990	$1,308	$90,517
TOTAL	$17,157	$426,418

On June 17, 1994, Clyde Orr's CPA made a formal claim for refund to the Internal Revenue Service seeking return of the amount wrongfully seized based on the tax returns. On June 23, 1994, the Internal Revenue Service denied Orr's claim for a refund—without explanation.

The difference between these figures and the ones "agreed upon" at the "last final agreement" nearly two years later was less than the likely value of the plane tickets and the trees cut down for the paper generated by the government's discovery efforts.

Not only did Clyde Orr lose his life savings in order to pay a non-existent tax debt; but he also was charged with early withdrawal penalties under the account with the insurance company in the sum of $21,545. He was subjected to the federal early withdrawal penalty of 10 percent which was $42,641; plus he would be required to pay taxes on the money in the year it was seized if there wasn't a settlement agreement!

In short, a fifty-eight-year-old Vietnam War hero and lifetime loyal citizen and taxpayer of the United States, for his failure to report and pay about $17,000 in income taxes (admittedly through his negligence, which was due to his failure to completely and fully understand the Internal Revenue Service Code and the Regulations), suffered severe federal retaliation. The government unilaterally, without warning and without cause seized over $426,000, creating an additional immediate tax liability of approximately $133,000, plus substantial penalties. He also suffered the emotional trauma of being well off one day and comparatively indigent the next day. As a side note, but as a related side note, Clyde Orr was kept out of the stock market for the entire year of 1995, a year in which the stock market and most mutual funds (his money was fully invested) brought in approximately 35 percent.

Nancy Spotter, Chief of the IRS Special Procedures Branch, in a June 23, 1994, letter denied the refund claim and advised Captain Orr that he had nine months to file suit for a refund or face permanent forfeiture of his money. Clyde Orr, pending the resolution of this matter, simply did not know how to proceed. He got behind on subsequent tax obligations.

On July 20, 1994, Captain Orr filed suit against the United States of America for a refund. An immediate request for mediation was made and an immediate request to open a dialogue was made. For reasons unknown and even after the discovery motions, perhaps unknowable, the United States government proceeded to defend its unreasonable position in this case based primarily on two entirely frivolous theories, which it pretended to the court it thought its research might demonstrate, those being to-wit: (1) That Orr was not a German resident during the tax years in questions; and (2) That he had received refunds for the tax years in question in Germany. The alleged refunds were money he sought deductions for. The government also disallowed credit for withholding it had received from Orr.

In April 1995, in a Motion for Summary Judgment, Clyde Orr swore under oath that he had, in fact, resided in Germany and that he had not received any refunds. The federal government's response was "...Defendant has undertaken efforts to obtain relevant documents from the German government...." The court felt the Motion to Deem Answers admitted was premature and denied Orr's Motion for Summary Judgment, but cautioned the government on April 27, 1995, in an Order of the Court that "...of course, if information comes into Defendant's possession, which renders a formal denial of a request no longer viable, relief under Rule 37(c)(2) may be appropriate."

At the time that the government made these representations of possibilities to the court, the representations were false. Clearly with the exercise of a minimum amount of due diligence, the government would have been in a position to acknowledge this. Why? First, the government had its own official records proving that Clyde Orr had been a resident of Germany. The government knew that Clyde Orr had received permission from the federal government to use the German base in Berlin as an American citizen domiciled in Germany, as well as other information detailed above. The federal government had copies of the W-2 forms demonstrating that money had been taken from Clyde Orr and sent to the federal government by Pan Am.

The tax treaty in effect between the Federal Republic of Germany and the United States of America allowed for a treatment by which Clyde Orr would pay 26 percent of his income earned as a German resident directly to the German government, but accepting that, which he did, the law forbade him from filing a German tax return or even requesting a refund. The federal government knew or should have known that Clyde Orr was a resident of Germany and further, that Clyde Orr could not have received a refund from the German government even if he had attempted to do so.

Let us say, for the sake of argument (presuming a reasonable person could accept the position of the government at any time), once Orr was deposed and produced additional documentation, the government's continued argument constituted an unbalanced examination of the facts.

The Deposition

Clyde Orr offered to fly into the office of his counsel and made the following offer: After the deposition his number cruncher would be available at the beck and call of the government, with the corresponding offer that the Internal Revenue Service would provide its number cruncher. In the event that the government counsel was convinced Orr had been telling the truth and had not fabricated the overwhelming documentation (such as letters, passport, and leases), then the complete settlement could be worked out, all the figures translated, and the appropriate refund made and given.

Unfortunately, at the last minute, Sobotka reneged and did not bring a representative from the Internal Revenue Service to help with the numbers. The deposition still proceeded, and on June 16, 1995, the deposition was taken at 9:30 AM. Orr unilaterally complied, and Snell was available and utilized by Sobotka for approximately six hours.

Before the deposition, I reminded Mr. Sobotka that while the court had denied Clyde Orr's Request for Admissions and Motion for Summary Judgment, the court had nevertheless issued what was tantamount to a stern warning, that the court would consider sanctions under Rule 37(c)(2) if the government failed to admit at a later date after an appropriate time to get information.

Clyde Orr had already stated under oath that he had been a resident of Germany. If Clyde Orr were not telling the truth to his government, that would be an act of perjury. Nevertheless, even though the government was still implying that this decorated war veteran had lied under oath, no Fifth Amendment rights were asserted, in fact they were specifically waived. A representation was made by me saying, "I'll quit practicing law if the government is able to prove that he was lying in that regard, do you follow? That's what I'm telling you and I'm saying that on the record too." I was frustrated by the delays and expense, and so were the CPA and Orr.

Sobotka, after an off-the-record discussion in which I requested that this case be wrapped up, that copies of the deposition be provided free to Captain Orr, and that both sides cooperate in order to conserve resources, conceded and replied, "Since it appears that you are trying to be cost-conscious...." (Sobotka did not keep his word to provide a copy of the deposition. Orr had to purchase one.)

Orr discussed a notarized statement by Elke Furck, Flight Administrator for Internal German Service for Pan American Airways in Berlin who ran the operation over there. Her notarized statement confirmed that Orr was based in Berlin from August 16, 1986, until March 31, 1991, and that he was registered in Berlin and Germany.

Orr also testified that: "At that time, if you were a resident, you had to register with the local police, where your apartment was, your address and so forth. You had to have a residency stamp put into your passport.... I was subject to German income taxes."

A letter, which had already been submitted to the government, was resubmitted as an Exhibit to the deposition at the request of the government and testified from. The letter was dated June 7, 1995, from Adele Askin, System Director of Benefits and Personnel Programs from Pan American World Airways. It also confirmed Orr's residency.

However, Sobotka then went on to ask a plethora of absolutely irrelevant questions (in addition to the ones that had completely proved the case for residency in the years in question). Most of these questions were irrelevant invasions of privacy. Documenting all of these would require a review of the entire deposition but a few excerpts will give you an idea of the abuse of the legal system by the prosecutor.

Sobotka: I don't know if this has anything to do with your case, but it's just a matter of curiosity that I have to satisfy myself with. Would there be any reason why your name would be on a sign or placard outside of an apartment in Germany today?

Orr: Well, I still maintain a relationship with the people. As a matter of fact, there is one German girl who is a German girl-friend and I still keep clothes over there, but that's just so if I go over to Germany and see her, I don't have to pack heavy.

Sobotka: So you do go back to Germany on occasion?

Orr: Since 1991, I have been back once, so not very often.

Sobotka: You are not actually leasing an apartment there? (Since this is not one of the years in question, since he was not claiming that he currently lived there, and since he had already testified over and over again and produced redundant information to prove that he had lived there through 1991 until leaving, this line of questioning seemed bizarre.)

224

Sobotka: This is going to show my ignorance, but I don't even know if the German people can vote at this time, so were you registered to vote in Germany while you were there?

Orr: No, you can't vote. They can. I can't.

Sobotka: They can, you can't.

Minns: I don't think a non-citizen can vote in any country.

Sobotka: So you didn't take any steps to actually become a citizen of Germany?

Orr: Oh, no.

The government's inquiry into whether or not Clyde Orr sought to become a German citizen demonstrates why we had the earlier off-the-record exchange, requesting that the government get to the heart of the matter and quit wasting taxpayer resources and Clyde Orr's resources. The entire exchange was an invasion of Mr. Orr's privacy and completely irrelevant.

Under a meandering quixotic interrogation, Clyde Orr stated that he was a loyal American citizen, that he was a card-carrying Republican, that he made donations to the Republican party, that he did not attempt to deduct them (There is no effort to deduct any of them on any of his tax returns.), and that he had no intention of becoming a German citizen. Rather than an inquiry as to whether or not he had lived in Germany from 1986 to 1991, the deposition transcended into a McCarthyesque-type of interrogation, which seemed to border on questioning Captain Orr's patriotism. Only Mr. Sobotka can explain the mental conclusions, observations, and goals that he was pursuing. While only Mr. Sobotka can answer those questions, a fifth grader could read the deposition and tell that they had no bearing on the lawsuit.

Sobotka: You have already told me you did not get involved in politics. Did you make any campaign contributions to any German politicians?

225

Orr: No.

Sobotka: What about contributions to political campaigns in the United States during that time period?

Orr: Quite possibly. I have always been a Republican support-er so I may have made political contributions to a political party of my choice. (This was just more redundant questioning, so I stepped in.)

Minns: Is that an issue that could be relevant in this case?

Sobotka: I think it goes to show on the question of tax home and things of that kind, place of abode and intent, things of that nature.

Minns: I'd have to disagree, but I'm not going to object. You can ask the question. He wanted to remain an American. He has always intended to return to the United States. These are not negative...."

As the deposition continued ad nauseam, Sobotka re-asked the same questions he had earlier asked about Pan American Airlines and the 26 percent German income tax and Elke Furck.

By some miracle, near the conclusion of the deposition, Sobotka stumbled into a relevant question. (Of course, he already had the answer sworn to on an Affidavit.)

Sobotka: Have you ever filed any sort of claim for a refund with the German tax authorities?

Orr: No, I have not.

That was the only question in the nearly six-hour deposition rel-evant to the second point addressed by the court. The deposition of Clyde Orr is interesting from a social aspect and it is also interesting from an aspect of examining government waste, but it was not inter-esting or necessary with regard to the lawsuit. It is helpfully redundant on the two subjects that the court addressed in its initial denial of Clyde Orr's Motion for Summary Judgment and in its insistence that the government obey the rules of evidence. If they found reason to change their position regarding these issues, they should have changed their Request for Admission answers.

No one, not even an indentured lifetime government bureaucrat, or a fifth grader (following the deposition and stacks of previously given and newly demonstrated exhibits), could have failed to admit that Clyde Orr was a resident of Germany from 1986 through 1991; but the government did!

As the Motion was drafted in March 1996, the government had still failed to revise its non-admission of this fact. Rather than file an additional Motion with the court and rather than fight, now that there was clearly no room for dispute of any kind whatsoever, I mistakenly continued to advise Orr to attempt to cooperate and negotiate. The CPA and Sobotka spent an entire day going over every single figure to make certain that there was an agreement to the penny. Private counsel and private CPA services expended approximately ten hours, respectively, in addition to all prior work, in order to educate Mr. Sobotka in the relevant nuances of the tax code. Mr. Sobotka, although he had previously agreed, failed to bring with him a number cruncher from the Internal Revenue Service.

On or about December 1, 1994, the parties each had filed a "joint" report concerning settlement discovery and case management. Letters were exchanged and attempts were made to satisfy the nebulous requirements of the government counsel, Sobotka. Following the deposition of Orr, the lapse of time made it painfully obvious that the promised cooperation and settlement was not about to occur. A rough draft of a Motion to Expand Discovery was prepared. The government had achieved all of its discovery, but Clyde Orr had agreed to postpone taking his discovery. Captain Orr's discovery would primarily have consisted of accumulating evidence as to the unreasonableness of the government's position by proving the government had violated

Rule 37(c)(2) because it had sufficient information and knowledge to admit or deny the Request for Admissions even before the lawsuit was filed. Furthermore, Orr would prove that the entire case was frivolous because the numbers had been substantially agreed to before the seizure, and would give rise to the potential for attorney's fees against the government at the statutory rate of seventy-five dollars per hour.

At this point and time, Snell and Sobotka had another complete and full agreement (the Internal Revenue Service had already come to a complete and full agreement) since the filing of the lawsuit. It was the opinion, fostered by Sobotka, that Sobotka's superiors had been unreasonable and had been the cause for the delay of the settlement. Nevertheless, we needed to move the case forward. Later Sobotka blamed Congress and then the shortage of co-workers and bad working conditions for lack of a prompt settlement.

History of Bad Faith Negotiations and Delays

The best evidence of the history of negotiating in bad faith, absurd delays, and poor conduct of the government is demonstrated by the correspondence, which was sometimes answered but often ignored and unanswered between the two parties. Most of the communications (with the exception of the time that the government was temporarily closed down), are between myself, as counsel for Orr, and Sobotka, acting as government counsel. It is my opinion that Sobotka was signing correspondence for other persons in the government, pretending to be the author, and I stated that this might or might not have to be determined at an evidentiary hearing of the court. What was certain was, that to that date, the government had delayed settlement.

Nearly all of these communications follow the June 16, 1995, deposition of Clyde Orr. Some pre-date it, but help explain the flow of events.

In a letter of April 7, 1995, I requested that the government agree to the Admissions. In a letter of May 4, 1995, from Mr. Sobotka I accepted an excuse for not responding to my letter. In letter of May 3,

1995, we informed opposing counsel of our understanding of German law. This was never responded to. The government never represented to the court that German law did allow for a refund.

In a letter of May 5, 1995, I requested that Mr. Sobotka tender to us the mysterious information from Germany that Mr. Orr did not pay taxes (referred to in the letter of May 4, 1995, from Mr. Sobotka). The case was allegedly settled and this information was never given. The reason? There was no such information.

In a letter of June 1, 1995, two weeks before the deposition, essentially, I told Sobotka, "you have never given us your evidentiary theory of the case except that you find Mr. Orr's position to be suspicious."

In a letter of government response of June 1, 1995, which purported to be signed by Louise Hytken [who allegedly was Andy Sobotka's supervisor], for the first time in the litigation, the government was now stating, "...we wholly disagree with your contention that it is undisputed that your client is entitled to a refund, and that only the computation numbers remains to be determined...." (Later this was re-conceded in October 1995, but Orr had not benefited from the concession.) "Finally, with regard to establishing a new date to meet and discuss settlement, we are willing to meet with you sometime in the next two weeks, however, we would have to discount any settlement offer for the fact that we have not yet completed our discovery on the various issues of this case. Accordingly, we suggest that a settlement meeting for sometime in early July is appropriate." In other words, the government was going to have the deposition June 16, and wait until July to begin settlement negotiations.

On June 6, 1995, we sent the government a letter of the secretary of the chief pilot demonstrating that Clyde Orr had lived in Berlin. On June 7, 1995, we received a Pan Am letter from Adele Askin, which was forwarded to the government and later attached as an exhibit to Clyde Orr's deposition on June 16. On June 7, 1995, we received a letter from Elke Furck demonstrating Clyde Orr had been based in Germany. Also on June 7, 1995, I sent a letter to Sobotka enclosing the information and attempting to set up the deposition at a time requested by the government indicating that I had called Sobotka again but had not heard back from him.

A June 14, 1995, letter from Louise Hytken (which may have been signed by Andy Sobotka) confirming that they will take the deposition but breaking the spirit of the agreement, letting us know that Sobotka was not bringing the revenue agent to the party. This was after Sobotka agreed to bring a number cruncher to the deposition and after Clyde Orr had gone through scheduling himself and his CPA to come to the deposition and all the expense that it entailed.

At this point in time, travel could not be economically stopped for Captain Orr (he had already re-scheduled and was off flight duty), and so the deposition took place, although it was set originally based on the assumption that we would be settling the entire case that day if we could convince the government that Captain Orr was not lying to them.

All of the following communications took place after the June 16, 1995, deposition.

My letter of June 28, 1995, that expresses the belief that the case is ready to be wrapped up (again) and that Snell and Sobotka have finished and that there is nothing left to do. The agreement was essentially the following:

(1) We conceded some penalties the government was arguably not entitled to collect in order to make the agreement go through expeditiously;

(2) We would waive any rights for attorney's fees for the frivolous position of the government and sanctions indicated as a possibility by the court;

(3) Clyde Orr would have sixty days after receipt to return his money back into a retirement account so that he would not receive the full early withdrawal penalty, and the tax obligations would then be abated until the money was taken out of said account. In other words, he would be put back in the position he was in before the seizure, except all taxes would be paid.

230

During the long discussions, delays and arguments and the government's "discovery," additional taxes had accrued. Captain Orr would pay those taxes by letting the government keep that amount. The disputed amount was in the neighborhood of one hundred thousand dollars of which approximately eighty-three thousand dollars had to do with funds that accrued after the seizure years in question and were unrelated to the case itself. (Except that without the case, they would never have been seized. The government had no authority to hold funds without an assessment.)

My July 13, 1995, letter where Orr requested the deposition of Charles Yahne and Shelley Prebble (the IRS number crunchers). Since the government had not settled the case and had not gone forth in good faith, even though the case had ostensibly been settled, it seemed necessary to go forward with a trial.

Captain Orr received a response allegedly signed by Louise Hytken (even though the letter had gone to Andy Sobotka). The response, unlike the government's previously slow responses, was sent out immediately, and threatened Orr with the termination of settlement negotiations if discovery continued. Since Orr had no money in hand and no final written settlement (only one that was promised), it made no sense and Captain Orr did not understand why he should not proceed forward to trial. It appears that Louise Hytken never saw, read, or proofread the letter or "her" response. It may have been drafted, prepared, and signed by Andy Sobotka, doing business as Hytken, i.e., his boss.

On August 17, 1995, we went to court and were issued the Court Mediation Order. Even though the parties had ostensibly settled there was no written settlement agreement and there appeared to be a complete halt to the process until the court ordered mediation. Ironically, the court ordered mediation after a settlement had ostensibly been made. Then Sobotka requested that mediation be postponed.

The delay of the mediation was not opposed with one proviso. That being, that the day for mediation would be used in an all day session with the number crunchers and Sobotka to hammer out a settlement since there were no remaining significant contested issues except adding up and subtracting the actual numbers. There was a small amount of potential negotiations on some of the penalties. Most of these were conceded to the government in an effort to settle the case. Again, Sobotka broke his word and failed to bring Shelley Prebble, the government number's cruncher. It should be noted that all meetings via phone with Snell and Prebble were productive, efficient and polite. Sobotka seemed to dislike this and appeared to keep the two experts apart.

On or about November 29, 1995, the government represented to the court that the case had been settled and that the parties would submit the dismissal documents once a check had been issued to Clyde Orr. The November 29, 1995, letter from Louise Hytken, purported to be prepared by Louise Hytken, is believed to have been prepared and signed by Andy Sobotka.

A December 13, 1995, letter of mine was a reminder to Sobotka that he had approved a settlement and the figures for December 2, 1995, and that nearly two more weeks had passed and there was no check and no closing statement.

Sobotka had decided that the program should be engineered in three stages: (1) Settle the issues on the years in question in the suit; (2) Settle the future tax issues; (3) Secure the agreement of the district director for permission to put the money back, without penalty, into a retirement account. I felt all three were necessary. A weary Captain Orr just wanted an end to the litigation; but Orr could have taken his money back and then had the future years reviewed. Sobotka apparently planned step one and then intended to avoid steps two and three, leaving Orr in limbo.

Although we were skeptical, we relied on Sobotka in good faith again. My letter of December 18, 1995, demonstrates our concern with the government's position. Sobotka had indicated that he had given the district director the closing statement and was waiting for it to be signed. Clyde Orr was desperate to get his tax situation resolved before the close of the calendar year 1995, since he had lost the entire year's interest on his funds and was afraid he'd lose even more. Everyone was led to believe that a resolution would occur. Sobotka had been complaining about the stress and the possibility of a government close down and blamed the Congress of the United States on his failure to proceed.

On December 21, 1995, I sent a letter to Sobotka, which was essentially the same as the December 18, 1995 letter that had not been responded to. There was a concern that it had not been received during the alleged shutdown confusion. Apparently, while Sobotka was working for the government, the December 18 letter never reached anybody, but when he was gone, the December 21 reproduction of the December 18 letter reached somebody and was responded to by somebody on behalf of Louise Hytken. It is the height of irresponsible conduct to have a civil servant signing something for someone else and not letting anyone know who actually signed it. How could Louise Hytken know who's signing for her? How can we know who is signing for her? In fact, you could not even locate the typist because the government in these letters generally leaves off the initials of the person who typed the letters. We perceived that most of them were created and typed by Sobotka. There is a code at the top of the December 22, 1995, letter from Louise Hytken that says, LCA:LPH:ALSobotka:jh. We can only speculate as to what that means. It may mean that Mr. Sobotka actually created it and signed it and just said that he was on furlough and not even in the office.

The government on December 22, 1995, when we asked whether they would oppose an entry of judgment and to set the record straight, opposed all of our potential motions. The letter complained that I did not respond to the court, informing the court that the settlement had not been completed, even though representation was made by the government that it had been completed.

There was no reason to embarrass Louise Hytken or embarrass

Andy Sobotka in court if the case was going to be settled shortly after the false representation of the government that it had been settled. The letter has a lot of other inaccurate statements that were addressed in my follow-up letter.

Another letter from Louise Hytken also dated December 22, 1995, stated that "we are transmitting with a notice of adjustment a treasury check in the amount of $189,900.48." The proviso was that we would dismiss our case with prejudice (i.e., end the case and bar all further litigation on the case). Unfortunately, this would not settle the case. The correct sum, even construing all the figures in favor of the Internal Revenue service was nearly $300,000. The attached Notice of Adjustment and the figures by the government indicated incorrectly a figure of $225,000 to be paid to Clyde Orr. In other words, the government stated that they should only have to pay back $225,000 and that they wanted a judgment entered dismissing the case with prejudice for a sum of only $189,900.48. We could trust them for the balance.

Contrary to the government's express written assertions to both the court and to us, the correct sums of money were not finally and fully agreed upon by the close of the calendar year 1995. The two other items, namely the closing agreement and the decision as to what amount, if any, would be allowed to be retained by the government for subsequent tax years had not been made. The year 1995 closed without the case being concluded. My office was closed on December 22, 1995, until January 2, 1996. (This fact had been previously relayed to Sobotka.) There was no way of knowing when the December 22, 1995, transmittal arrived, but it was waiting at the office when the office reopened.

A response was made January 3, 1996, to the government's letter and the check was returned to the government. The government's letter included a personal attack. A request was made to clarify the unsolicited personal attack. Two days later, I learned that the government had reopened the case and so on January 5, 1996, another request was made for answers. I noted that in nineteen years of practicing law, settlement discussions and negotiations had never continued this long after an alleged settlement had already been entered into. At this point in time, all the figures had again been agreed to but for some reason, the District Director claimed he had not received the closing agreement that Sobotka represented had been on the Director's desk since the previous year.

In fact, Snell contacted the District Director's office directly and asked about it and he was told they had no evidence of ever receiving the closing statement that had allegedly been given to them quite some time ago by Sobotka.

Rather than accept a facsimile of the settlement agreement, the government demanded that a new typed original be delivered by Federal Express to them. Compliance was made by copy of the letter of January 9, 1996. It was faxed first, hoping that this would be more efficient, so that if they wanted to change it in any way again, they would be able to notify me by the end of the day. I was in the office all day January 10, 1996.

Snell was notified January 10, 1996, that the agreement that had already been drawn up to the government's detailed specifications should be altered to read District Director on the signature line instead of Commissioner of Internal Revenue. The government refused to do this and demanded that we deliver the change by Federal Express. The request was immediately honored.

The closing agreement, which had been sent several times now, after Sobotka had been bypassed and the information given directly to the District Director, was again rejected with more changes requested.

My letter of January 16, 1996, in which I practically begged the government to call before delivering the agreement by overnight express again. I called them immediately upon faxing the January 16, 1996, letter but as was their custom, the call was not accepted.

In a January 18, 1996, letter we were told that the change from

235

District Director to Commissioner of Internal Revenue Service back to District Director needed to be changed back again to Commissioner of Internal Revenue Service, the same as the first time that we had sent it! It had to be delivered by Federal Express again. This time we decided that it was impossible to comply with the government's compulsive mood modification without retaining local counsel. (My office has worked in New Jersey, New York, Arkansas, Hawaii, Alaska, Oklahoma, Arizona, Delaware, Philadelphia, Massachusetts, and other places by facsimile, and without local counsel, for this type of transmission, but it was not possible in this case.)

On January 18, 1996, we informed the government we had hired local counsel in the Dallas/Ft. Worth area to do the typing. After retaining local counsel to type and retype and send by messenger service and re-send by messenger whatever the government wanted, and then flying Captain Orr back to Dallas *twice* to re-sign the closing statement with the District Director, the closing statement was signed on January 19, 1996, by the Commissioner (through an agent).

On January 26, 1996, I again asked Sobotka if he would give a date by which we would have our refund. He decided some of the figures on unrelated tax years needed examination.

We also asked him to send a new dismissal with prejudice accompanying the check. Obviously, we did not want to have an argument as to what papers should be signed in order to accept the check. We had already sent a package by Federal Express changing District Director to Commissioner, Commissioner back to District Director, and District Director back to Commissioner as the Internal Revenue Service yo-yo bounced us up and down. In the alternative, a Motion to Compel Entry of a Judgment was offered and an inquiry, as to whether the government opposed it, was made.

Louise Hytken, the apparent nom de plume for Andy Sobotka, responded to the January 26, 1996, letter with a January 29, 1996, letter saying that they would oppose our Motion for Sanctions, that they would counter the Motion with a similar request for sanctions, and finally requesting another delay until such time; your patience and cooperation are appreciated."

I responded to Louise Hytken's alleged letter of January 29, 1996, with my own letter of January 29, 1996, and in a last ditch effort to settle the case without a Motion, I sent a letter on January 31, 1996. It requested a decision, a time, and an answer summarizing some problems that had occurred over nearly two years of litigation over issues that were uncontested. Six patient weeks had transpired since January 31, 1996 on what was supposed to be an agreed-upon settlement. During those six weeks, Sobotka had not answered my letter of January 31, 1996.

An additional month of negotiations transpired between Snell and Sobotka recalculating the figures. Very little of this time was spent actually recalculating the figures. The agent with the Internal Revenue Service, Ms. Prebble, was apparently efficient, and wrapped up the recalculated numbers again. The delays were due simply because, according to the agent and Snell, the papers apparently sat unattended on Sobotka's desk.

This was actually the first time that the CPA had indicated anything remotely showing loss of faith toward Mr. Sobotka's intentions. The relationship over the two-year period of time with the CPA and Mr. Sobotka was one of attempted continuous cooperation. However, Snell's February 26, 1996, letter indicated that the CPA had lost his patience too. At this point, I had not received a response, orally or in writing, in six weeks to the January 31, 1996 letter and was unaware of any written response to the CPA's February 26, 1996, letter.

The Mediation History

The deposition of Clyde Orr occurred on June 16, 1995. At the time, it seemed plausible for settlement to have been effected that day and later at least within the next two weeks and, in fact, Sobotka had encouraged us to expect that. Nevertheless, it did not occur and separate joint status reports were filed on or about July 3, 1995. Sobotka, whose handwriting style is very similar to that of Ms. Hytken, stated, "...the parties have met and are presently discussing settlement amount and figures. Settlement is still likely and favored." One might wonder why it takes two weeks to discuss settlement amounts and figures, especially since the process had been ongoing more than two years prior to and during litigation. Meanwhile, the damages to Clyde Orr were not being discussed.

Following the court ordered mediation of August 17, 1995, contact was made with Sobotka in order to obey the court's order. So I sent a letter on August 23, 1995 to try to settle. No settlement had been effected and Sobotka gave no response to the mediation order of the court or responded to the letter; so I sent an additional letter on September 1, 1995. Sobotka then responded, requesting additional time to mediate. In the government's Motion they noted that they were reviewing Orr's formal offer of settlement. They failed to note that they had been reviewing it for well over a year. As an excuse they indicated that "review is not presently familiar with the facts in this case and, therefore, will need to be fully briefed on this case so that it can make informed decisions during mediation." One might ask why were they not familiar with the case? In any event, in the spirit of cooperation, the Motion by the government was unopposed.

Sobotka failed to return several phone calls and so it was necessary to tentatively set up the mediation process unilaterally, which I did in a letter of September 6, 1995. A qualified Mediator agreed to mediate and Sobotka finally returned a phone call and agreed to it. Although the government did make an agreement to pay for the lost time of Judge Clark, the mediator, the government never made any payment.

The mediation rules Judge Clark utilized required a summary. Orr sent this summary in a letter to Judge Clark of September 7, 1995. On that same date, the court granted the extension requested by the government to October 31, 1995. Since we did not have written confirmation of the new date, a letter was sent to Sobotka on October 16,

1995, asking for communication guaranteeing that the government would show up on October 24, 1995, for mediation. After agreeing to have the mediation on October 19, 1995, and obtaining a commitment by Judge Clark to be available, Sobotka requested a new time for the mediation and accordingly, the mediation was rescheduled for a third time to October 27, 1995. Four months had passed since the government had represented to the court that they were considering the settlement offer of Clyde Orr.

Finally, the mediation was put off altogether because Mr. Sobotka agreed (orally) on all the terms and conditions of settlement on or about October 27, 1995, after another all-day work session. The difference between the first settlement offer of Clyde Orr and the last settlement request and offer accepted by the government probably spans less than ten thousand dollars. The cost to Clyde Orr was several thousands of dollars in legal time, plus approximately one hundred fifty thousand dollars in lost revenues from the use of his mutual fund account during the calendar year of 1995.

The costs to the government was approximately twenty-four thousand dollars [8 percent of three hundred thousand dollars non-refunded money], plus legal fees and time. No member of the private sector under any circumstances, unless they were making an important legal point, an important principal of law, or an important moral point, would have wasted so many resources of both the government and the taxpayer. Any individual who ran a law practice that way would go out of business. Any corporate counsel who managed his corporate records in that way would be fired if the corporation survived his stewardship.

Sanctions should have been levied against the government counsel and the government for this type of conduct and these sanctions would ultimately inure to the benefit of the government. It would send a message that extreme government abuse and waste is not good. In litigation with the government, both sides must obey the rules! The whole court-ordered mediation process was avoided through subterfuge.

Requested Relief

When we went to court, Captain Orr respectfully requested that the pleadings of the government be stricken. This would enable him to receive the full amount of the seized money, plus interest. It would also enable Clyde Orr to prove up attorney's fees at the rate of seventy-five dollars per hour. There are no attorneys in federal court who charge as little as seventy-five dollars per hour in the State of Texas. The statutory allowable rate does not fully compensate a petitioner.

The complete and full recovery of the seized money would not make Clyde Orr whole. The striking of the pleadings would, however, allow the court to enter an Order that would promote as much justice as Clyde Orr could obtain under the existing statutes. As the alternative, but without waiving the foregoing requested relief, Clyde Orr requested that the court enter a judgment pursuant to the previously signed agreements of the parties, that a hearing be set, and that all of the signed documents be brought together for the court's immediate attention and interpretation. The parties were approximately four thousand dollars apart and Clyde Orr, would probably have been willing to have waived this, but since he had no settlement anyway (since the January 31, 1996, letter had gone unanswered for six weeks), he wanted the court to enter a judgment. Because of the enormous unnecessary delays, because of the violation of the federal rules and the local rules, because of the violation of the spirit of the court's mediation orders, and because of the dishonesty implied by the letters in the transactions that occurred, Orr felt that attorney's fees should be awarded and accounting fees should be awarded for all of the work done and committed in this case on his behalf.

As an alternative, if the court found that the case was not settleable prior to the discovery gained by the government in Clyde Orr's deposition on June 16, 1995, then all attorney's fees and accounting fees incurred following that day should be awarded against the government.

The case was finally settled by a refund of all money, interest, and penalties, and allowed the taxpayer to reinvest without penalty in a retirement fund. The court then ruled the issue moot and denied sanctions. Effectively, Clyde Orr got his money back, but the prosecutor got away with making his life hell for over two years for no discernable reason other than the prosecutor had the power to do so based on his assessment of Orr as "suspicious."

Chapter IX
Fred Ferber v. Rodney King

Few in public affairs act from a mere view of the good of their country, whatever they may pretend... fewer still in public affairs act with a view to the good of mankind.

—Benjamin Franklin

There really was a Rodney King and of course there really was a Fred Ferber. Fred was a tall thin Anglo artist. One of those talented guys who writes music, plays some music, writes lyrics, and thinks like an artist but hasn't hit. You've met these guys. On the whole you like them. They are smart, witty, fun, and usually good friends. Fred wrote jingles for songs and advertisements. He was happily married. Rodney was a big black man who hurt people. He was a criminal.

Fred had one real problem and one potential problem. The real problem was that the IRS wanted a million dollars from Fred that he didn't have. The potential problem was that his trial took place in the same courthouse as Rodney King. You could not go into a courthouse or talk about law from 1993 to 1996 without talking about Rodney King and O. J. Simpson.

On the day the O. J. Simpson verdict came in, I was in a trial in Cleveland, Ohio. It was time to give closing arguments. The judge and the jury were more interested in the O. J. verdict. Our judge told the jury that he wasn't like Judge Ito, the jurist in the King trial. It was a national obsession with many judges in America that they openly displayed their hostility towards Ito. They frequently let lawyers and jurors know that they weren't like Ito. They wouldn't let their case drag on forever. Some then proceeded to stop you from putting evidence in, just to show you and the jury that trials didn't drag on in their courts. (In Cleveland this was not the case. Our judge was very fair with both sides on the admission of evidence.).

Rodney King was beaten up in Los Angeles by several cops. However, one of the cops on the video (which nearly everyone in America saw) tried to protect King by pushing his head down. This cop was also indicted and he was found not guilty twice.

Essentially the Fifth Amendment, among other protections, was intended to shield people against double jeopardy. You could not be tried twice for the same crime. The federal government arbitrarily decided that many crimes were both state crimes and federal crimes. Therefore, if you got tried in both courts for the same thing it was all right as long as the names of the crimes were different. (The federal government called it a civil rights violation; California called it battery; hence, two different crimes, so there were two different trials.) Two cops appeared to be very guilty. They were found not guilty the first time and guilty the second time. OK. It is sad for anyone to be destroyed (not killed, but emotionally wiped out like in a big divorce, or going through lots of trials, or disease, or amputation) but if they are guilty of a crime, perhaps society can get on and forget that the rules weren't followed. My question is about the officer who risked his life to try (albeit only briefly) to stop the ruckus and was indicted twice. He was clearly innocent and found innocent twice. Does anyone care about his life being ruined? I guess not. I never heard anything about that on talk shows or in the courts.

One of my clients, Rap-a-Lot Records, Inc., released a record called F___(The F does not stand for Free) Rodney King that is critical of the guy. This took a lot of guts for an African-American company to attack Rodney King. Personally, while I don't think police should beat up suspects, I am not convinced that it is a good idea to make suspects multi-millionaire poster heroes either. The best reports of King's past included brutality and drugs.

This story, however, is about Ferber. No trial is run in a vacuum. It is run in a courthouse and in a country with lots of other cases going on at the same time. Fred's case was tried at the same time and in the same courthouse as Rodney King's second trial. Fred and I were less concerned with whether or not the King defendants would be convicted (or maybe even have a third trial a la Buford) than whether Fred would be found guilty of tax fraud, but it is not possible for rational people to ignore the environment. With a jury, of course, it might mean much more than a judge, but judges are human too.

Fred was accused of being the trustee of a business called Para Technologies. He was the trustee. Para Technologies was accused of not paying taxes of about a million dollars. It hadn't paid taxes. Whether it owed taxes or not is not relevant here because this chapter is about Fred. He was one of three IRS targets in this case. We will avoid most of the details, unlike other chapters, because they are overly technical, have almost nothing to do with Fred Ferber or Rodney King, and are still being litigated in part. You'll only get an outline of the case.

The man who set up Para Technologies was Tom Anderson. Tom was another artist but also a phenomenal businessman who entered into a series of trusts to protect "Mr. Smith" his partner in Argentina whose name must remain fictitious. Judge Jacob, our trial judge, allowed the record on this name to be sealed and he chose the name Smith as a pseudonym in the trial. Fred never wrote a check for Para Technologies, never made one penny of income on the project, had little or nothing to do with management decisions, but the IRS want-

245

ed him to pay taxes on transactions that he did not even know took place.

A ninety-day letter went out to Tom Anderson, Para Technologies, and Fred Ferber demanding that each one of them pay the full demanded million dollars. It also claimed that each had committed fraud. All three, as well as the attorney previously representing Para Technologies, were also under criminal investigation. Judge Jacobs, during the trial told the IRS that they might convince him all three could be responsible, but that they could not convince him the three should pay a combined $3 million if the government was only claiming $1 million.

The trial began Wednesday March 24, 1993, in the towering modern glass structure in Los Angeles named the Edward R. Roybal Center and Federal Building on Temple Street. We were on floor eleven and Rodney King and the police officers were on another floor. Everyday we went through TV cameras and newspaper reporters. The metal-detection security system was turned up so high that the metal in shoes, the metallic strip in a credit card, or virtually anything would cause the machine to go buzzing off. You had to get into the courthouse early to get through the lines at the metal detector. Everyone of the members of the trial team were approached by one or more papers and TV cameras for interviews until they found out we had absolutely nothing to do with the King trial.

Following the first King trial, when the police were found not guilty, Los Angeles was turned into a billion-dollar destruction-and-murder war zone. This time L.A. was supposed to be prepared with extra cops on the streets and extra diligence, in case the jurors let them off again and the war erupted again. I don't think the founding fathers anticipated that free speech would mean killing people, looting stores, and setting fires in populated areas to protest a jury decision, and then have the government violate the spirit of the double-jeopardy clause by having a new trial with a new jury to get things right.

We were in the courthouse and unanimously of the opinion that it would be a good thing if we could be out of the courthouse and out of L.A. before the potential second human earthquake. No one of course could predict that the jury would do as they were told this time: convict, and thus avoid the necessity for another rampant crime wave as a protest.

The problem with our evacuation plan was a man named Burns. Paul Burns was the lawyer for the IRS. Paul had an oval Santa Claus build with a strange extra jut coming out of his gut almost like a bit of an unborn unicorn horn trying to decide if it should come out or not. He wore a General Grant beard, which covered his face, and he talked with a bit of a nervous tick. His associate, an attractive attorney, Maria Murphy, unfortunately put in second chair to Burns (this means he runs the case; she helps), seemed to be mostly window dressing. I don't recall her doing anything except getting yelled at by Burns. It's possible of course that she handled all of the pleadings. Paul talked down to her like a sailor talking to the girls waiting at the shore for tips and partying. It was embarrassing to all of us. In front of a jury it would have cost him dearly but we were not in front of a jury. We were in front of a judge. Burns turned a two or three hour trial into a *much* longer ordeal. Every tiny unimportant issue would be argued into the ground.

I had not prepared the case for trial. Another lawyer did. A decision had to be made whether to go to trial or to ask for extra preparation time. We made the decision to go forward because we were set before Judge Jacobs. On a re-set in tax court you usually get another judge. Jacobs may be the fairest Judge in tax court—so we kept him and risked being less prepared. My associate Helena Papadapolous, had worked the file 24/7 the month before, and as it turned out, her month of pre-trial work prepared us better than years of pre-trial work prepared Burns.

Tax court has no jury trials. The judge is both judge and jury. Judge Jacobs was simply a nice man and a scholar. No point of law

247

was beyond him and no argument rejected without at least some reasonable discussion. He also pretty much let you know what he was thinking. He was thinking that lawyers should be polite to each other and professional, something that Burns with his abrasive attitude had trouble with.

In tax court you have stipulations to most of the evidence that will be reviewed by the judge and so the trial is a lot quicker. To stipulate simply means to agree that information is correct and that exhibits are before the court. Did Para Technologies get money? Yes. Stipulated. In a criminal case you do less stipulating because the burden of proof is on the government. You do not have to prove anything. In a civil case, the burden of proof is on the client. (Due to the Restructuring and Reform Act of 1998 this is no longer strictly the case. Theoretically, the burden has now shifted to the IRS.) Also the rules do not generally require you to agree in a criminal case. (Although often the government and some judges push you to agree.) In tax court you are required to agree to anything that will be proven. It saves time. You also do not necessarily need the dramatic impact that a jury might expect. I have tried two cases against Burns and both times he would not stipulate to things that he was required to stipulate to. Both times it got the respective judge cross. With Jacobs, getting cross simply means a mild request for cooperation.

Burns was very aggressive. He asked permission to start his case with a motion *in limine*. Basically this motion is one where you ask a judge to make a ruling before trial about whether or not evidence will be allowed in. What is the legal reason? The evidence probably won't be allowed in and if the jury even hears it they will be so prejudiced that the trial may have to be started over. With a jury it makes a lot of sense if you are right—but with a judge? Basically Burns was saying, Judge, if you hear this during the trial you will be so prejudiced that the government will not get a fair trial, so hear it now. Burns's conversation with Judge Jacobs was a lot of fun. I'll share it with you, though I did not participate. Some of the best work a trial lawyer ever does, and some of the hardest, is just shutting up and letting something good happen.

> Burns: I believe, based on my review of the documents, that Petitioners intend to take the position that those documents are self-authenticating as foreign public documents under Rule 902 (3) of the Federal Rules of Evidence. If that is their position, they're wrong, and all of the documents should be excluded because they simply do not comply in two very material respects with the requirements of Rule 902 (3). As a preliminary matter

> The Court: Well, let me ask a question before we get into all this. Aren't you making a big to-do over nothing in this? It seems to me that assuming that there are trust documents and that these trust documents are what they say they are, the government still isn't going to accept the fact that this income is taxed to those trusts. You're basically saying that the income is taxed to the individuals.

So what is the big deal whether these trust agreements are in existence or not in existence? I believe they are in existence.... What's happening here is that I think we're losing sight of the big picture. The big picture is, is the income taxable to the trust, or is the trust a corporation and the income is really taxed to these taxpayers? That's what the government's arguing.

> Burns: Well, with all—with all due respect, Your Honor, I don't agree with the court's characterization of it as a—as a—as an unimportant issue....

> The Court: Well, I'm not going to do that. I'm going to allow testimony in. It seems to me that the taxpayers have to have an opportunity to present their case, and what you're trying to do is the same thing as in this motion, is just win by not giving them an opportunity to present a case.

249

Burns argument started on page nine of the transcript and continued to page twelve. I am not going to go into the merits of the case against Anderson and Para Technologies. It would take too long and the issues are not common enough for most people to have public interest.

Ferber's case, the one we are focused on, was on the side. The issue here, which started the trial, was whether we could put on evidence of the existence of the trust. I intended to offer the records under the business records rule. I think I would have been successful, but with Mr. Burns's complicated explanation being overruled, I used the rule he had come up with for me by anticipating my offer. The nuts and bolts of this case for purposes of the book center on Burns and his personal attack on Ferber, when he had no evidence whatsoever.

In this chapter you get the ending before the case. Ferber won completely. The case against Para Technologies was dropped completely. (Burns made this decision). Burns won a judgment against Anderson for the tax (but all of the assets had already gone to Para Technologies) and Burns lost on all issues of fraud. The purpose of this chapter is not the ends but the *means utilized by the IRS* against a person they knew owed no money. They sought a $1 million tax liability against a man, knowing that in a fair trial they had no chance of prevailing.

There was evidence for Burns to present on part of his case, and he did, winning a legal draw against a person with no assets. I cannot fault him for bringing a case in which he won even a portion of what he was asking for, but others may say it was just a waste of the taxpayer's money to do so. I do fault him for putting Fred Ferber on trial at all when he knew he had no evidence at all and no chance of getting a judgment against him. Trial, you see, is a horrible experience. Only a very sick individual would force someone to go through the procedure for the heck of it.

After interminable argument over silly issues, Burns began his case with his first witness, a bank official, Ms. Fanaris. Her purpose was ostensibly to prove that bank records existed. They did. I agreed and did not require them to prove that. However, Burns wanted to put her on anyway. After looking at the records he offered, it seemed to me something had been handled improperly. The signature cards had been altered. Fred didn't remember if he signed them or not. He did remember that he had never used them.

Barbara Fanaris, having been first duly sworn, was called as a witness herein, and was examined and testified as follows:

Mr. Burns: Ms. Fanaris, what is your occupation?

Ms. Fanaris: Operations officer.

Mr. Burns: And by whom are you employed?

Ms. Fanaris: City National Bank.

Mr. Burns: How long have you been employed as an operations officer for the City National Bank?

Ms. Fanaris: Thirteen years.

Mr. Burns: What are your duties as an operations officer for City National Bank?

Ms. Fanaris: Right now I am managing the subpoena-processing department for City National Bank worldwide. We take all legal process and answer them, and—

Mr. Burns: How long have you—how long have your duties included that function?

Mr. Minns: Excuse me, Your Honor, in the interest of time, may I inquire if this is authentication? We're not objecting to any authentication—or if there's another purpose for this witness? I'm just trying to speed this up, if there—

The Court: I'd appreciate that.

Mr. Burns: I understood, based on my conversations with Ms.

251

Papadopoulos, that they were objecting to the authenticity of the signature cards on the accounts. [Helena Papadopoulos was my second chair. Her work in pinning Burns down before trial was nothing short of outstanding, and deserves a chapter in another book. Burns would claim we had not given him information. Helena would prove we had.]

Mr. Minns: Absolutely not. We would stipulate that she would probably say that they are authentic, and they came from the bank. I could take her two questions on *voir dire*, and the two questions would be whether or not she knows how those scratch marks on the signature cards got there—[*Voir dire* is a legal term that means that the judge hears some issue of fact that the judge must rule on as a matter of law alone or that requires his initial determination.]

The Court: Why don't we—why don't we let him *voir dire* the witness, and if he can satisfy himself, maybe we can save some time.

Mr. Minns: Do we have those two signature cards? If I could just see—could I just see the four documents, the only ones disputed. And for the Court's information, so the court knows exactly where we're going, the word trustee was scratched out and someone put in the word partnership. That's the only reason we're going into this. Have the documents been put before the witness?

The Court: They have not, as yet. Why don't we have the clerk identify these and mark these for identification.

Mr. Burns: My apologies, Your Honor.

The Court: Why don't we have the clerk identify—just mark these documents for identification purposes?

Mr. Burns: We'll have copies for opposing counsel and the witness in just a moment, Your Honor.

The Court: Well, that'll be fine.

Mr. Minns: I'm sorry. In order to expedite this, Your Honor, if the court please, we won't need the copies right now. I can approach the witness with these and ask my three questions while I'm over there.

The Court: Well, that'll be fine.

Mr. Minns: I'm showing first to the witness what has been marked PC, and there appears to be a card here, and there appears to be stars on the right of that, which looks like something has been deleted.

Ms. Fanaris: No.

Mr. Minns: No?

Ms. Fanaris: Those stars indicate there are no further signatures on the account. Also, it's a self-protection for the bank, that nobody can add a signature.

Mr. Minns: OK. On PD, and correct me if I'm wrong, but it looks like something's been whited out, and stars appear to be placed on it. Does that look like it's been whited out?

Ms. Fanaris: Yes. But I couldn't tell you why.

Mr. Minns: All right.

Ms. Fanaris: To be perfectly honest with you, it looks like—it looks like somebody gave us incorrect information about titles to the signer, and then corrected it.

Mr. Minns: And who?

Ms. Fanaris: I would have to see the original signature card for this.

Mr. Minns: All right. Does the government have the original signature card here?

Ms. Fanaris: No, they wouldn't.

253

Mr. Burns: No, we do not. Our—these copies originate from copies that were obtained by the Internal Revenue Service in response to a summons—

Ms. Fanaris: Right.

Mr. Burns: ...that was served on the bank in 1990.

Mr. Minns: OK. Only asking questions. So based on that, and based on her inability, without the original, I would—

Ms. Fanaris: See, it looks like they gave us the information that Kevin—

Mr. Minns: When you say they—

Ms. Fanaris: Whoever set up this account.

Mr. Minns: Excuse me. We don't want guessing. Only things you know for certain.

Ms. Fanaris: Sorry. It appears that incorrect information was given to us by the party setting up this account, and the bank tried to correct it. Like I said, I can I'd have to see the original signature card.

Mr. Minns: Well, help me on this one. It is also equally possible that the bank accidentally typed the wrong material, and corrected their own error?

Ms. Fanaris: It's a possibility. I don't know.

Mr. Minns: And the other thing is this. The—apparently the error was putting anything there, since the whiteout whited something out, and the stars, and put nothing there at all.

Ms. Fanaris: I can't answer that. I'm sorry, I don't know.

Mr. Minns: And underneath that, there's a handwritten thing that says secretary by—

Ms. Fanaris: Right.

Mr. Minns: And who put that in, and when was it put in?

Ms. Fanaris: I have no idea. It would have to be at the time the account was set up.

Mr. Minns: OK. Let me ask you again this question, and please try to relax. Here it says Frederick Ferber, which is typed in, and by it, it has "partner."

Ms. Fanaris: Um-hum.

Mr. Minns: And those are two different typewriter strokes, are they not? It's not the same typewriter.

Mr. Burns: Objection, Your Honor. It calls for—it effectively calls for the witness to be an expert on typefaces.

Mr. Minns: No. A fifth grader could tell this, Your Honor, but if she can't, we'll certainly accept her answer.

The Court: I'll let her. Can you tell whether it's the same typewriter or not?

Ms. Fanaris: It does not appear to be; the E's are not the same.

Mr. Minns: So this delineation that we're worried about here is—which are the two things that are in different type from the balance of the paper—"partner"—do you know if they were put on at the time that these cards were signed, or later? [Were they trying to call Fred Ferber a partner instead of a trustee? Income to a partner might belong to him and not the trust. It was a curious anomaly. Why would the word "partner" be there and who put it there? I knew neither Tom Anderson nor Fred Ferber did. The signature cards had been altered after they were signed.]

Ms. Fanaris: I can't answer that.

Mr. Minns: OK.

The Court: But these documents did come from the bank records?

255

Ms. Fanaris: Yes, they did.

The Court: And these are the photocopies of the originals?

Ms. Fanaris: Yes. I'm sorry, I—

Mr. Minns: And again, on what is marked PE—And it doesn't appear to be a government number on here, as the next one does, but says account number 07-222-874. Again, in a different type, there's the word "partner" by the names Tom Anderson and Kevin Ireland—and it's in different typewriter. Is that correct?

Ms. Fanaris: Yeah. I see what you're saying.

Mr. Minns: I have no objection to that. I don't want them to be entered with the words "partner" on there, and if the words "partner" are being entered, Your Honor, then—

The Court: Well, the word "partner" would be in the original document, would it not?

Mr. Minns: That's correct, Your Honor.

The Court: But the point of it is, we don't know when it was typed in.

Mr. Minns: That's correct, Your Honor. [It seems that Burns still wanted to imply a partnership that did not exist. Fred Ferber was never a partner, and, in fact, no one was. There was no partnership, only a trust. You can do business as a sole proprietor, or as a partner, or as a shareholder of a corporation, or just an employee, and with each entity your tax position will change.]

Mr. Burns: Your Honor, if I can suggest a solution to this problem we'll stipulate to the admission of the signature cards, Respondent's Exhibits PC through PF, for the limited purpose of showing who had signature authority over the cards, and we'll leave it to other evidence to establish what their capacities were.

256

The Court: Is that acceptable?

Mr. Minns: Absolutely, Your Honor.

The Court: Now, do you have any questions of this witness?

Mr. Burns: Just a couple more, Your Honor.

The Court: OK.

Mr. Minns: For the record, Your Honor, those stipulations were already made, so this was unnecessary to put in the evidence. I would request, if we'd gone to the trouble to stipulate to something, the government then not go ahead and try to prove it up; it just wastes time.

The next witness was Tom Anderson, the founder of Para Technologies, whose case we will only touch on. My favorite lines in the trial include the absurd eating questions of Mr. Burns.

Burns: Did you eat during 1987, Mr. Anderson?

Anderson: Yes. And the evidence of that is that I'm sitting here now.

Burns: Do you recall approximately how much you spent per month on food during 1987?

Anderson: No. I don't keep records of my food expenses, but I can say that my food expenses are minimal.... As a vegetarian my costs are lower than the average person.

Burns: Did you go to baseball games?

Anderson: No.

Burns: Did you go on trips?

Anderson: No.

In law this is what we call a fishing expedition. The judge probably would have sustained an objection but the arguments with Burns would have taken as long as the questions. I will generally let someone who is scoring no points keep doing so.

In a case where the government wants to show a high lifestyle or at least a lifestyle much higher than the income reflected on a tax return, then it makes sense to prove the taxpayer ate at the most expensive restaurants in town, even though he claims to have made only a thousand dollars a month; but to prove that he made enough to eat vegetables seems a little ridiculous in a case where the government is trying to show a couple of million in unreported income. Who cares? Even if Anderson had actually gone to a baseball game, would that have been evidence that might have convinced the judge he had made and presumably spent millions? While all this was going on Fred was sitting at the table wondering what these complex tax questions were? What was rule 902 (3)? Could that mysterious rule cause him to owe a million dollars in tax and be found guilty of fraud, even though he had not gotten a penny?

Tom Anderson spent half a day on the stand. After the initial ceremony and arguments it was about four in the afternoon when Fred Ferber finally was called to the stand. At five he was released.

After that hour, at the end of the day on the first day of trial, the case against Fred Ferber ended. Here's what happened.

Mr. Burns: Mr. Ferber, you were a signatory on Para's bank accounts. Is that correct?

Mr. Ferber: Yes.

Mr. Burns: OK. So you could have written a check on a Para bank account at any time that you thought it was appropriate?

Mr. Ferber: I had signatory. I could write a check. Yes. [He was not, however, a partner as implied earlier. There was not even a partnership. Someone cooked up something funny on the records.]

Mr. Burns: OK. Did you file a federal income tax return for 1987?

Mr. Ferber: No, I did not.

Mr. Burns: Why not?

Mr. Ferber: I was on the verge of bankruptcy at that time, and I had very little money. I didn't make enough to file.

The Court: You didn't make the threshold amount of money required to file a return? Is that your answer?

Mr. Ferber: Yes.

Mr. Burns: You didn't make $600?

Mr. Ferber: I borrowed money.

Mr. Burns: You also didn't file a federal income tax return in 1988. Is that correct?

Mr. Ferber: That's right.

Mr. Burns: Did you also make less than $600 in 1988?

Mr. Ferber: I was living on borrowed money at the time.

Mr. Burns: During those years you were occupying an apartment. Is that correct? So you were paying rent?

Mr. Ferber: Yes.

Mr. Burns: And you were paying utilities?

Mr. Ferber: Yes.

Mr. Burns: And you were paying for food?

Mr. Ferber: Yes.

Mr. Burns: Did you have a car?

Mr. Ferber: Yes.

Mr. Burns: Were you making payments on the car?

Mr. Ferber: I don't recall.

Mr. Burns: OK. Did you have insurance?

Mr. Ferber: Yes.

Mr. Burns: OK. And you had expenses for food?

Mr. Ferber: Yes.

Mr. Burns: And clothing?

Mr. Ferber: Yes.

Mr. Burns: And entertainment?

Mr. Ferber: Yes.

Mr. Burns: OK. What was your occupation in 1987?

Mr. Ferber: Songwriter.

Mr. Burns: And in 1988?

Mr. Ferber: Songwriter.

Mr. Burns: Refresh my recollection. Songwriters are usually compensated in the form of royalties. Is that correct?

Mr. Ferber: Yes.

Mr. Burns: OK. So you weren't receiving any royalties that point in time?

Mr. Ferber: No.

Mr. Burns: Where was the money coming from that you were living on?

Mr. Ferber: Some of it I borrowed. My wife stopped working. We just had a second child. And I was at a crossroads in my career. So Laura—my wife's parents offered to help us through that transition. And I made a little bit of money here and there with odd jobs.

Mr. Burns: But it's your testimony that most of your living expenses were paid for with borrowed funds?

Mr. Ferber: That's right.

Mr. Burns: OK. Did you borrow any money from Mr. Anderson?

Mr. Ferber: No.

Mr. Burns: Did you borrow any money from Para Technologies Trust?

Mr. Ferber: No.

Mr. Burns: Did you borrow any money from Atram Investment Group? [Atram owned most of Para Technologies.]

Mr. Ferber: No.

Mr. Burns: Did you borrow any money from Mr. Ireland?

Mr. Ferber: No.

Mr. Burns: Did you borrow any money from Mr. Smith?

Mr. Ferber: No.

Mr. Burns: Who did you borrow from?

Mr. Ferber: My father-in-law. My dad.

Mr. Burns: Are there any documents in existence that reflect those loans?

Mr. Ferber: Not that I know of.

Mr. Burns: So you never signed any notes?

Mr. Minns: Excuse me. Your Honor, again, he's not—

The Court: He can ask these questions, but it's not unusual that your parents or your in-laws will loan money without asking for a note. If that's—

Mr. Burns: It's unusual in my family, Your Honor.

Mr. Minns: That may account for Mr. Burns's character.

The Court: Well, my stepdaughters—I won't even use the word "borrow"—they get. So I guess it depends if you're fortunate enough or not fortunate enough to have parents who can help you out.

261

Mr. Burns: OK. Have you ever been the owner of a certificate of beneficial interest in Para Technologies trust?

Mr. Ferber: No.

Mr. Burns: Have you ever been the owner of a certificate of beneficial interest in Atram Investment Group?

Mr. Ferber: No.

Mr. Burns: Nothing further on direct, Your Honor.

The Court: Any cross-examination?

Mr. Minns: Yes, Your Honor. And it may be mostly direct, but I will promise the Court it's less that ten minutes. My entire case for this gentleman will probably be less than ten minutes. (To Ferber) I don't mean to embarrass you any more than the government already has—but economically, you're not—you may be a very good songwriter, but economically, you've not been extremely successful?

Mr. Ferber: That's right.

The Court: Financially successful. Artistically is a different story. [When the court repeats your arguments the trial is going well. I believe Judge Jacobs is a kind man and intended to emphasize what we all know. Good artists don't always make good livings. Van Gogh died poor.]

Mr. Minns: That's why I said economically, Your Honor. (To Ferber) Now, how many checks have you received—how many checks have you written, in your lifetime, from Atram checking accounts?

Mr. Ferber: I have no—none. Zero.

Mr. Minns: And how many checks have you written, in your lifetime, from Para Technology?

Mr. Ferber: I don't think I've written any checks from Para Technologies.

Mr. Minns: All right. Now, how many—how much money has come from Para Technologies into your pockets?

Mr. Ferber: Zero.

Mr. Minns: And how much money has come from Atram into your pockets?

Mr. Ferber: Zero.

Mr. Minns: At the risk of slight repetition, when the court asked you what benefit you were getting, you indicated none. Is that correct? You were doing this as a friend to the gentleman seated at the counsel table?

Mr. Ferber: Yes.

Mr. Minns: Now, do you recall a period of time in this case where you had no lawyer whatsoever?

Mr. Ferber: Yes.

Mr. Minns: And at that point in time, did this gentleman at counsel table, who's been asking you the questions—

The Court: Mr. Burns.

Mr. Minns: Mr. Burns.

The Court: And the person you pointed to before, so we have no misunderstanding, was Mr. Anderson.

Mr. Minns: Mr. Burns, did he have an occasion to call you on the telephone?

Mr. Ferber: He asked me to call him.

Mr. Minns: Did you do so?

Mr. Ferber: Yes.

Mr. Minns: What—

Mr. Burns: I think I—excuse me, Mike. I think I can speed this up, Your Honor. I'll stipulate that I had a telephone conversation with Mr. Ferber on December 18th of last year. [Burns suddenly got very interested, and wanted to stop this line of questioning in the worse possible way. I had no intention of letting him.]

The Court: OK.

Mr. Minns: And I can speed it up by asking my last question regarding that. (To Ferber) What did he say to you?

Mr. Ferber: What went on in that conversation was—we were talking about interrogatories, and I said to him, I said, I feel like I'm being dragged into this. You know I didn't receive any money from this. And he said, yeah, I know. We're just kind of holding you hostage, but the government has to get its money somewhere.

The record is dry here, but when Fred swore under oath that Burns admitted he was *holding him hostage* everyone in the courtroom froze and looked over at Burns, even the judge, and Burns turned red and looked at the floor. You could almost hear a bell go off in the judge's head; so I decided it was a good time to let Burns start burning himself and let the judge digest this blockbuster. I passed, with less than the ten minutes I had estimated.

Mr. Minns: OK. Pass the witness, Your Honor.

The Court: Any redirect?

Mr. Burns: Yes, Your Honor

Mr. Burns: Mr. Ferber, if you didn't receive any economic benefit I'm sorry, let me go back. The audit of Para Technologies began in early 1990. Is that isn't that correct?

Mr. Ferber: It's vague in my mind right now. Somewhere around there.

Mr. Burns: And sometime during the course of that audit, it expanded to become an audit of you as an individual?

Mr. Ferber: Yes.

Mr. Burns: OK. And you had the opportunity for a year to deal with the Internal Revenue Service. Is that correct? [Burns was stuttering a lot here, and it was hard not to laugh. Who would call dealing with the IRS an opportunity?]

Mr. Ferber: Wait. Let me backtrack. I don't know if it was an audit of me individually or not. I didn't get that.

Mr. Burns: OK.

Mr. Ferber: I got that it was surrounding whether I received money from Para Technologies Trust.

The Court: Mr. Burns, perhaps you ought to explain or—did you in fact, make such a statement that, yes, you know, we're holding him hostage?

Mr. Burns: I don't recall making a statement using those terms. [Here Burns starts to evade the question.]

The Court: But something—something in that regard.

Mr. Burns: And I'd like to think I wouldn't have. I may have expressed to Mr. Ferber—

The Court: That your case against him was not as strong as you'd like it to be?

Mr. Burns: We're getting into real 408 material here Your Honor, but, in the interest of time, I may have told Mr. Ferber that I didn't believe our case against him was particularly strong. That was probably intended to try and get him to exercise some leverage against Mr. Anderson.

The Court: I see.

Mr. Ferber: Those were his exact words.

The Court: Well, you've testified to that. I just want to get him—

Burns's next line of questions made it clear to me and I believe our Judge, that he had acted in bad faith, and was scared to death it wouldn't just be his word against Ferber, who was unshakeable, but that he had been tape recorded. I wish he had been; but Ferber's sworn testimony was as credible as a tape recording.

Mr. Burns: Did you record the conversation?

Mr. Ferber: No.

Mr. Burns: Did you take notes of the conversation?

Mr. Ferber: No. But I told Mr. Izen right after what you said. [Izen had previously represented Para Technologies. The tax court had taken him off of the case as a result of a motion filed by Mr. Burns.]

Mr. Burns: You told Mr. Izen?

Mr. Ferber: That's right.

Mr. Burns: Right after our conversation?

Mr. Ferber: Yes.

Mr. Burns: Three months after Mr. Izen had been disqualified from representing you in this case?

Mr. Ferber: Yes.

Mr. Minns: The record should reflect he still had not found counsel.

Mr. Burns: In any event, were you ever contacted by a Mr. Haberman from the IRS appeals office?

The Court: Let's go off the record for a moment.

Mr. Burns: OK.

(Discussion held off the record)

This was when Judge Jacobs first strongly suggested to Mr. Burns that he was concerned that there was the appearance of an *improper attempt to influence a witness's testimony* and perhaps the government might not want to proceed against Mr. Ferber.

> The Court: Back on the record. That this line of questioning can become very important in the event the court finds the government's case against Mr. Ferber is unreasonable, because there are sanctions such as attorney's fees, which can be awarded to taxpayers for unreasonable actions by the Internal Revenue Service, just as there are sanctions for taxpayers bringing frivolous suits in this court. So that's something that both sides ought to consider.
>
> Mr. Burns: I think I can address your concern with one question, Your Honor.
>
> The Court: OK.
>
> Mr. Minns: And when he's finished please let me respond.
>
> The Court: OK.
>
> Mr. Burns: You never laid your cards on the table to the auditor, did you?
>
> Mr. Ferber: I didn't talk with the auditor.
>
> The Court: Well, why don't we just say this. Why don't we—now that everybody knows what's happened with Mr. Ferber, the two of you might just want to get together this evening and decide whether you want to proceed against Mr. Ferber or not.

And one possible way of resolving the problem is no deficiency against Mr. Ferber and no attorney's fees for Mr. Ferber, because the only thing that we could do would be, of course, from December the eighteenth, whenever the government found out any of that sort of stuff. And, of course, they didn't have an opportunity to have him on cross-examination. This goes to credibility, of course. So that is something you might consider.

Mr. Minns: There is one other thing, Your Honor, and this is what I asked to make a record of. At the end of the government's opening, I discussed in front of—I'm sure he will agree to these exact words, and I will use them again with Mr. Burns. I said, Mr. Burns, from your opening you have absolutely no evidence. Therefore, we should not be proceeding against the gentleman—

The Court: Yes. I recall that. I recall that statement.

Mr. Minns: Yes. And I made that to him—there, over in the counsel room.

The Court: Well, you made it in open court. You made it in open court.

Mr. Minns: Yes, Your Honor. And I said to him that if you have no evidence, then it is your duty to dismiss the charges and not go forward. [I really wanted to go after Burns and the IRS for sanctions, but it was clear the judge didn't want us to. The only reason we were at this advantageous stage was because Judge Jacobs had been so fair, so I backed down, and took this victory without asking for sanctions.]

The Court: Well, he may decide to do that after listening to the testimony, because there's a big difference between having somebody under oath—believe in credibility under oath—and blanket statements. I think that, again, it's I'm not telling you both what to do. I'm just suggesting that you might talk in those terms.

That night Burns was in a panic to get me on the phone and settle. When I got back from dinner, I found six messages left by him at the hotel. The settlement was that he dropped Ferber from the case altogether.

The case proceeded against the others with government witnesses until conclusion and then months later the court ruled that Anderson owed a tax but had not committed any fraud. While

Anderson had no money (all the money went to Para Technologies, which was released from the suit) he still appealed out of principle. Para Technologies financed his appeal. I was brought into the case when Para Technologies lawyer was removed from the trial for a conflict of interest. He had drawn up the trust documents that the suit was based on. After the trial was over he took the case over again. If he wins it will be over. If he loses there will likely be a bankruptcy. No money will pass hands. Essentially, the government spent a great deal of money on a case from which it could not recoup any lost tax revenue.

The rest of the trial consisted of expert witnesses testifying to things that you could only be interested in if you owned offshore trusts.

Agent Camporeal, the revenue agent on the case, found it to be very suspicious that Anderson did not answer a letter that Camporeal mailed to the wrong address. He was also suspicious that Anderson had to pull out his social security card to give him the number when he asked for it. IRS agents often find ridiculous things to be suspicious of.

In tax court when the trial ends the judge often asks both sides to submit briefs, which Judge Jacobs did in this particular case, and so a record is made of the testimony and briefs are prepared to summarize it for the court and to include legal argument.

The only other Burns story I have, that is even more interesting, was against another California client whose wife was in a wheelchair with Burns trying to cause them financial harm. He did not succeed and the judge's words in that case were wonderfully strong. That was a complete rout of Burns and the IRS, unfortunately there is no record and that, of course, is another story. As a rule, tax court is a little like divorce court. You win part of it and the government wins part of it. There is no jury and both sides often say they won. In divorce court both sides get divorced so you can have two divorce lawyers who go off and each add another imaginary notch on their imaginary gun belt.

Fred Ferber's case is just another illustration of the arbitrary misuse of power by the IRS. Here the IRS harassed a relatively impoverished man for a million dollars, all the while admitting that they really had no case against him and were only using him as a catspaw against others. Just remember that these are your tax dollars at work in the hands of people like Mr. Burns.

We left the California courthouse before the Rodney King verdict came down and, relieved to get out of there, I returned to Houston.

Chapter X
The Salem Witch Trial Moved To Oklahoma

"A special court was bound to find culprits to justify its existence. And so it did. Its proceedings were outrageous. The more sturdy-minded among the accused, who obstinately refused to confess to crimes they had not committed, were judged guilty. Hysteria raged. Fourteen women and five men with unblemished records, had been hanged."

—Paul Johnson "Cotton Mather and the End of the Puritan Utopia"

In the decision to wrap up this book and put in the last story, I wanted one that was inclusive, that speaks to the evils of the Tax Code, and speaks to the evils of the IRS. For that reason, I am giving you the story of John Proctor and his wife, Jill Proctor, whose trial began on August 18, 1997, three hundred years from the date that another John Proctor was tried in Salem, Massachusetts for witchcraft.

John was a glass installer. He learned the trade from his father who learned the trade from his father. When his father died, John inherited his father's half of the business. He bought the other half of the business from his uncle C. P. Proctor for $20,000. He had to borrow the $20,000. Business was good. Ace Glass Company made good money.

John was one of those hands-on kind of guys who did the hard physical labor of his profession, along with a staff of people who worked with him in the business. As a result, he was in good physical condition, slim, lean, muscular and, if it wasn't for a large bald spot on the top of his head, you could have mistaken this forty-two year-old man for a twenty year old. He was married to my client, Jill Proctor, your basic homecoming queen type, who was a nurse and a professional photographer. They were high school sweethearts, married in 1975. They are still happily married today. They have two children, a son, Justin, who was getting ready for college, and a daughter, Kandis, who was a freshman in high school and an honor roll student, when the IRS auditing began. Jill was an active charitable member of the community who, among other things, handled a fundraiser for a paralyzed boy.

Unfortunately, no one is ever dealt all good cards in the game of life. Jill's mother and sister both became extremely ill. John's father died. Phillips Petroleum, a major employer of people in Bartlesville, Oklahoma, where the glass factory was, began to lay people off, and Ace Glass Company lost its luster. The Proctors discovered that a lot of their money appeared to be going to their bookkeeper, Susan Elliott. They brought this to her attention, she apologized, and they forgave her.

The uncle, C. P. Proctor, used supplies purchased by Ace Glass Company on his own jobs. Uncle C. P. turned the jobs in and kept 100 percent of the money, including the amount for the materials. Uncle Proctor opened up his own secret account under the name of Ace Glass Company even though he no longer owned any interest in Ace Glass.

Susan Elliott, the bookkeeper, was doing some other funny things. She set up a policy whereby all employees of Ace Glass could borrow money from the cash register and be on the honor system when it came time to repay the money. Since she declared herself to be an honorable person, she was one of the big beneficiaries of this policy.

John was a generous employer and, on occasion, when employees asked to be paid in cash, John would go ahead and do it. Of course that doesn't benefit the employer. One hundred percent of work compensation for employees is tax deductible. If you pay someone in cash, you save the 7.65 percent matching FICA (social security and Medicare) but you lose the deduction for the entire wage. The employee may benefit because the employee will then not have a record of having earned the money and may end up not paying any taxes on it. This was the case with the employees of Ace Glass Company for these occasional overtime payments. The transaction wasn't of any value, though, to John Proctor.

Finally, the Proctors were forced to lay off a number of employees. Business was that bad. Throughout all of this, Susan Elliott handled all the books and records for the Proctors. She also cashed checks made out to Ace Glass from time to time. All of the information given to the CPA came directly from Susan Elliott. In court, Susan Elliott testified that she had learned to imitate John Proctor's signature. "It would be the best but it was not the same," she would testify.

Two employees, Todd Thornton and Tony Stumpe, opened up Clearview Glass and became competitors of Ace Glass Company. Todd Thornton admitted that he took cash out of the company register. "It was kind of a given." Thornton, who left without giving notice to the company, always got paid overtime in cash. After he left Ace Glass, Mr. Thornton made obscene gestures at his former boss. On a bank glass job that Ace had installed, Mr. Thornton placed his own work advertisement on the window pretending that he had done it. During the trial, there was an amusing scene when Mr. Thornton was asked if he knew who did this. Initially, he couldn't remember who did it. Then when he was asked if he noticed that there was a camera on the bank property, he responded, "Yes, I do remember doing it now."

The other employee, Tony Stumpe, was fired for drinking and narcotics. Stumpe, while in a drunken stupor, accidentally shot himself. The bottom line was that while John Proctor hated to fire the man, he explained, "You just can't have a drunk man installing glass. It's dangerous." It wasn't very long after Stumpe and Thornton left that they started Clearview Glass Company. Susan Elliott, who had been laid off at Ace Glass, immediately joined them.

As the canceled checks and credit-card bills began to come in, John and Jill Proctor realized that they had seriously underestimated the amount of money that Susan Elliott had taken as "bonuses." They filed a criminal complaint for forging checks and credit cards with the district attorney's office. The district attorney, Rick Esser, after receiving the report from a police officer, elected to seek an indictment against Susan Elliott.

Susan Elliott contacted one of the top trial lawyers in the United States, Gary Richardson. Gary Richardson's son, Chad Richardson, a member of his firm, took her case. When I got involved, one of the first things that I wondered was how Susan Elliott could afford a nice home, a swimming pool, and the Richardson law firm. While the Richardson law firm is known for its great legal skill, it is not known for giving away its services.

Before Susan Elliott left Ace Glass Company, she went with the Proctors to their attorney, Ted Riseling. The Proctors, at that time, thought Susan Elliott was a friend. In fact, she was wired by the IRS so that they could eavesdrop on the conversation that she and the Proctors had with their attorney. There was nothing incriminating said at the meeting even though the Proctors told their attorney everything they knew and even though Susan Elliott was there for the purpose of getting incriminating information. Susan Elliott continued to tape record conversations with the Proctors.

IRS agent, Gary Benuzzi, had told Susan Elliott in advance that there was going to be a meeting with Ted Riseling and the Proctors. How did he know? Susan Elliott confirmed with him that she knew about the meeting so they wired her up. How many people in America know that there are circumstances by which they can go into an attorney's office for consultation and be secretly tape recorded by government agents?

On May 26, 1995, nearly a year after Susan Elliott had been dismissed, the Proctors filed charges against her. The IRS seized most of the incriminating evidence. The district attorney, Rick Esser, requested cooperation between both governments (the feds and the state of Oklahoma), but Benuzzi refused and the documents were not turned over until after the statute of limitations passed. At trial, the government talked about the indictment. Susan Elliott testified that it was all based on lies.

The defense wanted to put the district attorney, Rick Esser, on the witness stand so the jury would know that it was he who had made the decision to indict Susan Elliott, and so that the jury would further know that the IRS had helped Susan Elliott by hiding evidence. Letting the jury hear only that my client, Jill Proctor, had filed a criminal complaint against Susan Elliott was an unfortunate decision by the court. Nevertheless, Judge Terry Kern is known as an evenhanded judge who generally allows a defendant a level playing field.

Ted Riseling's battle plan before trial was to fly to Washington, D.C., and lay all the cards on the table, and try to convince the people in Washington not to go forward. In a criminal tax case, you have the right to approach the government in Washington and ask them to overturn the decision of the local people on a tax prosecution case. It is one of the very few crimes where that is so. However, in every case that I am aware of, Washington simply rubber-stamps the decision by the local people to prosecute. I counseled the Proctors that they should not spend the money. It should be saved for the trial. Even so, the Proctors were so certain the case would be tossed out, they insisted on the Washington effort. Ted also felt it was worth the long shot.

I was told Mr. Riseling, who used to work for the IRS, routinely got concessions in Washington. I told the Proctors I never had, and Riseling should go alone. Instead we both were requested to go. It turns out Mr. Riseling had never won one of these before either, so I took the lead once we got to Washington. I paid half the cost of my plane ticket to Washington. In Washington, we argued vigorously that this case should be thrown out. Ted was an effective helpful second chair. When we left, we knew we had done a good job and Ted was optimistic. I was not. How do you convince the high school bully to punish himself? You have to do it or let him off. The procedure is one where you argue against the government to the government, then lose and go home.

About the only thing that was accomplished in Washington was that we gave away our defense plans, so the other side changed the attack from an income-tax-evasion case to a gross-receipts case. What's the difference? In an income-tax-evasion case the defendant may do everything in his or her power to avoid paying taxes but, at the end of the day, if beyond a reasonable doubt, they don't owe any taxes, then they haven't committed the crime of income tax evasion. There is no crime of attempted income tax evasion. There are, however, crimes that sound like attempted income tax evasion. A gross-receipts case simply means that you put the wrong amount of money on the tax return. In this case, since the money received had been used to pay overtime to employees, it was all deductible. It was a wash.

Even if the money had been properly put on the Proctors' tax returns, even if it was supposed to be on their returns and not the corporation's returns, it still would have been a wash because they still would have been entitled to a deduction for the employee expense. In other words, you cash a check for five hundred dollars. You hand the five hundred dollars cash to employees for overtime. The five hundred dollars is completely deductible and zeros itself out. There is no income.

When we lost in Washington, the Proctors informed me that Mr. Riseling had convinced them to hire other local counsel. I later learned that all these efforts and all the other counsel had cost the Proctors about $25,000 that we could have used in defending the case itself. A couple of months before the trial setting, the Proctors contacted me again. The local attorney they had hired to work with Riseling told them honestly that he did not understand the case and did not understand what a defense would be. Ted told them that there was no possibility of winning now and advised both of them to plead guilty. One thing was certain, $25,000 poorer, having given up the trial strategy, and after hiring counsel who told the government he wanted to plead guilty, the case was much different than it had been.

Riseling had conducted a confidential meeting to discuss strategy with the informant in the room. He was then given the clients unrealistic expectations about Washington. He then arranged for a new lawyer to take over. Together, after collecting the money, the two let the Proctors in on the bad news: "You have to plead guilty, and we're out of money."

I received some heart rendering pleas to get back on board and steer the sinking ship. I reluctantly agreed to do so but only if I could drop the dead weight overboard and hire my own local counsel. Just like the Bussey case, I hate taking over after someone who doesn't know how to steer a ship has run it aground and put a few holes in it.

After interviewing a number of very good attorneys, I found Stan Monroe, the president of the local criminal defense bar, and one of the top criminal defense attorneys in the state of Oklahoma. While Stan had an extensive and successful criminal practice, he had never handled a tax case and so he was willing to severely reduce his normal fee for three reasons: one, he wanted to translate his considerable criminal defense skills into the tax ring and, two, he believed in the Proctors and, three, he told me he wanted to try a case with me. Both of us got a significantly reduced fee up front and agreed that there would be no other fees until the end of the trial.

You really know now all the basic facts of the case. All the employees were stealing from the Proctors. The former employees set up a competing glass company. IRS agent Gary Benuzzi sent letters out to over a hundred of the Proctors' customers notifying them that the Proctors were under criminal investigation and the balance of their business diminished greatly. Gary Benuzzi seized information that the district attorney, Rick Esser, wanted in his case against Susan Elliott.

The turmoil at home was unavoidable. Children suffer horribly in these situations. The parents suffer and it is hard for families to stay together. Their daughter went from the top of the honor roll in her freshman, sophomore and junior years to significantly below average and borderline passing at times in her senior year. When she went to school, other students would ask questions about her parents' honesty. The investigation had lasted nearly as long as her high school career. Of course, IRS press releases demonized these wonderful people just like Cotton Mather had done to John and Goody Proctor three hundred years ago. The witch hunts of government never end.

All three former employees testified against the Proctors. Gary Benuzzi, the IRS expert, testified against the Proctors. A handwriting expert testified, among other things, that John Proctor had signed a check even though John was out of the state at the time. The handwriting expert's courses, none in college on handwriting, were primarily seminars on how to testify.

There was an important issue under another important case, *Daubert,* in which experts are supposed to be qualified. They are supposed to tell you the method by which they reached their conclusion. The handwriting expert did not give us a report telling us how he reached his conclusions and Gary Benuzzi was not put on as an expert. He was put on merely to testify under oath that the Proctors owed money that they hadn't reported on their tax returns. Could a non-expert read and interpret ten years of bookkeeping, decide which line it should be put on the tax return and whether or not it was deductible? I don't think so. Nevertheless, both of these experts were allowed to testify to their opinions.

Gordon Cecil and John Russell, assistant U.S. Attorneys, were opposing counsel. In the twenty-four years that I have been practicing law, I almost never have an honest assistant U.S. attorney and an honest special agent for the IRS on the other side. By the same token, at least half of the time, one of them will be honest. Most of the time, the honest party is the assistant U.S. attorney. This is a generalization but I don't think it's unfair. Most of the mean aggressive bullies have, also, been extremely dishonest. In my opinion, Gary Benuzzi actively helped Susan Elliott avoid the consequences of her own actions and actively hurt the business of the Proctors. Strangely, this guy was one of the few IRS agents who had been working there long enough for retirement and didn't retire because he apparently enjoyed his work so much. I have nothing but contempt for him. He was able to testify under oath to God that the Proctors were legally responsible for putting the corporation money on their tax return because they had cashed the checks and it didn't matter that they had used all the money for corporation purposes.

On the other hand, and I know my clients will be a little disappointed, and I don't blame them, the two assistant U.S. attorneys conducted themselves with honor and decorum. While I am disappointed that I was not able to convince them to drop the case, they both showed a measure of integrity in the prosecution of it. You can't expect anyone to like the people prosecuting them.

One factor that I had not thought about was the effect that the Oklahoma bombing had on just about everybody in the state of Oklahoma. I later learned that aside from our case, every criminal case in Oklahoma federal court that was tried to a jury out of Tulsa by the defense was lost until Stan Monroe broke that streak himself several months after our case.

When the jury was selected, we were pretty happy with the exception of one person. We had a woman who was a professor who was married to a minister and who had said she did not like taxes but "we all have to pay them." It's a bad attitude for a tax juror. It's not as bad as "I hate people who get away without paying taxes," or "Anybody that doesn't pull their weight needs to go to jail," but it's pretty high up there.

All tax cases are tough. However, I had a good team put together for this one. I had great clients with great character. I had a top-notch local counsel. I had some horrible facts against me but that is always the case in a tax trial, particularly when the IRS has the liberty to make the facts up as they need them. I always counsel clients that it's an uphill battle but I win a bunch of them, maybe as I've been told, more than my share. With a good judge, a good client, a good local counsel, a high school student at home, and horrendous villains leading the attack, I expected to win.

I was wrong. We lost. The court entered a verdict of guilty on August 28, 1997, my 46th birthday.

On December 12, 1997, Jill Ann Proctor was sentenced to eighteen months of actual time and twelve months of probation. The judge added about six months because of the criminal complaint that Jill had filed against Susan Elliott for obstruction of justice. At the same time, her husband was convicted and sentenced to the same exact time. If you want a heartbreaking experience, then try watching a sweet seventeen year old girl who never thought her mom and dad would lose, try to understand they are heading for federal prison.

Judge Kern graciously allowed Jill to stay out of prison until June 5, 1998 so that she could stay with her daughter Kandis until she graduated from high school. Because of the judge's mercy in that situation, Jill Proctor was able to struggle with her daughter and, together, they made certain that she graduated from high school although not in the upper echelon where she should have graduated. Rough finances and emotional drain forced her to cancel plans to go to college.

Our notice of appeal was filed on December 19, 1997, the date of the final judgment and sentencing. We had to wait however until the transcript was ready before we could file an appeal.

John Proctor went straight to jail. Jill Proctor stayed out of jail begging and borrowing to make the payments on the money she had borrowed against the house. Meanwhile, we waited on the transcript. The transcript is the typing of the entire trial. You can't file your appeal until you have the transcript. The government then files a response and the appellant (defendant) has the right to make a final reply to them.

I received the transcript sometime in April of 1998 and rejected all new business during the month of April. I had to make a choice. I could not take the calls, which generally are anywhere from a third to half of my criminal tax practice, for new business and at the same time get ready for a summer trial that I had and also prepare the Proctor brief.

You do your best to learn the entire transcript, even those portions that you will not be quoting from because the other side may be quoting from them. I try in my briefs to cover both sides of the argument so that the judges will know that I am asking for fairness and justice and that I am being even handed in what I represent to the court, and that it is truthful and accurate.

In trial, the government goes first and last. On a criminal appeal, the defendant gets to go first and last. In a criminal tax case appeal, the "jury" consists of three judges. You are told who they are going to be about two weeks before the appellate argument, if one is granted.

We asked Judge Kern to recognize that the Proctors were indigent, but he disagreed. For that reason, Stan and I had to decide whether or not we would represent them on appeal for nothing, including paying our own costs to go to the appellate argument or leave them to their own resources. Both of us agreed to handle the appeal for nothing.

Handling an appeal correctly means reading anywhere from ten to a hundred cases, which can range from two or three pages to fifty pages a piece, and reading the transcript, which in a week long trial is about a thousand pages, and then forming your reasons for the appeal.

After that, you pull the pages that you've marked out of your transcript, study them and write the first rough drafts of your appellate argument. The appellate argument is a small book generally around fifty pages that you put together and publish out of your office. Then you wait for the government to respond and you print another smaller book replying to them.

If you are fortunate, the court rules that your case has some merit, at least enough to listen to you, and they will set it for oral argument. They assign a time, fifteen or twenty minutes, sometimes a little more, for each side to talk to the judges.

Jill went to jail on June 5, 1998. I filed a motion with the court to allow her to stay out of jail while the appeal was pending. Two judges who were randomly selected ruled against us. Oral argument was set for September 24, 1998.

The Tenth Circuit Court of Appeals is stationed out of Denver, Colorado but covers many states including Arizona and Oklahoma. The Tenth Circuit elected to have this hearing in Oklahoma City so I flew directly from Houston to Oklahoma City. Stan drove up from Tulsa the night before the hearing and met me. We re-read our joint briefs, re-read portions of the transcript and case law and made our plans until late in the night.

Our three judge panel consisted of Judge Paul Kelly who had been appointed by Bush in 1992, Mary Briscoe who had been appointed by Clinton in 1995, and William Holloway, Jr. who had been appointed by Johnson in 1968.

Both Briscoe and Kelly had been two of the three judges who had voted on the recent *Clifton* case. In the *Clifton* case, our same judge, Judge Kern, had said materiality was a question of law for the judge and not the jury and that even the difference of one dollar would be enough to convict on. The three judges ruled that he was wrong, that it was not for the judge to decide, that it was for the jury to decide but they agreed with the definition similar to the one that Judge Kern had given. They said that materiality was anything that affected the return itself. They also however adopted the *Uchimura* decision out of the Ninth Circuit in California. In *Uchimura*, the court ruled that materiality was a two-prong test: first the government must prove that there is a mistake on the tax return, and second, the government must prove that it is material. The jury decides both issues.

I did not know how Judges Kelly or Briscoe would feel about that. Part of the *Clifton* decision went with us and part of it went against us. They ruled that the judge had made a mistake in the *Clifton* case, which had been ruled on months after our case was tried, but which was pending on appeal while our case was in trial but that there was no grounds for reversal because the trial lawyer had not objected at the time of trial. In the Proctor case, Stan and I had objected.

During oral argument, Judge Kelly asked me a point about my brief. I had said in the brief that the instructions required even a dollar to make a finding of guilt. If you did that, you might as well take the word material out. I argued that materiality should not be supported by a mere dollar as a matter of law. Judge Kelly inquired: "What if that dollar pushes the taxpayer up to the next highest bracket?" I had to agree. I responded: "Good point, judge." In that case, the jury should have the right to decide if that dollar is material. In fact, take the analogy a step further to the one in the Proctor case. What if there is a hundred thousand dollars but there are more than a hundred thousand dollars in deductions? So, the Proctors would not owe one penny in tax? Wouldn't that be material?

Judge Kelly interrogated Stan and me a great deal on the issue of materiality. There were only two issues that were brought up by Judge Holloway. First, he asked if the materiality objection that I had wasn't just to the definition. He said it wasn't really an instruction, was it? My response was that it was a definition but was also an instruction. Whatever the judge tells the jury is an instruction and they are required to obey it. The actual law is that the jury can legally say "not guilty" no matter what the facts or the law if they so choose. That makes the jury as powerful as Congress and the president on the day of trial. The only other remark by Judge Holloway was that the obstruction of justice increase in the sentencing made no sense to him. Judge Kelly nodded his head almost in disgust over the extra six months for obstruction of justice and, when we walked out of there, we felt pretty certain that we had at least two votes which would lower the sentence. We could not read Judge Briscoe's reaction.

Months later a verdict came down. The court regretfully did not lower the sentence and sustained the convictions. We lost. The court did rule that our clients should get costs for court-appointed lawyers retroactively of about $2,500. Stan filed for his nearly two years ago and still hasn't been paid.

I haven't gotten around to filling out the forms. They take more than $2,500 of work to file. The fair market value for appellate work is around $25,000.

To say that the Proctor case was a gross miscarriage of justice would be an understatement akin to saying that the Grand Canyon was a hole in the ground. The IRS agent intruded on the attorney-client privilege, illegally withheld evidence to protect his snitch, and then deliberately ruined the Proctor's glass business by notifying their customers of alleged criminal improprieties. He did it simply because he had the power to do it. It is about time we, as the people of the United States, rein in the power of the IRS so these abuses cannot continue. And the best way to rein in the IRS is to choke it to death.

Chapter XI
One Hundred Tax Secrets

There is one difference between a tax collector and a taxidermist— the taxidermist leaves the hide.

— Mortimer Caplan

If you have read my book *The Underground Lawyer*, a lot of these tips are not secret anymore; but I have put together this list of ideas, some common—some uncommon, that some people have paid hundreds of thousands of dollars for and for want of these tips occasionally have done time in prison. There is no particular order or emphasis intended. There is a heavy emphasis on conflict because that is the area of my expertise.

1. The IRS has separate divisions. The three most prominent are the examination division, the collection division, and the criminal investigation division. Examination determines whether you owe money and how much. Collections attempt to collect on the debt. The criminal division puts people in jail.

2. CID stands for criminal investigation division. The special agent, who works with CID, has the job of bringing criminal charges against citizens.

3. You have the right to know if the agent investigating you is trying to collect money or put you in jail. His statements won't necessarily let you know this—he may lie. His badge will tell you if he is an agent for the CID.

4. Agents carry badges for identification and must show them to you on request.

5. Sometimes agents deceive the interviewee and pretend they are civil when they are criminal. Check their badge.

6. You have the right to record any interviews you give. In some states you can't do so without notifying the other party. In some states you can't record over the phone. Federal tax law does not prohibit recording, in fact the 1988 Taxpayers Bill of Rights specifically allows it. In Texas, you can record secretly. In Florida, you can't.

7. Sometimes agents lie about what you said (See Buford and Spulak) so a record of the conversation on tape is sometimes your only solid evidence.

8. The most important goal for the special agent is a conviction. Be on guard. Incriminating evidence may lead to a charge even though you are not guilty of anything (See Buford and Spulak). When a special agent shows up you need to contact an attorney.

9. You have the right to remain silent if you are being criminally investigated or have a reasonable fear of criminal ramifications. Your silence cannot be used against you in criminal court. To invoke it just say; "I should consult an attorney before talking to you." (See Buford.)

10. There are a lot of people working in the IRS who are just plain nuts. (See many chapters.)

11. There are newly revised statues to protect innocent spouses; but they have more holes in them then swiss cheese. If you are going through a nasty divorce it could be a bad decision to file jointly. Many divorce lawyers don't handle this very well.

12. The statue of limitations on most federal tax crimes is six years.

13. The date for statue of limitations does not start in the calendar year of the tax return, but the day it is filed or should be filed. Example: Tax year 2000....Filing date due April 16, 2001 (the 15th falls on a Sunday)....Six years later is 2007 April 15th.

14. If you file late, the statute may start late.

15. If you don't file, the start date is April 15.

16. An audit must take place within three years of the filing of the tax return unless fraud has occurred or is alleged.

17. It is common practice to give the IRS extra time to audit you with a voluntary waiver.

18. Most of the time, if you don't give the waiver the statute passes because they don't react on time. Many people have lived with tax audits over their heads for a decade or more by simply agreeing to let them go on and on.

19. There are essentially two types of tax practitioners: Adversary and amiable. The adversary wins cases in front of jurors or administrators or judges. You hire him if you have or expect a conflict.

20. The amiable works over and over again with the same agents and has to get along with them. He is likely to also be a tax preparer. Since most of his living is settling, he may not be up to a good fight.

21. The IRS can audit or tax all of a preparer's clients by using his social security number to pull all his clients' returns. This can effectively put him out of business, so by temperament and fear he may not be your best choice as lead counsel in a contested case.

22. Sometimes it is better to go to court and lose than to let the proceedings drag on for a lifetime. This is of course is a personal judgment call.

23. You do not necessarily have to pay all of the tax you owe. People make legitimate offers to compromise tax debts every day and reduce

their debt. On rare occasions, large debts have been settled for as little as a dollar. Make certain, however, your "offer" doesn't look like an inappropriate suggestion, i.e., a bribe (See Spulak). A settlement of 10 percent on the dollar is not impossible, but it is unusual.

24. If you are not found guilty of fraud you may wipe out your taxes by filing a bankruptcy under certain limited rules and strict guidelines. Two bills to limit this were vetoed during the Clinton administration. A third is probably on its way.

25. Civil fraud means extra penalties, generally found by a tax court judge.

26. Criminal fraud means jail potential. Generally it is found by a jury.

27. It is common practice for the IRS to ask for more money than you owe and then bargain down unless you just agree to the inflated amount, which is also common, or just default, which is also common.

28. Many field and office collection agents are not born in the United States, speak poor English, and have no idea how to interpret the laws they work under. Some might have trouble getting a job in a convenience store.

29. Anyone under any scrutiny or fear of evaluation by the IRS should send their returns by certified mail, return receipt requested.

30. In a criminal tax trial it is very common for IRS agents to lie under oath.

31. In a criminal tax trial it is very common to face your own CPA as a witness against you.

32. Your records and statements to your accountant are not completely privileged communications. They may be used against you in a criminal case.

33. There is no amnesty program by the IRS. It is all negotiated.

34. You do not have to go personally to an audit of your taxes. You

may have an enrolled agent, a CPA, or an attorney go in your stead.

35. You shouldn't go to an audit. All you can do is give them additional information to use against you.

36. An enrolled agent (EA) is a person (citizenship is not required) who took and passed a two day intensive exam on federal tax forms. He is not licensed to give financial advice, but then most financial advisors have no licenses.

37. Some EAs may avoid taking the exam if they formerly worked at the IRS. They may be better prepared to help you politically with a particular agent; but they may not know anything about taxes since they have not taken the courses or passed the exam.

38. A CPA has taken an exam which contains a lot of financial accounting that is unrelated to taxes. They also train specifically in taxes.

39. There are lawyers specializing in criminal tax defense who have never won a criminal jury trial in their career, and they are very expensive, and they usually have great credentials.

40. The majority of the men sitting on the tax court bench used to work for the IRS.

41. If you pay the tax the IRS says you owe and sue for a refund you are entitled to a jury trial and the interest that accrues may be refunded to you if you win. This is one of the last tax shelters around.

42. CPAs and EAs can take the tax court exam and get a limited license to practice law in the United States Tax Court; but most of them don't know this. Lawyers often prefer it this way.

43. Citizens who earn income overseas are required to file tax returns; but most don't.

44. There is a foreign tax deduction available of $70,000 a year; but if you don't file in a timely manner you lose it. Of course that may be negotiated. (See Orr.)

289

45. If you receive a ninety-day letter in the mail from the IRS and do not file a petition in tax court opposing it within ninety days you lose. Ignorance is not a defense.

46. If the IRS mails it to your last known address (or says they did) it counts even if you never got it. One airline pilot got a judgment against him when the letter was delivered to his next door neighbor. The neighbor, after opening the letter, had a heart attack and died. Six months passed before his widow got the letter to the pilot. Tough.

47. Ignorance is a defense to a tax crime. It is not a defense to owing money. (See Buford and Absent Minded Professor.)

48. Americans living overseas can negotiate their tax debt away; sometimes for pennies on the dollar.

49. IRS agents refuse to give allowed deductions every day. You simply appeal to the appeals officer. You need to object in writing. (See Hobbs.)

50. The Taxpayer's Advocate provided for in the Taxpayer's Bill of Rights II can stop IRS collections. The ombudsman, provided for in the Taxpayer's Bill of Rights I, could stop IRS collections temporarily when you make a complaint. They have a form 911 for this purpose. It remains to be seen if the change will have any value. A blind person or a quadriplegic who they thought would seek publicity against the IRS would be most likely to get temporary service in the past. In 1988 when the first act passed, the IRS seemed to be trying a little at first but the effectiveness vanished by 1989. In 1998 and 1999, they started smiling again, or was it baring their teeth?

51. For large complicated returns it always makes sense to hire a CPA or EA.

52. If you have a particular question that you think may cross the line you may want to consult a lawyer first and use the protection under the Fifth and Sixth Amendments. These amendments together create attorney client privilege. The Fifth gives you the right to remain

silent. The Sixth gives you the right to counsel. Together they give you the right to ask a lawyer about specific things and keep the question confidential.

53. The lawyer cannot, however, help you commit a crime.

54. If the lawyer prepares a tax return for you he changes hats. He is not a lawyer anymore. He is a tax preparer and you may waive the privilege. He could be tempted to sell you out to protect himself.

55. A lot of well meaning lawyers don't know this. They think they are in a confidential meeting with you. Later they may end up on the stand testifying against you. Since many do not go into court they have no idea what can happen or what the rules are. Whoever signs your tax return is your preparer, not your Fifth Amendment lawyer.

56. IRS agents have posed as priests and lawyers. You just get stuck. There is no protection if you rely on the wrong person.

57. Before the local IRS can charge you with a tax crime they need permission from district counsel in Washington D.C. You have a right to protest this and either appear in Washington or have a lawyer do so.

58. If you do, whoever appears on your behalf may say things, and those things may be used against you.

59. The agent against you may have committed a crime. It's not uncommon. This may be used against him in court.

60. There are a lot of retired IRS agents who have seen the light and make effective advocates in private practice.

61. Some, however, still haven't figured out they have switched sides.

62. Most lawyers have no background in tax law and are as afraid of the IRS as you are.

63. The IRS frequently targets specific groups of people. In recent years lawyers have been targeted, especially lawyers in small or solo practice firms. They usually leave big firm lawyers of one hundred or more alone. The IRS loves to ruin Medical Doctors and even jail them. They usually never see it coming until the cell door slams shut.

64. The IRS often targets specific accountants or CPAs and may even audit all of their clients.

65. It is illegal for an IRS agent to divulge information about you publicly. He can be sued. The exception is in a bonafide case where disclosure is necessary to prove up the case or conduct an investigation. This is a fine line and most judges lean towards the IRS.

66. Everything is potentially negotiable; even when they say it isn't.

67. Every citizen has an Individual Master File in the IRS computer in Martinsburg, West Virginia, and you are entitled to see it. You may write for it under the Federal Freedom of Information Act. They may decline only if there is a current criminal investigation going on; but even that limited information may be helpful in your defense.

68. If you do, ask for the ADP Code book with it, or it won't make any sense.

69. Failure to file tax returns are the easiest cases the IRS ever has to try.

70. Failure to pay taxes are the toughest cases they try.

71. The penalties for not filing are far worse than the penalties for not paying.

72. Federal law is slightly different in every state on taxes because the origin of the income is interpreted differently and the ownership of the income changes from state to state. Example: In a community property state like California the money belongs to both husband and wife. Both may be charged. However, while New York is not a community property state, if you sign the return, you may be held liable.

73. If you hire an attorney for a criminal tax case (this in fact applies to all criminal cases and to a lesser extent all trial cases) check out his/her track record. If the lawyer doesn't have any trial or appellate victories for the defense (some ex-government lawyers have a lot of convictions but it is much easier to convict someone than to win an

acquittal for them) get a substantial discount from them and buy an extra toothbrush.

74. You can't get out of death or taxes; you can just limit each and postpone both. Even if you never filed an income tax return or paid an income tax directly you still pay lots of taxes to the feds every time you fill your car tank with gas.

75. If you have the money you are always better off paying a disputed tax and then getting it back; unless there is absolutely no chance you can lose. The penalties for non-payment and interest often will exceed the tax debt by a multitude.

76. Never trust the figures that the IRS says you owe. They are wrong as often as they are right and there are no shortage of dishonest people working in the IRS.

77. Every year there are hundreds of promoters selling new promotions, silver bullets, to protect you from IRS agents or shelter your income (keep you from paying taxes). Many are con artists. Silver bullets kill werewolves. The IRS is an organization of blood suckers, vampires, so the bullets don't work. Many of these customers will lose their homes and businesses, or even get indicted. It is often better not to be the adventurer trying out a new shelter that has not been tested in court. Someone else will risk their home and retirement to test every new theory. Why not wait and see what the courts say?

78. There are books and government forms that say or imply that compliance with the tax code is voluntary. Nothing could be further from the truth. The people who say that are either mistaken or lying. Income taxes in the U.S. today are no more voluntary than the draft was during the Vietnam War. (See Williams and Laschon.) "Taxes are enforced exactions, not voluntary contributions." said Judge Learned Hand.

79. The federal government does not need an income tax to exist or operate. Most of the time this country has been in existence there has been no direct tax on the citizens.

80. A license to practice law, an EA designation (enrolled agent), or a CPA designation only demonstrates that tests and courses have been taken. These are the three licenses that allow someone to negotiate for taxpayers with the IRS. Many in each field are incompetent.

81. Final deals with IRS agents need to be put into writing as soon as possible. Sometimes you can't get them to put it in writing and that should make you concerned. Oral agreements aren't worth the paper on which they aren't written. They are not enforceable (See Orr Chapter).

82. The statute of limitations for refunds is two years from the date the tax is paid. All W-2 withholding is deemed paid by April 15th of following the tax year. In other words, your 2000 W-2 withholding is deemed "paid" April 16, 2001 (April 15th falls on a Sunday).

83. Almost everything you do each day, certainly every check transaction, credit card transaction, long distance telephone call, and financial application with banks, is recorded and the IRS has access to it.

84. The IRS offers rewards to people who turn in friends, neighbors, and family for tax delinquencies of up to 10 percent of a portion of what they collect. There are very few people who turn in their neighbors and most of them never get a penny of the money promised. Some of them end up getting audited themselves. If you sleep with the devil expect to get burned.

85. The IRS has ten years to collect the tax you owe (from the date of assessment). After that, unless you have done something to extend the time, which many people do, the debt usually becomes unenforceable.

86. For civil purposes tax records should be kept for at least three years. For criminal purposes they should be kept at least six years. To be cautious it makes sense to keep them until all property relating to them has been sold or transferred and three years have passed. How do you figure that out? The best rule is to keep them and leave them for your heirs. You never know when they could be needed or what new laws Congress may pass making them relevant.

87. A tax lien will survive bankruptcy against the property on which it was placed.

88. IRS agents violate the law everyday. Some don't care and some simply don't know. After all, the code is so complicated that the men and women who wrote it don't understand it. The former commissioner of IRS, Joseph Nunan, was convicted for income tax evasion. He kept no records and claimed he didn't understand the law.

89. Your attorney may hire accountants to analyze your tax position. As long as they work for the lawyer the information and work product is privileged. If they come up with something you do not want public you seal it, or as long as it is not under subpoena, you can destroy it. If the work is filed with the government then the accountant is no longer protected by the attorney client privilege. You may want to hire two: one for advice and counsel under the lawyer's control and one to file a tax return.

90. Income taxes are evil. If you haven't figured that out you missed all the important chapters. You should not encourage government to tax income. If you live in the United States, live in one of the states which do not impose a state tax on individual income. They are: Alaska, Wyoming, New Hampshire, Tennessee, Nevada, Washington (Is this why Bill Gates lives there?), Florida, and Texas. Granted, Texas has some high property taxes; but they are not as intrusive as filling out the income tax forms and giving them to government.

91. If you make even $50,000 or more, tax planning will probably save you some money. Spending $20 on a computer program to play with your own ideas and then taking them to an EA or a CPA makes a lot of sense. Also, for professionals who work by the hour you may save yourself money. Even for a very small wage earner using the wrong form can cost you money. Between the computer program and a professional you are more likely to get it right.

92. The IRS gives free tax advice. (See Buford.) Often that is more than it is worth. They don't warrant it (unless it is in writing, which is not easy to get) and you can still be penalized for their negligence.

93. Everything you read about taxes anywhere, even in this book, must be read with concern and suspicion because the laws change every minute and the effectiveness of advice on specific information may diminish with time. General information shouldn't. For example, IRS agents often lie. During the twenty-four years of my practice to date this is something on which I have been able to rely.

94. Ultimate tax shelter. Most of these are sold by con artists. People (and companies) who are required by U.S. law to pay U.S. federal taxes are: all U.S. citizens. All who are living in the U.S. and earning money in the U.S. If you are not a U.S. citizen, and you don't live here or earn money in the U.S. you don't have to pay U.S. taxes. Every year U.S. citizens expatriate. That means they leave the U.S. and renounce their citizenship. Several billionaires have done this to avoid the huge estate tax when they die (only if you leave more than $600,000 in your estate). Both the Republicans and the Democrats have suggested legislation to tax these people before they leave. At the time of the printing of this book that has not been done. This is not an option for people who work for a living; only for the independently wealthy or those with some type of iron clad (I'm not sure it exists) job opportunity abroad. You need to have citizenship somewhere else before you do it. You will never again get to come home without another passport from another country. You will not be a U.S. citizen again. My preference is against this form of "tax shelter" but I am opposed to the government making it difficult to do. I don't want the U. S. to become an iron curtain country trying to keep people and currency from leaving. I want the U.S. to remain a country of preference to most people.

95. The U.S. is one of the only countries in the world that taxes its citizens on money earned outside the country.

96. The ownership of foreign banks is one of the last remaining foreign tax shelters. Recent tax laws have been implemented to tax U.S. citizens on foreign holdings in many situations even when the citizen does not actually receive the money. Banks are an exception. You can

probably figure out from the stories which clients this could have been an option for. The bank must actually be a bank and not a shell. This allows citizens to accumulate offshore money tax free.

97. It is foolish to consider any of these "Super Shelter" options unless you are already using IRAs and 401-Ks and other local shelters to the max. Anyone earning money abroad and making less than the amount which our government allows us to take tax free would be really foolish to entertain one of these options. If you live and work outside of the United States your first $70,000 of income is deductable.

98. A corporation or company or partnership or any other business is required to withhold taxes on its employees and these are called trust funds and are filed on a Form 941. If you work for the company and have signature authority on any of its accounts, and these funds are not paid over to the IRS, you may be held liable for them personally. A bookkeeper, a way-down-on-the-totem-pole vice president, any signature on the account, even if they don't have access to the checkbook and even if they have never used the checkbook, may be held civilly liable for failure to pay the tax penalty.

99. Since 1913, you have had an attorney-client privilege and tell an attorney anything you wanted as long as you didn't involve an attorney in a criminal conspiracy about what you had done and hadn't done and be completely protected.

100. The Second Circuit Court of Appeals, out of New York, had a similar privilege for CPAs. That privilege was stricken down. The IRS Restructuring and Reform Act of 1998 added a number of new protections including the presumption in civil courts in favor of the taxpayer. They have also added a CPA confidentiality rule. However, the confidentiality is limited to civil cases and does not extend to the portions of the CPA file which are necessary to prepare the tax return. In other words, if the IRS changes its investigation from civil to criminal, the CPA privilege is avoided. The CPA uses the information in

the preparation of a tax return or if it is in the tax return file, it is quite likely also to be avoided. What's the privilege worth? It is worth being very careful about if you want to rely on it. The kinder, gentler IRS, the same agents who trampled on constitutional rights and lied under oath are now required to be kinder and more gentle. Beware. To some extent the messages are being received and it is a little easier environment in which to work. However, if you let a mass murderer, mass rapist out of prison, and ask him to sign a paper that he will be kinder and more gentle, he might break his word. IRS agents who are accustomed to lying under oath and ignoring the law are not likely to suddenly stop doing that simply because they are told to stop doing it.

Epilogue
Not Quite Everything You Ever Wanted To Know About Write-Offs, Deductions, Shelters, Trusts, Offshore Banking, Perpetual Travelers, Personal Privacy and the Future of Taxes

This chapter is in no way intended to serve as an encyclopedia or a major treatise on these extensive subjects. My purpose is simply to give you a broad overview of what these things are. This section will detail how they work and how they don't work. It will also explain which parts are legal and which parts are not.

Governments have always lived on taxes. The government does not create, it takes. Workers have always sought to keep as much of the fruits of their labor as they can. Average United States citizens are a captive audience for the tax man. All of their wages are reported to the government with W-2s, W-4s and 1099s. They work from nine to five and have income tax taken out before it gets into their pockets.

Of course, wherever you find a system of control as strict as the IRS, you are sure to find dissenters as well. There are a million and one ways in which the general populace tries to get out from underneath the taxman's yoke. A common tactic among the more clever dissenters out there is to look for deductions, shelters, trusts, and other ways of lowering or eliminating their legal obligation to pay taxes. What follows is a brief examination of some common ways to avoid or reduce taxes.

Write-offs and Deductions

One of the best write-offs that exist today is simply earning all your money in another country. Uncle Sam allows you a $70,000 deduction for the first $70,000 in income. You have to be very careful about it. Live too many days in the USA or file papers late and you could end up broke or in court like Captain Orr.

The simplest forms of tax deductions are the ones afforded the entrepreneur. For the citizen who runs his or her own business a half a day of work often means 9 AM to 9 PM. This citizen has more opportunities to reduce taxable income than one who works a regular 9 to 5 job. Any expenses related to the business becomes deductible. For those who run a business from their home the most simple things such as phone service and electricity are deductible, as they are necessary to run your business. Additionally, company benefits are largely deductible.

Unfortunately deductions do not always work in favor of the average citizen. There was, for example, a certain bill passed through Congress to allow a specific women in the Dallas/Fort Worth area to pay less probate tax.[9] I don't have anything against Mrs. Ballard; but wouldn't you like a $12,000,000 deduction too? It seems that the moral of the story is that fairness does not always enter into the equation where tax deductions are concerned. Money and political influence often have as much to do with your tax status as do actual laws. Furthermore, there has not been a tax bill in the last fifty years which had the exact ramifications and repercussions that the politicians promised it would have.

Tax Shelters

A tax shelter is something that shelters your money from taxes for a period of time or forever. Capital gains is an interesting example. Bill Gates is the richest man in America. His wealth is stock. The

9. The bill was passed to save Geraldine Ballard, a rich widow, $4,000,000 in taxes. For more details and the first paragraph, see pg. 350 of *The Underground Lawyer*.

capital gains laws allow him to sell stock (if he has owned it more than a year) and pay only 20 percent of the profit in taxes. That allows him to be in one of the lowest tax brackets of anyone in the country. If he pays himself a salary, he shoots up over 40 percent (with social security and medicare) to one of the highest tax brackets in the country. The point is that converting the value of your labor into a capital event can cut your taxes in half. It hardly seems fair that labor is worth less than capital, net dollar for dollar?[10]

I have chosen this illustration intentionally making it over simplified. It is better today to sell property than to sell labor. Of course, in the smallest tax bracket is the best way to sell anything. Turning labor, like Gates did, into capital, is a great shelter and an even better tax bracket adjuster.

The most absolute tax shelters are buying government bonds that allow you to have tax-free income. Obtaining money in a personal injury case is mostly tax free (the income portions and punitive damage portions are not). The most popular tax shelters today are 401Ks and IRAs. This money accumulates and as long as you follow the rules (whatever they are now or in the future, which could change) you never have to pay taxes on it. Unfortunately, never is often a subjective word for the government. Many are concerned that when Congress sees a whole bunch of money in the Roth IRA program they will simply change the rules and tax it again anyway. I hope not. Nevertheless, when laws change any shelter can disappear overnight.

Trusts

The trust holds money or invested property for a trustee as outlined in the trust agreement. It is advisable to have an experienced professional who is well versed in current tax rules and regulations (which are so complex they merit an entire volume to cover thoroughly) to set up the trust.

10. The upshot is that in April 2000 his net worth dropped from one-hundred-billion to forty-nine billion, due in no small part to the government suing him using, of course, our money.

One purpose of the trust may be simply to avoid probate. You can start a revocable trust where you put your money in a trust which you can cancel at anytime during your life. When you die your heirs (the beneficiaries of the trust) get the money as outlined in the trust agreement. They do not have to go through probate, which may avoid extended legal battles over your estate and the publicizing of who in your estate gets what. However, Uncle Sam will tax your estate on that as though it is still in your name. That is the difference between a revocable trust and an irrevocable trust. An irrevocable trust means you cannot get the money back. It also means it will probably not be taxed as a part of your estate. A revocable trust means you can get the money back, but it still remains a part of your estate for tax purposes.

The Multiple Trusts

Multiple trusts are sometimes set up for the purpose of avoiding—or in a case of the illegal trust, evading—taxes.

An example of a multiple trust would be if you had $100,000 that you want to put in a trust for four children. A $100,000 trust would be taxable as it is higher than what tax laws allow to be given as a gift and remain tax free. Instead you would establish four separate trusts for smaller amounts to avoid extra taxes.

As mentioned, many abuse multiple trusts as a means of evading taxes. They do this by establishing one trust and making the beneficiary of that trust another trust. In turn, the same person who established the first trust would be the beneficiary of the second trust. This creates a circle in which all parties involved claim that the other is responsible for any taxes incurred. This is tax evasion and is unlawful.

Almost every theory for multiple trusts that I have seen for tax purposes in the United States fails. Some fail because they aren't done correctly. Others fail because they lack the political or legal clout of a major corporation. Most probably they will fail because the IRS has made such trusts a target which will not survive legal scrutiny.

If your goal is to wave a red flag in hopes of getting the IRS's bull headed attention, a system of complex trusts will certainly do the trick. I have handled trials where IRS agents actually said that trusts were illegal. In such instances I show them the blank form 1041 and ask why the federal government creates a form for the perpetuation of crimes. Their assertion, of course, is ridiculous.

Nevertheless, attempting to arrange one of these trust schemes is like tattooing "I hate cops on your forehead," it is sure to draw the attention of the authorities. If you are lucky you may go through the rest of your life without finding that IRS agent who is looking for a quota of people to attack with these particular types of trusts. But more likely you will spend a large portion of your income, time, and personal freedom fending off the IRS.

I have seen many scam artists peddle these trusts for as much as $50,000. I've also seen people purchase them for $20 out of a book store and fill in their own forms on the computer. The State Bar of Texas very recently sued a service which created a computer disk which helped people create their own forms. The bar won. The defendants lobbied the Texas legislature to change the law. The bar doesn't want non-lawyers to buy the same forms lawyers buy and sell to clients. Eventually, lawyers selling basic forms a computer can easily generate will go the way of the horse and carriage and become tools for the tourist or the eccentric wealthy only.

Moving Your Money

There have been public debates about Mexican citizens not being able to take their money out of Mexico. American citizens can take their money out of the country. They just have to tell the government about it. It is a sad and horrible intrusion into our personal rights. The government is passing new laws every day which intrude on the privacy of American citizens and to force banks to report occurrences. These are the types of laws that the United States and many former supporters of the Geneva Convention once protested concerning the Iron Curtain countries. In one of history's humorous twists, many of the former Iron Curtain countries have less strict currency transaction laws than we do today. For that reason and others many companies like to move offshore.

Offshore

Having your business operate offshore is an effective way to reduce your tax bill as well. One extreme (not to mention bewildering and clever) example of how this works can be found in Shell Oil's business plan. Shell Oil Company is a Dutch company. They trade it in the United States. It has a big home base in the Netherlands, Antilles. If you were to go to the Netherlands, Antilles and watch a trial, Shell never loses; they essentially own the island. The Netherlands, Antilles is what is called as a tax haven country. They have tax secrecy laws. They have no juries.

Lets examine two ways that the Shell corporation could do business.

Example One: Shell earns $1 in the USA. Shell pays 40 percent in taxes. Shell's net after taxes is 60¢.

Example Two: Shell USA earns $1 in the United States but spends 40 percent on offshore expenses. Shell USA borrows $2 from Shell Antilles at 10 percent. This constitutes 20 percent of its cost of doing business. Shell Antilles, borrows the $2 from Shell Panama at 9.5 percent. Shell USA makes a contract with Shell Panama at 20 percent to provide merchandise, contacts, and expertise. Shell Panama contracts with Shell Isle of Man at 19 percent to provide everything it provides Shell USA.

Confused? That is understandable. The bottom line is this: 40 percent of Shell USA's expenses are from doing business with its offshore subsidiaries. This lowers their net profit of $1 to 60¢ before taxes. They pay the same 40 percent in tax, but do so on the reduced profit. This leaves them with a 24¢ tax bill as opposed to the 40¢ paid in example one. Considering the amount of money Shell brings in, this is a substantial savings.

How do they get away with this? Well, as a general rule, Shell

Antilles and Shell Panama will say they don't do business in the United States. However, the U.S. government will claim they *are* doing business in the United States and want to tax them. If the IRS wins this battle and Shell Antilles has to pay taxes on the profits of its 20 percent and Shell Panama has to pay taxes on the profits of its 20 percent. Here's the trick, Shell Antilles doesn't make much profit because most of it is made by Shell Panama who is charging a huge interest rate for the money offshore. Shell Isle of Man, therefore, is making most of the profits. Shell Isle of Man and Shell Panama have no relationship to the United States whatsoever and pay no taxes in the United States. This complex scheme lowers the Shell Corporation's taxes and raises their profits significantly.

This form of "creative" but legal tax planning was put out of the reach of American citizens when Congress, during the Reagan administration, changed the law. If American citizens who own stock in offshore corporations did not pay taxes after the new law was passed they would be held personally liable for the amount of unpaid income to the corporation. This effectively made these types of structures illegal. Does that mean that large international corporations do not get the benefit of it? Of course not. It means that individual U.S. citizens don't get the benefit of it. Big Republican changes with a Democratic Congress shafted the little capitalist but protected the big corporate structures.

One large exception to the new legislation is offshore banks. An American citizen can still own interest in an offshore bank and reap tax savings and tax benefits from accrued income. However, it cannot be a "shell" bank. The bank must actually do banking business and have a motive for making a banking profit.

Lots of people all over the world prefer to live in one country and have their money in another country. They do this because the country that has the money is very friendly to the money, knowing they only have temporary use of it and that it can be wired out in an instant. Money in the country is good for the economy even if the government can not tax it. Many governments, such as the Cayman

305

Islands, make a large portion of their revenue by charging franchise fees for offshore corporations and banks.

What is the advantage of having an offshore account? If you are an American citizen, they require you to report it, so it doesn't protect you from the eyes of the government.[11] It does, however, protect the funds from an illegal seizure by the government. Of course an offshore account can't protect your physical body from seizure by the government. The United States once held the heavyweight champion of the world, Jack Johnson, in prison as ransom for offshore money. He had to pay it to get out.

American citizens are taxed on their income all over the world. The United States is one of the very few countries that does this. In recent years some very wealthy citizens have given up their citizenship and become Jamaicans' or Costa Ricans' so that when they died the government would not charge it's excruciatingly high death tax. (Mrs. Ballard simply got the law changed to lower her tax but most of us don't have a personal friendship with the former speaker of the house.) If you do not live in the United States and you do not have money or possessions in the United States and you are not a citizen of the United States then the government has very little control over you.

Perpetual Traveler

The perpetual traveler, who has been written about in a series of books by W.G. Hill (undoubtedly not his real name), is the individual who does not live in the country where he has his passport and does not have his money in the country where he lives. Since no country enjoys jurisdiction and control over his body and his money, and since his investments are not in the same country that he lives in, he generally pays little or no income tax. If you don't have to live off the income of your personal labor, but can live off the income from investments, and if you are content with not staying in any country for six months or

---

11. This assertion presumes that you follow the law. Thousands of citizens don't because: (a) they don't know they have to, or (b) they don't care.

more (that is the general time rule about when most countries demand jurisdiction over you and call you a tax risk) you could avoid the payment of income tax forever. (Or at least until so many people become perpetual travellers that the governments of the world decide to crack down on them. Though, that's not likely to happen soon.)

The perpetual traveller is often richer than the average citizen. Generally these people pick up the bills, obey the laws of the countries they inhabit, and are a beloved and sought after visitor. Everyone, and every country, likes the guy who picks up the tab. Without him civilization goes into the sewers.

In general, an American citizen who wanted to become a perpetual traveller would be better off giving up their citizenship. However, giving up your citizenship is an extremely drastic step. There are literally millions of people on this planet who would like to take your place as a citizen of the United States of America. For many, the United States is arguably the best country to live in the world. That can certainly change. In fact it is changing. Our great advantage has been a high-level of freedom. If this country continues to weaken constitutional protections of free speech, free press, capitalism, and free circulation of money, this country could be less free than former Iron Curtain countries. In fact, more than one Polish-American citizen has returned to Poland for its recent economic freedoms. More than one American citizen has sought Israel for its religious values, its tax holidays available to new citizens, and its personal protection for the Jewish people. More than one person has sought Irish citizenship, especially writers and artists because they are not taxed at all on their Irish art as a matter of public law and policy.

Today borders are very important. A U.S. passport is one of the most coveted in the world. However, it comes with a huge tax—all U.S. citizens are taxed on income made world-wide. Many U.S. citizens have given up their citizenship to stop filing tax returns. This is downright foolish if you don't have another passport in the vault, as you need one to travel.

Money Laundering Laws

There are very few laws and statutes used more improperly than the laws on money laundering. In order to stop drug dealers who would take their drug money to buy legitimate businesses for the purpose of laundering money, the United States government created forms for reporting cash. Unfortunately, the majority of the people, "caught" by these forms are honorable individual citizens like Dr. Bussey, the dentist who liked to deal in cash.

The law has even been modified to include cashiers' checks or money orders. The government continually re-works the definition of money. Not just Federal Reserve notes; but bank notes.

Every bank in the United States and every individual in the United States is required to fill out a CTR form (Currency Transaction Report) anytime they receive ten thousand dollars or more in cash. As a general rule lawyers would tell their clients, "Don't give me ten thousand dollars in cash, give me nine thousand nine hundred dollars. You don't want the form to be filled out do you?"

In fact, bank tellers often tell their customers, "Give me nine thousand dollars and come back through the drive in and give me the other thousand. You don't want the form to be filled out do you?"

That of course caused a road block in letting the government know everything about everyone with ten thousand dollars in cash and that was changed by making it illegal to tell people how to avoid the law. The new law is still routinely broken. Most bankers and lawyers don't understand it can be illegal to truthfully tell your client how the law works...if you are trying to help them avoid it.

The problem of course is that it restricts your rights to get legal counsel and it restricts freedom of speech and freedom of press. It restricts the flow of truthful information.

As far as I know of the writing of this book it is still legal to tell you what the law is in writing.

The one thing the law shouldn't be is ridiculous and when these fine points are pressed the law becomes ridiculous. In the words of a

308

Charles Dickens character "If the law says that: the law is an ass."

While expanding its effort to control the trafficking of money for drugs, government creates an ever expanding web of laws that we must follow and conform to on threat of imprisonment. Of course the people who are most likely to be imprisoned are the very small drug dealers on the street, and the small drug users, and harmless idiosyncratic individuals. Not the people who are wiring billions of dollars across international lines daily. Though I don't condone the use or sale of drugs, I recognize that the drug war is in essence a war against the personal privacy of the citizens of this country. The actual sale of drugs is largely unaffected.

Privacy

Generally the purpose of shelters, offshore banking, and becoming a perpetual traveler is to save your income and protect your privacy. Many of them however become conversation pieces which lead to trouble. Your unused "offshore trust" sitting on the coffee table can become a blackmail device in a lawsuit against you.

An acquaintance who recently wrote a best selling book entitled *Hide All Your Assets and Disappear*, has a saying that he repeats many times and bears repeating in this chapter: "Three can keep a secret if two are dead."

There are very few governments that allow you to have privacy. There are very few situations when you actually have privacy. Do I resent it? Absolutely. Can something be done about it? Yes. You can write books, lecture, protest, and vote for government officials that oppose the violations of your human rights of privacy. I've done all of the above.

In the alternative you can pack up and leave. Just bear in mind all governments are interested in what you have to say, what you do, what you know, and what you own. If you own stock in a legitimate offshore bank that bank can generate income As long as you don't get that income back you don't have to pay taxes on it. Rest assured that when you do get it back you are legally required to pay taxes.

Thousands upon thousands of people in the United States don't file tax returns. Those who have never filed tax returns are required to do so if they earn income. Nevertheless, if they don't get the W-4s or 1099s, don't use regular banks, or deal in cash, they are practically invisible. The government wants to stop that. It's hard to tax and control invisible people. On the other hand, it is hard for invisible people to be active citizens. If you own or operate vehicles, own real estate, or vote, you are not invisible. The sacrifice in my opinion is not worth the reward. That is not to say I don't respect the brave individuals who are supremely conscious about their privacy. I do. I am just not willing to make the trade that they are willing to make and I have to recommend against it, especially if they have small children. The overwhelming majority of them have family problems and financial problems. I say the overwhelming majority because I know people in the underground who seem to be quite happy, quite prosperous, and always have cash to pick up a meal. As big brother gets bigger and bigger this is going to be harder and harder to do.

Money and the Future of Taxes

What is money? The dollar, cent, pound, ruble, kopeck, centavo, peso, franc, lira, mark, schilling, drachma, and yen are all *forms* of money. But that doesn't answer the question.

Money is the greatest invention in the world for assessing value. As it turns out it's also the greatest invitation in the world for assessing taxes. We grow accustom to the units we deal in and learn to believe in them, but it's only a game. Our unit, the dollar, is only as valuable as our belief in it and imagination.

When crops were taxed at ten percent, the assessor had to carry the crops off. The first modern form of money was coins in weighted gold. This was easier to carry than bars of gold. In the United States, banks created paper money. The paper represents promises to pay gold. This, of course is even easier to carry.

310

What constitutes a dollar has changed radically three times in the last century. When the government took it over, it issued dollars backed by gold. Ultimately, the government lowered it to dollars backed by the promise to pay silver; and finally, during the Nixon administration, the silver was taken away. Today the U.S. dollar is backed by a promise to pay paper.

Income is really the creation of value, not neccessarily the accumulation of money. The difference is that value in the form of money is much more easily taxed.

The European Union's new money, the Euro, goes into paper and coin this year. Up until now it has been the world's first purely computer money. It too, like the Japanese Yen and the United States Dollar is backed only by government promises. The competition between the three giant types of money will be interesting to watch and all three will be doing their best to tax the money.

The airlines have created frequent flyer miles—a new currency. They are a new bargaining chip in today's divorce courts and, at least for the moment, non-taxable. Credit cards create "money." All of these things indicate that our concept of money continues to change with time and technology. The ways to create, use and trade "income" are growing and will continue to grow exponentially in the future.

The next step is that the government will try to translate all of this potential "income" into normal, taxable, "money." People will move this "monopoly money" around and try to interpret it to either avoid or lower the government value, or keep it under the government radar screen, to limit the taxation of it. Money that is harder to tax than dollars, or taxed at a lower rate, will go up in value.

The methods of taxation are going to change tremendously. The one rule that will not change is this: Most people will try to pay the smallest amount of tax possible. They will be limited only by their willingness to do this and their imaginations.

Governments will test national and international borders as vigorously as they have always tested them, in hopes of finding a way to

collect more taxes, to levy taxes, to make the taxes politically acceptable and then to spend the bounty. In turn dissenters will find new
ways to circumvent tax laws. Inevitably currency and laws will
change, but essentially the game will remain the same.

343.7304 Minns, Michael
MIN   Louis.

How to beat the IRS.

Wallingford Public Library
Wallingford, CT 06492

A2170 455949 6

WALLINGFORD PUBLIC LIBRARY
200 NO MAIN ST
WALLINGFORD CT 06492

BAKER & TAYLOR